J.K. LASSER'S
✚ GUIDE TO ✚
BUYING YOUR
FIRST HOME

JOE CATALANO

Prentice Hall
New York • London • Toronto • Sydney • Tokyo • Singapore

2nd Edition

Prentice Hall General Reference
15 Columbus Circle
New York, NY 10023

Library of Congress Cataloging-in-Publication Data
Catalano, Joe.
    J.K. Lasser's guide to buying your first home / Joe Catalano.—
2nd ed.
       p.   cm.
    Includes index.
    ISBN 0-671-88066-7
    1. House buying. I. Title.
HD1379.C37 1993
643'.12—dc20   93-27415
                                           CIP

Manufactured in the United States of America

1 2 3 4 5 6 7 8 9 10

Contents

Introduction   *1*

PART ONE: SELECTING THE RIGHT HOUSE FOR YOU

Chapter 1   You Can Do It!   9

Chapter 2   Determining How Much House You
              Can Afford   *23*

Chapter 3   Determining Where to Live   *37*

Chapter 4   The Type of Residence That's Right
              for You   *49*

Chapter 5   Bargain Alternatives for Cash-Tight
              Homebuyers   *67*

PART TWO: FINANCING YOUR HOME

Chapter 6   Where to Get a Mortgage   *89*

Chapter 7   Getting Over the Down Payment Hurdle   *113*

Chapter 8   Government Help   *129*

Chapter 9   Creative Financing   *187*

PART THREE: GOING FROM HOUSE SHOPPING TO
              HOUSE CLOSING

Chapter 10 The Best Time to Buy a House   *203*

Chapter 11 Do You Need a Broker?   *217*

Chapter 12 Inspecting the Home You Want   *227*

Chapter 13 Choosing a Good Attorney   *239*

Chapter 14 Negotiating the Purchase Price   *255*

Chapter 15 The Closing   *273*

Dedication

To My Parents

Acknowledgement

I would like to acknowledge all the people who took the time to share their expertise and experiences with me.

Introduction

Congratulations! You've picked the best time to be out home shopping since 1976. Why?

A combination of the lowest interest rates in two decades and home prices that have declined in many areas of the country from their highs last decade has enabled the greatest number of people to buy their first home since 1976, according to the Chicago Title and Trust Company. First-time buyers accounted for 47.7 percent of all homes sold in 1992, up from 45.1 in 1991 and 41.9 percent in 1990.

Owning a home is the dream of almost every person. For some, it's the fantasy of several acres right on the water where the setting sun can be watched while sipping cocktails on the deck of a contemporary beach house. For others, it's relaxing on the 56th floor of a residential tower in a major city while the rest of the world bustles along below. And for still others, it's a roomy colonial in a suburban neighborhood with a pool and big backyard for the kids. Whatever the ultimate housing dream, the goal is the same: to own something that grows in value as time goes on and to be free of paying rent to a landlord.

But unless they win a state lottery or inherit property from some long-lost relative, the first home most people entering the housing market today end up owning probably won't be the one they'll be living in when they retire or, for that matter, 10 years from now despite lower home prices. Your first home will probably lack many of the amenities and the location you ultimately want. But as broker Bonnie Lazar put it, the first house you purchase should be "one that satisfies your needs and starts building equity so you can go on to the next stage."

You should feel good about starting your house-hunting expedition today because you have a better shot at achieving your goal now than at any time in the booming eighties. A study done several years ago by Harvard University showed that the rate of homeownership among people between the ages of 25 and 34 had declined from 52.3 percent in 1980 to 45 percent in 1988. In another study, done by the National Association of Home Builders, first-time buyers made up less than 30 percent of those who were purchasing homes in 1988.

The decline during the eighties occurred because income didn't keep up with the rise in home prices. The median price for a single-family home in the United States rose from $66,400 in 1981 to $96,700 by the end of the decade. But according to the National Association of Realtors, its first-time buyers index is now at its highest level in years. How long the market will favor buyers is hard to say. The median price for a home in the United States is again on the rise, jumping 4.3 percent to $103,400, in the last three months of 1992, from the same period the year before. However, during that same period, prices were still dropping in some areas, particularly in California and parts of the Northeast where prices had jumped the greatest in the mid-eighties. For example, prices were down 1.5 percent in Los Angeles, .5 percent in New York City and 3.2 percent in Springfield, Massachusetts, in the last three months of 1992. Plus there's no telling when interest rates will get out of hand again, popping mortgage rates to 16 percent or more, as happened in the early eighties.

While forecasting the future is difficult, most economists think that as the country lifts itself out of the recession, home prices should climb only about 2 or 3 percent a year. Of course, that's a national average. Some areas will see further declines while others experience a more rapid property appreciation.

Although the eighties economy was soft, it did give first-time buyers time to save money for their down payments. And for those who may not have yet put together the 20 percent down needed to get a conventional mortgage, there's more good news. During no period in recent memory have lenders come up with more programs to help first-time buyers with closing costs and low down payments than exist today.

Yes, lenders are scrutinizing borrowers more closely than ever. They want squeaky-clean credit that demonstrates promptness in paying bills. They also want to see a low amount of debt. But by the same token, "there's a wider variety of [special mortgage programs] today [to help first-time buyers] than there has ever been before," said Carolyn Weber, vice president of Century 21 of the Northeast. Both government and private lenders have come up with, and continue to come up with, programs that make it possible for more people to purchase a home.

After speaking with hundreds of brokers, attorneys, lenders and other real estate experts over the years, there seem to be 12 common mistakes made by first-time buyers. They are:

1. Shopping for a home before knowing how much you can afford.

2. Not realizing how mortgage interest tax write-offs can help you afford a home.

3. Not setting aside enough money for closing costs.

4. Wanting your first home to be the showcase pictured in your dreams.

5. Relying too much on the advice of friends and relatives rather than professionals.

6. Not looking at all of the different types of mortgages available to a first-time buyer today.

7. Not giving a current landlord enough notice that you're leaving your rental unit and, as a result, losing one or two months' security.

8. Not having a home inspected by an engineer before closing on it.

9. Not choosing the right attorney.

10. Relying on a real estate broker as your only source of information.

11. Not realizing what a bad credit rating can do to your chances of getting mortgage.

12. Not having the contract of sale checked by an attorney.

The goal of this book is to twofold: to examine these mistakes, as well as others, and help you avoid them; and to guide you through your first homebuying experience so that it can proceed as smoothly as possible.

Despite prices that have dropped since they peaked last decade, home prices still remain high. Chapter 1 begins with actual examples of people just like you who have beaten the odds and bought their first home. Some did it with financial help from their parents, while others did it on their own using savings as well as hard work in fixing up beat-up homes.

From there, you'll see how to determine which home and neighborhood is right for you. When budgets are tight, often compromises have to be made. Chapters 2 through 4 will help you determine which requirements you should give up and which you should not budge on.

Since finding the right home is only part of the search, Part Two of this book gets into financing the property you find. While some buyers think only of 30-year fixed-rate mortgages for financing a home, today there are a variety of products ranging from adjustable rates—where the mortgage rate can change every year—to convertibles, a term that may seem like a description of a car now but will be explained as you delve deeper into the upcoming pages. Many of the newest loan programs available are also detailed.

Part Three takes you from house shopping to the final closing day. Questions that will be explored include when the best time to shop for a home is, whether you should use a broker and how to determine whether the home you're buying is in good shape and worth the money. How to choose a good real estate attorney will also be discussed, as well as what happens on that final day when you close on the house you've bought (this is the closest you'll ever feel to being a philanthropist who just sits there writing and signing checks to all those who request one).

What this book won't discuss are convoluted schemes to buy homes that work for perhaps six people in the whole country. Too many books are available that promise to help you buy a home with nothing down at ridiculously low prices involving complex schemes that are not only hard to pull off, but often risky. The issues and tactics discussed here are the ones that people use every day.

Buying a home is involved and confusing, and it will probably help accelerate the number of grey hairs that find their way onto your head. But after reading the following, the process should be less painful and be an experience based on knowledge rather than confusion.

Part One

SELECTING
THE RIGHT HOUSE
FOR YOU

Chapter 1

YOU CAN DO IT!

You CAN do it! Whether you're single or married, if you really want to buy a home, it is possible despite what statistics, real estate brokers, or anyone else tells you.

As proof, look at Doug and Heidi Vandewinkel. After four years of searching and saving, they managed to purchase a three-bedroom ranch for $115,000 in one of the most expensive markets in the country. But as they and other successful first-time buyers will tell you, it isn't easy. You have to really want it and be willing to make sacrifices during the entire lengthy process. "The big question for us," said Doug Vandewinkel, "was determining what we could accept, meaning what we could afford."

Both Heidi and Doug wanted to live near where they worked. But the neighborhoods surrounding their mutual offices were way out of their price range which they estimated to be about $120,000. One of the first homes they looked at was only a block from the apartment they were renting, an area they both enjoyed living in. But the house was priced at $180,000 and had less space than their apartment. After seeing the property, the couple felt they should leave the market for a year to put together a bigger down payment.

When they returned to the hunt 12 months later, they began searching in neighborhoods about 40 minutes from where they worked; these were areas where homes were going in the price range that their combined incomes could afford. They looked not only in communities that were well maintained, but also in neighborhoods that had been neglected, but were starting to come back and would be the type of place they wanted to live in five years from now.

"We saw things that a squatter wouldn't have been happy living in." "They were in our price range, but not in our dignity range." One home was only a year-and-a-half old. It had no landscaping, which Doug and Heidi said they could live without. But when the broker took them inside, they noticed that the home's roof was about to cave in. So much for that prospect.

Reality of what the couple's dollar could buy quickly set in. At the same time, they were facing the vicious cycle many firsttime buyers encounter. To buy a home, you need a down payment. But it's hard to make headway towards saving for a down payment when you're also paying rent each month and home prices are rising (as they were when the Vandewinkels were in the market).

So they did what a lot of first-time buyers do—they went to their respective families and asked for whatever financial help they could get. At the same time, they decided to put off having children until they not only had a home of their own, but were also back on their feet financially. After getting some money from each set of parents, Heidi investigated below-market, state-backed loans which, at that time, had a 7.25 percent rate of interest. (How these are obtained and what states have them will be discussed in Chapter 8).

When they found that their combined incomes fell within state requirements, they applied and were accepted for the loan. They now intensified their search for the right property using brokers from three different real estate offices to help them find something livable in their price range. After seeing a dozen houses in one weekend, they found a ranch they liked for $115,000. The home doesn't have a basement and it has less space than the couple ideally wanted, but it's theirs.

In order to buy a home, a first-time buyer should evaluate what he or she really needs and then be willing to make compromises as he or she realizes what the dollar can actually buy. Your first home won't be the castle you eventually want to stay in until you retire or die, but buying something is a way of getting out of the rent cycle and starting to accumulate equity so you can later begin trading up and ultimately move into what you really want.

Likewise, the bigger the down payment you can put together, the better off you'll be. When the Vandewinkels felt they didn't have enough money saved, after their first few months of searching, they withdrew from the market to save even more.

When it comes to putting together a down payment, no one probably had more foresight than Edgar Sanchez. "I knew that someday I would want a house," Edgar said. So he began saving for one while still in his teens, starting with money he earned while in high school. By the time he was married to Maria and ready to buy, Edgar, now in his mid-thirties, had $68,000 saved.

He looked at more than 35 homes, some of them falling apart, before he realized that his original price range of $250,000 would not get the type of home he wanted—something in move-in condition in a good neighborhood. So he and his wife began saving more by cutting back on a lot of things and watching their spending even closer than they had been, which wasn't easy considering the couple had two children. Eventually the Sanchezes found a home they liked costing $285,000. After being in the home for a couple of months, Edgar said that it was tough going and that the family was still pinching pennies. But at least his family had gotten the home it wanted.

Now when Tom and Michaela Taylor were out buying their first home seven years ago, $285,000 was way above the level they could afford. Inexpensive was the operative word for the then newly-married couple on their search. And the only way they could afford to buy anything was to go with a handyman special, which in real estate parlance means "the house is falling apart."

The house they eventually settled on "was a disaster," said Michaela, as she showed pictures of a building some might have thought should have been condemned rather than sold to a nice young couple like the Taylors. "We were even hesitant about buying it," Tom added. "But by buying our house in the shape that it was in, it allowed us to own something. If we had bought one that was move-in perfect, we probably still wouldn't own a house." They made an offer $15,000 less than the current owner was asking. To their surprise, the seller accepted it.

"When we brought in an engineer to inspect the place, he said it was a walking museum," Michaela recalled. Plumbing and other fixtures were decades old. "We had carpenter ants as well as crickets in the kitchen that were as big as mice. We had the exterminator coming in once every two weeks." He was starting to become a member of the family.

But while things were old and rundown, the engineer told them that the house was physically sound, which prompted them to go ahead with the deal.

Every corner of the house needed work. It was, however, livable which was important because, while fixing up the house, they had to live there; they could no longer afford to pay rent to live in an apartment elsewhere. They quickly discovered that living in a house that's being remodelled is not as easy as it sounds. Dust from walls being torn down gets into everything, no matter how tightly covered it is. Complicating the task further was that they were both working full time so they could meet their monthly mortgage payments, while also paying for the growing construction costs. Each project was done during evenings and on weekends.

And if something could go wrong while remodelling, it did. Tom remembers buying a washing machine for the house and then finding that it wouldn't fit through the basement door. Who thought of measuring the doorway opening before buying the appliance. After all, he was a novice carpenter, not a professional. "To get the washing machine in, I had to take the flooring off the front porch and lower it in," Tom explained. "Now I know why there were three other washing machines down in the basement when we bought the house."

Then there were the new pine floors that the Taylors laid down only to find that none of the doors in the house could be opened afterwards. "I had put all the floors down with the doors shut." "When we went to open one . . ." The doors had to be removed and planed to clear the new flooring.

Today, *nearly* the entire 95-year-old house is completed. (There will always be something to do.) The couple knew only a little about remodelling, but with the help of books, friends (including one in the construction business), and the use of some professional help (to do things such as plumbing), the couple managed to turn their small budget into a home that has since seen considerable appreciation in value.

While the Taylors were willing to use sweat equity to get the home they wanted, Diane Degl and Kenneth Uher decided this wasn't the route for them. After being turned off by the condition of some of the handyman specials they were being shown early on, they decided they wanted something as close to move-in condition as they could get.

Diane and Kenneth, in their early 20s, had recently become engaged when they decided they didn't want to start married life in a rental. They wanted the American dream of a single-family home from day one of their new life together.

Kenneth had actually started saving for the down payment even before the joint decision to buy was made. When he discussed the idea with Diane and she agreed that owning was the way to go, Kenneth made his fiancee pay off all her credit cards and then give them up. Whatever was purchased from this point on was to be paid for in cash. If they didn't have the money in hand, then they wouldn't buy it. And if they did have the money, they would always ask themselves, "Do I really need this?" Austerity was to be their new way of life.

But even though they were feverishly stashing cash into the bank, Diane said she began to have doubts if the two would ever own anything. She said she was amazed at the prices that sellers were asking for their homes and the poor condition some of the homes were in. "One lady was trying to sell a house that had a hole the size of a car in one wall." And the owner was asking $135,000.

Reality soon set in that the house they would eventually buy would not be move-in perfect. The couple also realized they couldn't live in any of the neighborhoods their parents and their parents' friends now owned in. All the homes they looked at in these areas were just way out of the young couple's price range.

What finally gave Diane and Kenneth the ability to buy the home they are now living in was a generous cash gift from Diane's grandmother. Both bankers and real estate brokers say that, besides savings, financial assistance from a relative is what makes a majority of young people able to buy a home today. It helped not only the Vandewinkels and Diane and Kenneth, but also John and Maureen Kessler.

When they first began looking for a home, "We gave up a few months later," Maureen said. "Everything was out of our reach and we decided we had to save more." Eventually both sets of parents helped the couple's savings mount faster by making cash donations (which they intend to pay back) adding up to $15,000.

But while gifts are nice, Maureen found that lenders only allow borrowers to use a certain percentage of donated or gifted money for their down payments. On a 10 percent down or less loan, at least half the down payment has to come from the buyer's own savings. With a 20 percent down mortgage, most lenders want to see at least five percent of the down payment coming from the buyer's own savings. This proves to the lender that the borrower is able to manage money and save enough to help make his or her housing dream happen. For the Kesslers this meant that even though mom and dad were extremely generous, the couple still had to save up a tidy sum of money on their own.

The Kesslers' house ended up costing $190,000—more than they had originally intended to spend—and it still needed at least $30,000 in work, such as redoing the driveway. And while they looked long and hard for the perfect house, even after purchasing the one they eventually settled on, Maureen sometimes thinks they should have looked even longer and harder. Self-doubt starts setting in when you're making the biggest purchase of your life.

One of the Kesslers' friends recently bought a home for $40,000 less than the Kesslers were paying for the home they were about to close on in two weeks. And all their friends had to do to their home was change the wallpaper.

Guilt about buying too early was also compounded by other opportunities that had been presented to the couple in years past. They had found a waterfront home several years ago priced at only $95,000. The owner was even willing to hold the mortgage at an attractive rate of interest. But the Kesslers weren't married yet and they had nothing in the way of a down payment saved. Time went on and after they had been married almost a year, another deal came their way—a $120,000 home not far from the water. But again they weren't ready. If only you could go back in time like Michael J. Fox did in all those *Back To The Future* movies and snag the deals you passed up.

Maureen's home-hunting expedition has proven one thing to her—that you shouldn't go out and be tempted unless you've got enough cash saved and are ready to move on the first good deal you see. Looking before you have the necessary funding only leads to frustration, anxiety, and disappointment. She also noted that had she and John been able to save a larger down payment, it would have helped reduce the $171,000 mortgage and nearly $1,800 monthly mortgage payment they now have to make.

Maureen's parents have said that the house she and John bought is not in the greatest area. They're also amazed that the driveway needs work and that the home needs a new roof among other things. But Maureen noted that her parents are measuring her home against what they could have gotten for $190,000 when her parents were home shopping several decades ago. They failed to measure her home against what other buyers are getting for the same price today.

While in the back of Maureen's mind she's wondering if she and John will make it—their mortgage payments are triple the $600 in rent they used to pay—she said that "as scared as I am, I am happy."

The home is in a good school district and, hopefully, when they have to pay their parents back, they'll have the money. The good thing about home ownership is that the mortgage interest is deductible which allows the couple to keep more of their income to help pay monthly payments and expenses.

One thing home hunting did do for Maureen Kessler "was help me learn the lingo quickly." You find out what lock-in rates and convertible mortgages are very quickly. (These will both be explained thoroughly in later chapters). The more knowledge you have, the better off you are.

What helped make Michael and Kathleen Tripptree's first-time homebuying experience better "was that we were fortunate enough to find a woman who worked at the bank (where we were getting our loan) who explained everything from mortgages to closings," said Michael. "Without someone to help educate you as you go along, buying a home becomes a lot harder affair."

Some first-time buyers said they relied on brokers. Others said they followed the advice of bankers. Still others turned to family members who had already been through the home-buying process for advice. (As you'll see later, some experts believe relying too heavily on brokers or family members can do more harm than good in your search.)

The Tripptrees had looked for about a year before finding a home they could afford. Halfway through the search, Kathleen became pregnant. This taxed their limited resources even further. "When we were renting," Michael said, "life was pretty comfortable. If something went wrong, you called the landlord." Before buying, Michael, a fireman by profession, wrestled with the fact that once he owned his own home, if something went wrong, he would be the one responsible for fixing the problem as well as paying for it.

While becoming the property's landlord didn't have the greatest appeal to Michael, his realization that his rent checks were not leaving him with anything he could really call his own, ultimately convinced him home ownership was the only way to go. And with his crazy sleeping hours—his shift as a fireman is always changing—a single-family home meant that no one would be living above him making noise as he tried to sleep days when on a night shift.

He knew home prices were high in the area he was looking in. But getting a 7.6 percent state-backed loan requiring only five percent down helped. Another thing aiding the couple was luck. You can shop around and look forever, but somehow, some weird twist of fate causes you to stumble onto that one home that fills your needs and also fits your budget. Others called this luck, the persistence of shopping around.

The $113,000 home the Tripptrees ended up buying needs work. "But you learn to be handy." And even after being in the home for a year now—with a new daughter sharing their lives—they are still watching where every penny goes.

Sacrifice is the word heard most often by the first-time buyers who have beaten the odds and bought their own home.

"We became known as the tightwads," said Lynn Wood, as she explained what she and her husband Randy did to save up the money they used for the down payment on the home they eventually bought. "As soon as we got married and decided we wanted a house, that's when our lifestyle changed."

The couple did little dining out. They also stopped meeting friends for cocktails. When they did socialize with other couples, more often it was in their own apartment or at someone else's place. Going to the movies was also curtailed. To find out what had befallen the lead characters in the latest Batman or Rocky sequel, they waited until it hit the videotape market and then rented it. They also stopped going on vacations. "We'd bring lots of people to the airport, but never went anywhere ourselves."

At the same time, they began looking at what was on the market. Brokers tried to discourage them. At best, they only had 10 percent to put down instead of the customary 20 or 25 percent many conventional mortgages required. One broker even told the couple, "forget about buying. Think about saving for another five years." At one open house, a broker told them, "no one buys a house today without 25 percent down."

These types of comments dampened their home-buying enthusiasm somewhat, but it didn't kill the urge entirely. They believed they could get what they wanted with the under $20,000 they had saved.

And then one day, after about ten months of searching, the couple stumbled upon a beautiful three-bedroom, one-bath home that an older couple had put on the market. Lynn and Randy made an offer, a few thousand dollars below the owners asking price, that was accepted. They immediately went to contract to buy the home with visions of moving vans and carpet colors dancing in their heads. But just as they thought their search had come to an end, a snag developed. The bank that was making the Woods' mortgage sent an appraiser out to the home, as is the case with all loans being made by bankers. The lender does this to make sure that the home it is making a mortgage on is worth the price being paid by the buyer. This way, if the borrower defaults on the loan, the lender knows it can still get its money back if the home has to be sold.

To the Woods' surprise, the bank said the home didn't appraise out; it was not worth the bargain price they thought they were paying. This meant the Woods' would have to: accept a smaller mortgage amount—which their budget didn't allow; get the seller to reduce the price of their home—which the seller already felt was a rock-bottom price; or pass on the house. The Woods' had no choice but to painfully take the last of the three options presented to them.

"But thank God we kept up our hunt," Lynn said. They eventually wound up with a four-bedroom home, costing $144,000, that had two full baths, a garage, a finished basement, a large patio with an awning, a nice-sized yard, and located in a much better neighborhood than the home they had almost bought.

Now friends come by who are still renting and, the Woods' said, "they're eating crow." Their friends look at what the couple got and ask how they did it forgetting about the times they would come by to share a pizza instead of dining out in some trendy neighborhood bistro.

When you're a first-time buyer, "You have to be patient. Don't listen to what other people say. There ARE good deals out there. You just can't say, 'I want to buy a house,' and then expect to move in three months later." Every cent that was used to buy their home came from the couple's own pockets. There were no gifts from parents. That money came from working and economizing, by not going to movies, buying less new outfits, and other penny-pinching tactics. "There are lots of other people besides Randy and me who have succeeded and done it without the help of friends or relatives." Buying a home on your own with just the money you've saved *can be done.*

Perhaps the greatest example of what Lynn Wood is talking about is Margaret Metayer. Not only did Margaret buy a home without taking gifts from anyone, but she did it as a single person and at the age of 45.

After renting all of her life, eight years ago Margaret realized that if she didn't get out of her apartment soon, she would never be able to buy something. So Margaret began saving her money in earnest five years ago after returning from a European vacation—a sort of farewell to frivolous spending trip. This was to be her last vacation to anywhere for awhile, as well as the start of a careful accounting of where all her money was going.

To help accumulate money faster, Margaret took on weekend and evening private nursing assignments on top of her full-time nursing job during the day at a hospital.

During this period of saving, she sat down and calculated how much she would need to buy the type of home she wanted. She didn't want a handyman special that needed another $20,000 worth of work. Realizing that homes in better condition cost more, she upped her budget and looked for even more ways to save. "I probably could have bought something 10 years ago," she said, "but I was having too good a time vacationing." Now she was making up for all those years she didn't put anything away.

She stopped going to stores just for entertainment sake. These are the trips on Saturday, when you have nothing better to do, and you go down to the local mall to kill a couple of hours wandering around window shopping. Of course, while you're at the mall, you have lunch and invariably end up buying things that seem like great bargains at the time, but that you really have six more of at home. Now, if Margaret needed something, she'd jot it down on a list, go to the store, buy it, and then immediately leave the premises. And whatever she did buy, she paid for in cash. Her credit cards were all stopped so that finance charges of 15 percent or more would not have to be paid.

The hardest part of the whole experience was finding a home within her $115,000 budget that she really liked and that didn't need thousands of dollars in work. She finally settled on an area, about an hour's train commute from her job, that had a number of homes selling within her price range. She also looked for a broker that she liked who she felt would aid her in her search.

After three years of saving, searching and agonizing, she found a three-bedroom home with a large kitchen and a big backyard for $110,000. "I liked the house when I saw it." She paid an engineer to inspect the premises and, after getting a clean bill of health from him, closed on the property and moved into her new home.

"I have no money in the bank now, but at least I have a house." It will probably be two or three years before she's back on her feet, because it's even harder to save after you've finally gotten your home. Expenses are high and there's so much to maintain. For example, she had just paid $400 to have her 75-foot by 200-foot backyard cleaned out.

She will continue doing extra weekend, private nursing work, and watching where her money goes. But despite the past and future sacrifices, "I'm enjoying it. I have to give myself credit. It's a great feeling knowing I did this and did it by myself. You just have to have faith. You have to believe you can do it, say you want it . . . and you will."

TIPS FROM FIRST-TIME HOMEBUYERS

1. Be persistent. Believe that you can buy a home and it will happen.

2. Start putting together a down payment as soon as you can. The bigger it is, the easier it will be to get a mortgage and the smaller your monthly mortgage payments will be.

3. If you're short on cash and handy, buy a home that needs work. But remember, fixing the home up will consume many weekends and evenings and put a drain on your weekly cash flow.

4. When shopping for a home, tell everyone you know that you're in the market and look everywhere. Don't limit your search to just one or two neighborhoods.

5. Ask yourself what you really need in both the house and neighborhood.

6. Be flexible and willing to make compromises.

7. Focus all energies on getting a home and scrimp, save, and cut back to get it.

8. If you find something you like, but it's priced just beyond your reach, make an offer you can afford. You'll be surprised what a seller—especially a desperate seller—is willing to accept.

9. If you use a real estate broker, use one you feel comfortable with and who will take the time to explain things to you. But don't rely strictly on the advice of the broker. Confer with other professionals such as an attorney and lenders.

10. Check into low-interest state-backed mortgages (detailed fully in Chapter 8).

Chapter 2

DETERMINING HOW MUCH HOUSE YOU CAN AFFORD

Chapter 1 has demonstrated that people just like you can—and have managed to—buy a first home even in the United States' most expensive markets.

So now you're ready! You want to go out there, take on the market and see which of the homes currently for sale in your area you can snag and close on. Your enthusiasm is admirable. But before you run out and start house hunting, you really need to determine how much home you can afford to buy.

"People literally go out and break their own hearts," said Paul Havemann, vice president of HSH Associates, a mortgage research firm. For instance, they may find a three-bedroom ranch overlooking a lake that they love. It has ample closets, a spacious kitchen and just about everything else they've been looking for in a home. But when the pair go to get financing, they learn their combined incomes can't afford the asking price of the property. What first-time buyers have to do before doing anything else, Havemann said, is either have a lender or real estate broker figure out how much house they can really afford to buy.

When you go to buy a TV set or other item, if you don't have the cash in your wallet, you charge it. With a home, when you're cash poor, you get a mortgage. And just as a bank issuing you a

Adrienne yearly gross ≈ 33,600   per month = 2750

Charlie   "   "   ≈ 33,000 $5500

33,000 / 66,600 ≈ $66,000   28% = $1540 ≈ $66,000

piece of plastic money imposes a credit limit based on your income, a mortgage lender will likewise impose a limit on you.

This limit is based on your income and calculated using two numbers that will haunt you throughout your home search: 28 and 36. What do these numbers mean?

According to Barbara Becker, a former mortgage company vice president, a lender won't allow any more than 28 percent of your monthly gross income to be used towards paying principal, interest, property taxes and home insurance. If you put less than 20 percent down, this 28 percent will also include the cost of private mortgage insurance, or PMI. Principal is the amount of the loan you've borrowed and is paid back monthly (although biweeklies do exist) for the duration of the loan term, with 15, 20 and 30 years being common terms. Interest is what the lender charges for the privilege of borrowing the firm's money. This will be added to each monthly payment. Property taxes are what you fork over to your local government municipalities to pay for services such as garbage pickup, schools, snow removal and items that differ from area to area. These taxes can be paid directly to the government municipality by the borrower. However, many lenders like to pay these bills directly and incorporate the cost as part of the monthly mortgage payment (more on how this works in a later chapter). Home insurance (protection for your home, much like the insurance you buy to protect your car) can be paid directly by the borrower to the insurance company or tacked on by the lender to your monthly mortgage payments.

The average lender usually wants the borrower to put 20 or 25 percent down when buying a home. This is so a borrower has a cash stake in the home (called equity) and won't walk away from it the first time some kind of financial problem pops up. While certain lenders won't budge from this rule, there are banks willing to make loans with only 10 or even 5 percent down. But because the lender is taking a greater risk, said Jack Eleford, a past president of the National Association of Mortgage Brokers, the firm will want you to take out private mortgage insurance.

PMI is protection for the lender in case you default. But the premium—to every homebuyer's delight—is paid by YOU, the

Private Morgage Insurance

-$5000

borrower. The cost is up to 1 percent of the mortgage amount borrowed, payable upon closing on the home. Additional monthly premiums are due thereafter, paid as part of your monthly mortgage, until the loan balance drops below 80 percent of the home's value, explained Hal Levine. Levine, a vice president with Commonwealth Mortgage Assurance Company, a PMI firm, noted that the PMI monthly fee is based on the size of the mortgage and PMI company used. Some lenders, however, use the guidelines set by the Federal Home Loan Mortgage Corporation (Freddie Mac) and the Federal National Mortgage Association (Fannie Mae), secondary markets that buy loans made by other lending institutions. Their guidelines allow PMI to be dropped after two years if the principal falls below 80 percent of the home's current market value.

Some lenders around the country self-insure their mortgages instead of using an outside PMI company. Instead of a monthly premium, the interest rate may be about 1/2 percent higher than the rate charged on loans requiring a minimum of 20 percent down.

Which brings us back to 28/36. Remember that 28 is the percentage of your monthly gross income that can go towards principal, interest, property taxes and PMI. The latter number, Becker explained, is the total amount of debt the lender will allow you to have including the total mortgage payment you'll be taking on. This total debt can be no more than 36 percent of your gross income.

Debt is considered car payments, unpaid credit card balances or outstanding student loans, among other things. But, Levine pointed out, if a loan has less than 10 months to go on it, debt usually won't be figured in. Lenders said that when looking at income, it didn't matter whether borrowers were married or unrelated. What did matter when qualifying people was the total income of the parties signing the mortgage agreement.

The main thing lenders are looking for when making a loan, especially one with a 5 or 10 percent down payment, Becker said, is "squeaky clean credit and stability of income." But lenders like Gerard Troha, district manager for Continental Capital, a mortgage banker, pointed out that not all mortgages made are cast in the

28/36 mold. Some lenders, as well as new mortgage programs introduced by the secondary market, allow either number or both numbers to be higher, as will be seen when specific types of mortgages are discussed in later chapters. In addition, some state and federally backed government loans, such as Veteran's Administration mortgages, allow higher ratios.

The current trend among lenders is to do whatever they can to make financing more accessible for qualified first-time buyers. The only hard and fast rule about mortgages is that guidelines are always changing, so it pays to keep up with what's going on by reading the real estate section of your local newspaper each day and paying attention to radio and news broadcasts.

CREDIT RATINGS

One common mistake first-time buyers make, said Bob Herrick, owner/broker of Century 21 Herrick Realty, is not realizing how important their credit rating is. Maybe you were late in making a couple of car payments last year. You ended up paying a late fee when you finally got around to remembering to send in the bill. What first-time buyers don't realize, Herrick said, "is that those late charges can come back to haunt you when you go to apply for a mortgage."

According to Herrick, if a lender doing a credit check finds you failed to pay a couple of car payments on time, a red flag goes up in his mind. It shows that you might be a bad credit risk. You can end up either being turned down for the loan or asked to pay a much higher interest rate than someone with good credit.

Mortgage lenders, Eleford added, want to see that a borrower has a history of paying back the loans taken out in the past. The lenders examine whether there are any defaults on your record or suits resulting in judgments levied by past creditors.

If you've never borrowed money, some experts recommend taking out a small loan when you begin to think about buying a

DO YOUR OWN CREDIT CHECK before HAND

house and then paying it back promptly. This helps establish a good credit rating.

But sometimes there can be mistakes on the credit reports lenders use, said Havemann. This is one reason lenders are required to make credit checks using two different credit reporting companies. There are a lot of people with similar names around the country. They are cross-referenced by social security number, but even so, it's not uncommon for wrong information to end up in the wrong file. As Havemann noted, someone with the same name as you may have terrible credit and be unable to get a loan to buy a $50 dollhouse, let alone a $50,000 condominium. This is why Havemann and others recommend doing your own credit check BEFORE you apply for a loan. The process is simple. A credit report costs about $20, Havemann said, with firms performing this service listed in the phone book under "Credit Reporting Agencies."

According to one of the country's leading accounting firms, a few of the major credit-reporting agencies in the United States are:

- Equifax Inc., 5505 Peachtree-Dunwoody, Suite 600, Atlanta, GA 30358 (phone 404-885-8000).

- TRW, Inc., Consumer Relations Office, Orange, CA (phone 714-991-6000).

- Trans-Union Information Co., P.O. Box 9119001, Chicago, IL 60611 (phone 312-645-6008).

Check your local Yellow Pages for additional credit-reporting companies.

If a mistake is found in your credit report and you can prove it, it must be changed, Havemann said. If the mistake is not changed, by federal law you can have your own statement explaining the mistake amended to the report. One other thing worth noting is that if you applied for a loan and were turned down for poor credit, federal law says you are entitled to a free copy of your credit report from the lender who rejected the loan.

Another check a lender will make is to see how promptly you pay your rent each month if you are currently residing in a rental apartment, Becker said. Lenders also look at promptness in paying phone, electric and other monthly bills.

One piece of advice heard over and over is that once you have established a good credit rating, you should pay up all your credit cards, pay off your car loan and eliminate as much debt as you can before applying for the mortgage. This shows the lender that more of your money will be available for paying your monthly mortgage.

INCOME AND OCCUPATION

When it comes to how much money you earn, lenders are not only looking at the bottom line, Eleford explained, but how long you've worked at your present job. Lenders usually want to see three or more years at the same job. It shows stability.

However, if you did switch jobs, this can work in your favor too. If you went from a low-paying job to a higher-paying one over the last few years, it shows you are advancing in salary and position, Eleford said.

According to Levine, chances are the lender will contact your employer and try to find out about your chances for a raise, your opportunities for advancement and whether or not your particular division or skills will be phased out in the company. Cash gifts from a relative can be used to help make your down payments. However, when putting 10 percent down, lenders say they would not allow more than 5 percent of the money to come from a gift. On a 5-percent-down loan, Levine said, no gifts can be used. All of the down payment must come directly from the borrower.

One other factor looked at, according to a now retired lender, is whether the home you're buying is a two-family residence and one-half of the property will be rented out. That rent will be taken into consideration when calculating how much loan you can afford. But, pointed out real estate broker Bonnie Lazar, you have to make sure the residence is considered a legal two-family home within the community where it is located. Lenders won't consider the rental income if the apartment is not recognized as legal, since at any point it could be eliminated—if a neighbor complained or local government officials cracked down—and the income would be gone, making it more difficult for you to meet your monthy mortgage payment.

OTHER FACTORS EXAMINED

When determining whether or not to make a loan, Becker said, "a lender uses any other information he or she can get his or her hands on." Her former firm, like others, examines other investments the borrower may have that contribute to income. Also looked at is whether the borrower receives any stock dividends, money from a trust or any other regularly scheduled cash flowing into his or her hands that can be counted on to help pay the monthly mortgage.

The general rule of thumb for determining how large a mortgage you can carry is usually twice your annual salary, said Jerry LaSurdo, former chairman of the board for Green Point Savings Bank, who noted, "You're looking for trouble if you go beyond that."

$= \$132,000$

Despite warnings like LaSurdo's, many first-time buyers, Herrick said, "are pushing to the limit what they can buy." But push too much and you may get in over your head. Lenders realize this and, as a result of the recent rash of savings and loans failures, many lenders are looking longer and harder before making mortgages, Havemann said. The slower appreciation in home prices—as compared to the 20 percent or more annual increases seen in some areas of the country during the last decade—is also making lenders more conservative, he added. Should the borrower default on his or her loan, the lender wants to make sure there's enough equity in the house that the institution will be able to recover the outstanding loan balance.

And beyond the lender, if PMI is required, the company issuing that insurance also has to approve the loan, Levine pointed out. That company is underwriting the mortgage, saying to the lender that if it fails, they will make up any loss to you. Giving the lender this guarantee, Levine said, means the company also wants to examine the buyer's financial profile to make sure he or she is a worthy credit risk. If the PMI company doesn't like what it sees, even if the lender approves your application, the loan won't be made. Likewise, because so many loans are bought by the secondary market (like Fannie Mae and Freddie Mac), their guidelines have to be followed too. If a lender ignores one of the rules, and what he's done isn't caught until after selling the loan, the buyer of that mortgage will require that the lender take the loan back, said Stephen Sorahan, president of Sterling Mortgage Corp., a mortgage broker. For this reason, all underwriting rules are followed very carefully. Even a bank that keeps loans in its own portfolio will still follow Fannie and Freddie's guidelines in case the lender decides to sell the loan at a later date.

So, in effect, what the experts are saying is that your application has to meet the approval of not only the lender you're directly dealing with, but also the secondary market and a PMI company.

INTEREST RATES

Of course, one important factor figuring into how much house you can afford will be the rate of interest being charged on the borrowed money. As the chart accompanying this chapter shows, the lower the interest rate, the more money you can afford to borrow because your monthly payments will be smaller.

For example, $100,000 borrowed at 9 percent on a 30-year fixed-rate term requires monthly payments of $805. Increase that interest rate 1 percent and the payment rises to $878—a difference of $73 each and every month, or $876 a year! Experts have said that each time mortgage interest rates rise by 1 percent, about 1.5 million homebuyers get shut out of the market.

The trick, of course, is trying to borrow when interest rates are at their lowest. This requires keeping an eye on the economy and constantly paying attention to what rates are doing. Most daily newspapers list current mortgage interest rates at least once a week, usually in their real estate sections. It pays to follow how rates are moving.

And if you have been following rates, you will have noticed that in the first quarter of 1993, they hit a 21-year low. As stated in the introduction, this has allowed a greater number of people to become first-time buyers. How long rates will remain low is anybody's guess.

FIGURING OUT HOW MUCH YOU CAN AFFORD

So how much home can you afford?

You can use Jerry LaSurdo's simple formula of twice your annual income. Or you can follow a slightly more complicated, but somewhat more precise, formula compiled from different accountants as well as Paul Havemann. Make a list of all your regular income (including everything discussed before). Multiply this times .28 (the first number of that 28/36 formula). Next, add up the monthly property taxes in the area in which you are planning to buy a home (a broker is helpful for getting this) and the amount of homeowner's insurance payments (call a home insurance agent for this figure), along with monthly installment payments you now carry on a car or credit cards. Subtract this from the income figure.

Then multiply your monthly gross income by .36. Subtract from this your monthly real estate tax, homeowner's insurance payments, monthly installment payments and PMI payments (this number can be gotten from a lender or real estate broker). The lesser of the two amounts tells you approximately how much in the way of a monthly mortgage payment you will be able to carry.

A tip: Many brokers and lenders can calculate this for you on computers in their offices, provided you supply them with fair and accurate information, Herrick emphasized.

TAX BENEFITS

Once a person roughly calculates how much he can spend on mortgage payments, by either going to a lender or broker or figuring it out himself, he get nervous about whether he wants to commit that much of his income every month to housing, said Donald Henig, a former president of the National Association of Mortgage Brokers and president of his own firm, Island Mortgage Network. Some people really want to buy a home, but they don't want to see every spare piece of change they own going into paying for it. But what many people forget, he said, are the tax benefits that home ownership brings. Both mortgage interest and property taxes are deductible from federal and state tax returns (if your state has an income tax). This, in effect, is giving you more money to spend on housing each month. Herrick noted that in their excitement to sell a home, brokers often forget to remind the buyer that deductions for mortgage interest and property taxes will increase the buyer's take-home pay.

To figure out how much more money you'll have to throw into your housing budget, take your current tax return and recalculate it figuring in deductions for mortgage interest and property taxes—using schedule A on your federal return and basing it on the house you are considering purchasing. After doing the calculations, divide the tax savings by 52. This will give you an idea of the extra money home ownership will add to your weekly budget, Henig said.

One other thing you should do after buying the home is go to the payroll department where you work and increase the number of deductions you are declaring, Lazar said. The more deductions you put down, the less money will be taken from your pay. Calculate the number of deductions based on the weekly savings you'll have from home ownership. "Why not get the tax benefits monthly rather than at the end of the year?" Lazar emphasized. Instead of getting a refund weeks after you've filed your income tax return on April 15, by increasing your payroll deduction, you can latch onto that money every week and use it to pay your monthly mortgage payment. Noted Henig, it is better that the money go to work for you than sit in Uncle Sam's coffers. Mortgage interest and property tax deductions reduce some people's federal taxes so much that he knows of cases where people with large mortgages have actually increased their payroll deduction withholdings to 12 or 13 dependents, returning them a nice piece of change each week!

MORTGAGE PAYMENT FACTORS
(per 1,000)

Int. Rate (%)	15 years	20 years	25 years	30 years
6.000	8.44	7.17	6.45	6.00
6.125	8.51	7.24	6.52	6.08
6.250	8.58	7.31	6.60	6.16
6.375	8.65	7.39	6.68	6.24
6.500	8.72	7.46	6.76	6.33
6.625	8.78	7.53	6.83	6.40
6.750	8.85	7.61	6.91	6.49
6.875	8.92	7.68	6.99	6.57
7.000	8.99	7.76	7.07	6.66
7.125	9.06	7.83	7.15	6.74
7.250	9.13	7.91	7.23	6.83
7.375	9.20	7.98	7.31	6.91
7.500	9.28	8.06	7.39	7.00
7.625	9.35	8.14	7.48	7.08
7.750	9.42	8.21	7.56	7.17
7.875	9.49	8.29	7.64	7.26
8.000	9.56	8.37	7.72	7.34
8.125	9.63	8.45	7.81	7.43
8.250	9.71	8.53	7.89	7.52
8.375	9.78	8.60	7.97	7.61
8.500	9.85	8.68	8.06	7.69
8.625	9.93	8.76	8.14	7.78
8.750	10.00	8.84	8.23	7.87
8.875	10.07	8.92	8.31	7.96
9.000	10.15	9.00	8.40	8.05
9.125	10.22	9.08	8.48	8.14
9.250	10.30	9.16	8.57	8.23
9.375	10.37	9.24	8.65	8.32
9.500	10.45	9.33	8.74	8.41
9.625	10.52	9.41	8.83	8.50
9.750	10.60	9.49	8.92	8.60
9.875	10.67	9.57	9.00	8.69

cont'd

Int. Rate (%)	15 years	20 years	25 years	30 years
10.000	10.75	9.66	9.09	8.78
10.125	10.83	9.74	9.18	8.87
10.250	10.90	9.82	9.27	8.97
10.375	10.98	9.90	9.35	9.05
10.500	11.05	9.98	9.44	9.15
10.625	11.13	10.07	9.53	9.24
10.750	11.21	10.15	9.62	9.33
10.875	11.29	10.24	9.71	9.43
11.000	11.37	10.32	9.80	9.52
11.125	11.44	10.41	9.89	9.62
11.250	11.52	10.49	9.98	9.71
11.375	11.60	10.58	10.07	9.81
11.500	11.68	10.66	10.16	9.90
11.625	11.76	10.75	10.26	10.00
11.750	11.84	10.84	10.35	10.09
11.875	11.92	10.92	10.44	10.19
12.000	12.00	11.01	10.53	10.29
12.125	12.08	11.10	10.62	10.38
12.250	12.16	11.19	10.72	10.48
12.375	12.24	11.27	10.81	10.58
12.500	12.33	11.36	10.90	10.67
12.625	12.41	11.45	11.00	10.77
12.750	12.49	11.54	11.09	10.87
12.875	12.57	11.63	11.18	10.96
13.000	12.65	11.72	11.28	11.06
13.125	12.73	11.80	11.37	11.16
13.250	12.82	11.89	11.47	11.26
13.375	12.90	11.98	11.56	11.36
13.500	12.98	12.07	11.66	11.46

Chapter 3

DETERMINING WHERE TO LIVE

If finances didn't have to be taken into consideration, most of us would probably choose to live wherever our fantasies took us—on a farm, near the water, or in a penthouse apartment overlooking a major city.

But dollars and cents are a reality for most of us when buying a home. And when it comes to picking a neighborhood, the oldest real estate principle of all comes into play—that of location! Location! Location! The more desirable the area, the more homes will probably cost. Nearness to the water, type of view, and proximity to major centers of employment are just some of the factors that contribute to driving up the cost of housing. Likewise, a neighborhood away from everything, right behind a factory complex or in an area that has become rundown or has a mediocre school district can decrease the price of housing.

In determining where to live, the first thing you should consider is how far you're willing to travel from your new home to work each morning, said Lazar, a former president of the Long Island Board of Realtors in New York. Since most of us spend at least five days a week going to and from our places of employment, you have to honestly look at yourself and examine your personal stamina of how far your body can tolerate commuting every morning and afternoon. Some people can do two hours each way without even thinking twice about it. They can live in a remote suburb, far away from the major city they work in and not mind the long commute. On the other hand, others are drained and miserable after only traveling a half-hour.

Once you figure your commutation tolerance, from there, personal tastes set in. If you have kids, schools become important. If you love the outdoors and gardening, then you may want to be in an area that enables you to buy a home sitting on a bit of property so you can plant a garden.

Sometimes, when couples walk into Lazar's office and tell her what they want in the way of neighborhood, she finds the wife listing one set of criteria and the husband another. It's as if each were buying a separate home instead of one together. Her advice to couples: before going out to house hunt, sit down and put together a list of items that you both want your neighborhood to have. In fact, everyone buying a home should do this—arrange the list with what you want most at the top and then place the second most important item next and so on down the line until everything you want is jotted down on that piece of paper in descending order.

One mistake many brokers find first-time buyers making when coming up with a neighborhood is concentrating too much on the quality of schools in an area. Yes, good schools do help sell a home in the future. But they often drive up the price when your initially purchasing a property. If a young couple buying their first home doesn't have any children yet, then the quality of the schools shouldn't be of prime concern. Even if the couple ends up having a child several years after moving in, explained Linda Albo, owner of her own ERA real estate office, by the time that boy or girl is ready to be enrolled in kindergarten, it's more than likely that the family will probably be moving on to their next home. Statistics show that seven years is the average length of time a family spends in a home.

First-time buyers Caroline Trautmann and her fiancee Edward Wills, Jr., found themselves wrestling with this quality of schools problem. They had found a brand new home that they liked, and also could afford, in an area that pleased them for the most part. However, the one thing that did bother them was that the schools in the district were not the best. They were to be married and close on the home seven months after signing the contract of sale. Despite the less-than-great schools, Caroline said that she and Edward went ahead with the purchase because she figured that at her age, 25, and the financial stage in life that the two were in, they most likely wouldn't be having a child for at least four or five years. It would then be another five years before that child would be ready to attend kindergarten. By then, she said, the school system could be entirely different from what it is today, especially since the area was enjoying an increase in population and development.

What buyers have to ask themselves, said broker Herrick, is how long they expect to live in the house. Despite what statistics say, if a couple sees themselves staying a long time and expanding the home as their family grows, then the quality of the school district becomes more important.

However, the idea of a first home, Lazar said, "should be something that satisfies your needs and allows you to build up enough equity so that you can go on to the next stage." It shouldn't be viewed as something that you will live in for the rest of your life. As you grow older and your family expands and job status changes, so will your housing needs. With an increase in income and a change in job position, the type of home you'll need later on in life will most likely change from what you need today. Years from now, you'll probably want more amenities, more space, a different locale, and other things that your income isn't able to afford in this first home.

A Neighborhood Like Mom and Dad's

Which brings us to another common mistake first-time buyers often make and that's in trying to find a home in the same type of neighborhood their parents are currently living in. Yes, the area mom and dad currently reside in is wonderful. Everyone has well-groomed lawns, it's in a quiet part of town, and shopping and the major highways are not too far away.

But in all likelihood, your parents moved into this lovely neighborhood a number of years ago and only paid a fraction of what that home is worth today. In some areas of the country, such as California and the Northeast, in the mid-eighties homes were increasing in value by as much as 20 and 30 percent a year. Because of this appreciation (and just general appreciation tied to inflation in most areas), a number of people who bought their homes years ago probably couldn't afford to purchase the very home they're living in today, numerous brokers pointed out.

However, noted Albo, "there's no harm in looking in the neighborhood your parents currently are living in." You may be a doctor just out of medical school and have the income to afford a lesser house in the area. Or you may find a desperate seller offering a great deal. Anything is possible. Once you know how much house you can afford, there's nothing wrong with looking in any neighborhood if it meets the qualifications you set down on your laundry list. Likewise, not every parent traded-up from one house to another every five years. Some parents may still be living in a very affordable area where their offspring could easily buy a home.

For the most part, however, most brokers are in agreement that the majority of first-time buyers will probably find that they just can't come up with the dollars needed to buy in the locale their parents currently reside.

ZEROING IN ON THE RIGHT NEIGHBORHOOD

So, how do you zero in on the neighborhood that's right for you? "It's a decision that's personal in nature," said broker Robert Olita.

First Northern Mortgagee Corp., a mortgage banker, suggests starting with all the things you both like and dislike about the place you're currently renting a home in.

Want specifics?

If swimming is one of your main interests, said Marie Costello, owner of her own self-named brokerage firm, then you'll want to find a neighborhood that's near a lake or the ocean. If this location is beyond your buying power, then look for an area that has some kind of community pool nearby. For others, fishing, sailing or tennis might be very important to their lives and having access to places where you can partake in these sports, not far from home, is of major importance. For still others, the proximity to supermarkets, a giant mall, or some other form of shopping is essential. If you don't drive, having these within walking distance (or within access of public transportation) begins to play a more important role.

For example, a single man in the process of buying his first home was moving from a rental apartment in a large city where he had grown accustomed to walking to a nearby bakery every morning for freshly-baked bread and pastries. When it came time to finding a home in the suburbs, high on his list of things he wanted in the area was a bakery at least within walking or driving distance of his home.

Tour the Area

Once you've sat down and decided what the neighborhood you want to buy in should have, the best way to get a feel for certain areas as you shop around is to spend time in the communities, said Charles W. McGill, owner of two real estate offices.

Broker Bruce Torrani, owner of Century 21 Fisher-Friendly, agrees and suggested that a person grab a good map of the area and drive around. Look at how the homes are kept up, the types of stores in the area, and the proximity of police and fire departments to the neighborhood. Every so often, get out of your car and walk around. Have lunch in some of the local restaurants. Walk into the shops. Talk to store owners. Buy a copy of the local paper to see what's going on.

Also stop and talk to the people out raking their leaves, watering their front lawns, and walking their dogs, McGill said. Ask them what they think of the area and what they like and dislike about living there. If you have cultural interests, ask if there are any museums, concert halls, or movies nearby. Talking to people in the area is essential. He recalled the time he was looking for a home in Florida. During one of his neighborhood drive-throughs and chats, he discovered that a new sewage treatment plant was about to be built on vacant land near where he was seriously considering buying a house. This made him look elsewhere.

If you do have children, said Steven I. Lieber, president of a property management firm, hang around the neighborhood when the school buses are dropping kids off. Talk to the parents and ask what they think about the schools.

In addition, said attorney Myron Cohen, "go down and visit the school when it's open." You'll be able to get a first-hand look at the students enrolled, classroom sizes, and condition of the building. Also speak with some administrators and ask about curriculum and what percentage of the students drop out and what percentage go on to college. You might also inquire what awards the school has recently won.

If you have a child that excels in a certain sport, said Costello, make sure the school has a team competing in that activity. Costello recalled a couple whose son was an excellent swimmer who had won all sorts of awards on his last school's swim team. In showing the family around, she immediately had to eliminate some homes because the school district didn't have a pool or swim team.

Likewise, Cohen said, if you have a handicapped child, look to see how the school is set up to accommodate these students and what the curriculum is for them.

If religion is important to your family, Costello said, visit the houses of worship in the community and talk with the rabbi, priest, or minister. Attend a religious service and talk with some of the parishioners. When she was considering a move several years ago, "every week we went to a different church until we found one that felt comfortable." The clergy is also a good source for directing any general questions you might have about the area.

Crime has also become a major factor for many when deciding where to move. If you're unsure about how safe an area is, check with the local police station. One woman who had been searching for a first home for a number of years thought she had finally found an apartment in a co-op that she could afford. She liked the building and the unit very much. However, because she had crazy working hours, where she found herself coming and going at all hours of the day and night, safety of the neighborhood became a major item on her home-shopping list.

When she checked with the local police about how safe the surrounding area this co-op bargain was in, she learned that the rate of car thefts in the building's parking lot was high. This was the result of a low-income housing project located not too far from the building, the proliferation of drug sales in the area, and a fairly high crime rate. The woman immediately fell out of love with the bargain-priced co-op and continued searching elsewhere.

Which brings up one fear that some people have, and that's buying into an integrated neighborhood. Some people have certain built-in prejudices and only feel comfortable living in an area populated by people of their own race, color, or ethnic background, broker Herrick said. But there are terrific and safe integrated neighborhoods all over the country. Herrick finds that some buyers "give up a radical amount of house just to live in a non-integrated neighborhood." Instead of getting three-bedrooms and 2,000 square feet of living space for $120,000 in an integrated neighborhood, some buyers would rather spend $140,000 for only two-bedrooms and 1,200 square feet of space to be in a non-integrated area. This is a personal decision that only a buyer can decide for himself. But if the area is well-maintained, fits your needs, and can offer you more house for less money, then it's a home and area you should seriously consider.

Property Taxes and Beyond

Another item about a neighborhood you should check into is the property taxes. These dollars collected by the local municipality is a factor of life that helps pay for community services. But if you're on a tight budget, a big rise in taxes from one year to the next could make the difference as to whether or not you can afford the home. It may be worth your time to check with appropriate city, town, or village agencies to find out what the property tax rates are. Also ask how much taxes have risen in the past 10 years and what they are expected to do in the future.

While visiting these government offices, you also may want to ask about zoning in the area. Certain areas will be zoned just for commercial properties (such as factories and office buildings), while others are zoned residential (for single-family homes and apartments). If there are large tracts of empty land in a neighborhood, finding out what they are zoned for is important. If zoned commercial, this could mean that instead of more homes going up, one day there could be a large factory rising on the site or even, as McGill found in the Florida neighborhood he was looking in, a sewage treatment plant.

A visit to the local chamber of commerce, McGill added, is also worth scheduling. Here you can learn about nearby recreation facilities and other local attractions as well as any annual events that might be held nearby or within the community. The chamber of commerce staff might also be able to answer any other questions you've come up with while riding around the area. (Whenever cruising a neighborhood, it's always smart to jot down questions you may have while they're still fresh in your mind.) If the chamber of commerce can't answer your questions, then they most likely will be able to point you in the direction of someone who can.

CHOOSING BETWEEN HOUSE OR LOCATION

After you've finally zeroed in on one or two neighborhoods and several homes, if you have to choose between one particular house and one particular location, Herrick said that there's one rule of thumb worth noting: you can always fix up a home. What you can't repair is the neighborhood or location. This doesn't mean that you shouldn't consider an area that has seen better days and is now coming back. Great bargains can be gotten in gentrifying neighborhoods (as these areas on the mend are called). This is discussed in greater detail in Chapter 5.

But if you're choosing between two homes and one of the houses is not as nice as the other, but it's located in a better area, you should probably pick the property that's better located. While you are buying this home for your own pleasure and enjoyment, it's nonetheless a first home that you'll be trying to build equity up in and sell one day down the road. Good location always helps sell a house faster.

You can redo a house to a certain extent, within the limitations of your budget, but you can't redo the location, added broker Albo. For example, you can't plant a field of 100-year-old pine trees if that happens to be the charm of one area over another.

LONG DISTANCE MOVES

Now, sometimes a person is moving hundreds of miles from where he or she is currently living. How do you cruise a different area every weekend you may be wondering?

First, read as much as you can about the area in trying to decide where you want to move. Often, it's a job that relocates you, so there's a smaller area to concentrate on. Next, stay in a hotel for as long as you can while visiting the new area, said broker Carl Riese, co-owner of Realty World Segal-Riese Associates. Then, proceed to make your neighborhood checks. If you can't zero in on an area to buy in immediately, the smartest thing to do may be to rent an apartment or house in the vicinity when you first arrive. After getting a feel for the area, then you can buy something.

If you don't want to waste money on rent, but think you have some inkling as to where you'd like to live, Riese advises to consider renting a home with the option to buy. This is where a portion of your rent each month goes towards the purchase price of the home. Other details about doing this are described in Chapter 9. But the advantage here is that it puts you on the road to owning while also giving you an out in case you later discover you either don't like the area or find some place that you prefer better.

**QUESTIONS YOU SHOULD ASK YOURSELF
ABOUT NEIGHBORHOODS
YOU ARE CONSIDERING BUYING IN:**

What is the longest period of time I am willing to commute to my job each day?

Will I be living here long enough to take advantage of the schools?

Since I have children, or believe I'll be using the area schools sometime in the near future, what is the reputation of the district?

What types of stores—such as supermarkets, bakeries, mega-malls, or small groupings of shops—are the ones I absolutely must have nearby?

Are the stores in the area in my income level or is the merchandise too expensive for me to be able to afford, meaning that I'll have to shop outside the neighborhood?

Are cultural facilities important to me and if so, how far are they from the area and what types are there?

Is public transportation important to me and, if so, is it conveniently located to the neighborhood?

What are the community services—such as ambulance, fire, and police—like?

---

cont'd

What recreational sports are most important to me and are these facilities nearby?

Is there a house of worship in the area?

What is the crime rate in the area?

What are the property taxes like in this neighborhood and how much have they risen in the past 10 years and how much are they projected to rise in the future?

Are there big pieces of undeveloped property in the area and, if so, are these parcels zoned for commercial or residential use?

Do I prefer a rural or populated area?

Does the area have a reputation for fast or slow snow removal in the winter?

Is cable TV important to me and can homes in this area be hooked up to it?

What is the ethnic make-up of the community?

What is the cost of home insurance in the area?

Can I be happy living in this community?

Chapter 4

THE TYPE OF RESIDENCE THAT'S RIGHT FOR YOU

Once you've zeroed in on the neighborhood you think you want to settle down in, there's another choice you have to make—the type of house that you're going to buy.

Twenty years ago, when people moved on from their parents' home or a rental, it was usually to another single-family residence. But today, a first-time buyer can also purchase a unit in a condominium, a co-operative or a homeowner's association (also known as an HOA). You will also sometimes hear the term townhouse. This is a multi-level unit belonging to one owner and usually found in either a condominium or homeowner's association.

Having grown up in a single-family home, most people know that with this form of property you own title to both the land and the home. Whatever changes you want to make to the structure can be done subject to your own finances and sometimes local zoning (for example, some areas around the country won't let you build up more than a certain number or feet or build out past a certain point to the end of your property line).

But condos, co-ops and homeowner's associations are different forms of ownership, each having its own set of restrictions and rules. In general, each form is a community made up of many owners. Condos and co-ops can be highrises, with units stacked one on top of each other, or in a complex of several different buildings or even individual, detached units, much like a single-family home. An HOA can't be two separate owners living one on top of the other, explained Douglas Kleine, former director of research for the Community Associations Institute based in Alexandria, Virginia. It can be a multi-level townhouse, but each unit must sit directly on its own deeded ground. And while many may think that condos are the oldest form of the three types of ownership, the HOA is actually the granddaddy, dating back to the early 1800's, Kleine noted, adding that condos really didn't start appearing until the 1960's.

Today, it's estimated by the Community Associations Institute that one in eight Americans lives in some form of community (condo, HOA or co-op) governed by a board of directors. The board is made up of homeowners, watching over the community's finances. This body also sets and enforces rules and regulations for unit owners. This popularity has developed in part, Kleine said, because multi-owner dwellings usually cost less than a single-family home and require less maintenance on the part of the owner. There are, however, areas of the country where a condo or a co-op can now cost not only as much as single-family homes, but a great deal more.

EXAMINING THE DIFFERENCES IN OWNERSHIP

So what are the differences between a condo, a co-op and an HOA? Based on interviews with attorneys, brokers, insurers, association organizations and others, the chart below was put together to help you differentiate between the three forms of ownership as well as list the pros and cons of each:

What You Own

Condo: As with a single-family home, you receive a deed and own title to the unit. You also own a percentage of the common areas, such as the recreational facilities, sidewalks and laundry rooms. You may or may not own the land beneath your unit. In some associations, that land may belong to everyone in the community. You would have to check the offering plan or selling prospectus to be certain.

Co-op: What you are actually purchasing here are shares in a corporation—much like buying shares of stock in General Motors. The number of shares you own is based on the size of your unit. Instead of a deed, the association gives you a proprietary lease, which lists the rules of the co-operative and allows you to live in the unit. Besides the unit, your shares also give you part ownership of all of the common areas in the building or complex, such as the recreational facilities, hallways and land beneath the co-op.

HOA: This type of ownership is similar to that of a condo. You receive title to your unit and usually to the land beneath it, as well as to the back and front yard area surrounding your unit. You may also own a portion of the common areas, such as the recreational facilities. The offering plan or association's bylaws will spell out exactly what you own outright and what you share.

What You Must Maintain

Condo: You are responsible for everything from the sheetrock in (in other words, the interior of the unit, including the floors, the appliances and your possessions). Water pipes and electric wiring found behind the sheetrock is the association's responsibility unless, when redoing a unit, you change or upgrade the wiring or plumbing. These items then become your responsibility. There are sometimes variations to this; check the condo's offering plan.

As for the exterior, the association will maintain this as well as cut your lawn, clear your sidewalks of snow in the winter and maintain the streets.

Co-op: As with a condo, you are responsible for everything from the sheetrock in. Water pipes and electric wiring, found behind the walls, are the association's responsibility. Some co-ops do, however, make the owner responsible for the piping and wiring if they are changed or upgraded during a renovation done by the unit owner. Others make you responsible for water pipes and electrical wiring no matter what. Check the proprietary lease or offering plan for each party's exact responsibilities. The exterior is also maintained by the association.

HOA: Owners are responsible for maintaining the building and its interior. Sometimes, exterior maintenance is provided by the association. Usually, maintenance for all common areas, such as recreational facilities and sidewalks, is provided by the association. Again, check the offering plan or association bylaws.

Property Taxes

Condo: A unit owner pays his or her own property taxes directly to the municipality.

Co-op: Property taxes are included as part of the monthly maintenance fee (see below for what else this fee includes).

HOA: Property taxes are paid directly to the municipality by the unit owner.

Monthly Maintenance Fees

Condos: Because the association is maintaining your lawn and other common areas, it needs money to foot these bills. It gets this money by charging each owner a monthly maintenance fee (also sometimes called a common charge). The amount of the fee is usually based on the size of the unit; the bigger the unit, the higher your fee will be. How this fee is determined will be spelled out in the prospectus. When budgeting your expenses, it's safe to assume the maintenance fee will go up each year. In general, however, condo maintenance fees are lower than those for co-ops.

Co-op: As with a condo, co-op owners will have to pay a monthly maintenance fee to cover the association's expenses. However, the monthly fees in a co-op are much higher because they usually include property taxes and the cost of carrying an underlying mortgage on the building or complex itself. This mortgage usually comes about as the result of a conversion (of a rental building into a co-op) and of the developer placing a mortgage on the building and passing it on to the owners. The mortgage on the building may also be the result of the co-op board taking out a mortgage to help pay for major repairs to the property (such as the installation of new windows or a new heating system) instead of assessing each shareholder a specific amount. A condo is real property. Each owner can mortgage his or her own property, but the common areas cannot have an underlying mortgage placed on them by the board. Repairs must be covered through an assessment of each owner or by building up what's known as a reserve fund, where a small percentage of each owner's maintenance fee is placed each month. A co-op will also try to build up a reserve fund so that, should a major repair come, it will not have to assess owners a special fee or put an additional mortgage on the building.

HOA: A monthly maintenance fee will also have to be paid here, but it may be the lowest of the three forms of ownership depending on the types of services offered by the association. If exterior maintenance of the unit, as well as lawn cutting and snow removal around the unit, are not included, maintenance fees will be quite low. Here too, the monthly fee is spelled out in the offering plan. In nearly all instances, the maintenance fee will be the same amount for every unit owner regardless of the home's size.

Board of Directors

Condo: To look after common areas in a condo there will be a board of directors made up of unit owners. The bylaws of the condo will spell out the powers that the board has as well as how many homeowners will make up the board. It is usually comprised of five, seven or nine homeowners, one acting as president and another as vice-president, with others holding such offices as treasurer and recording secretary.

Co-op: As with a condo, there is a board of directors to look after the common areas of the co-op and to set rules. In general, a co-op has many more rules and restrictions than a condo. The board can decide to restrict everything from allowing pets in the building to requiring that children not be allowed to play on the grounds. The board is made up of unit owners. All rules are spelled out either in the association's bylaws or the proprietary lease each shareholder receives.

HOA: There is also a board of directors to look after the common areas of the HOA and set policy for the community. As with a condo, there are fewer restrictions than in a co-op. Rules will be spelled out in the bylaws.

Right to Rent the Unit

Condo: Owners usually can rent their units out, but some condo boards will exercise what's known as the right of first refusal. This means that the tenant the owner has selected to occupy his or her unit must be interviewed by the condo board. If the board doesn't like the tenant, it can turn that person or couple down. However, the association must then pay the owner of the condo unit the agreed-upon rent (or find its own tenant to put in the unit) for the duration of the lease that was being offered the perspective tenant.

Co-op: Many co-ops don't allow shareholders to rent their units. If they do, the board has the right to turn the tenant down for any reason, other than discriminatory ones, without explanation to the unit owner. When the real estate market is slow, making it harder to find a buyer and sell the unit, some boards ease up on their "no-subletting" policies and allow unit owners to rent their apartments out.

HOA: You usually can rent your unit as you see fit.

Selling Your Unit

Condo: You can sell your unit to anyone you want, whenever you want. Some condo boards, however, do exercise their right of first refusal. If the buyer is turned down by the board, the association must then purchase the unit from the condo owner at the price that the owner and his or her buyer have agreed upon. The board will then try to get its own buyer for the unit. This is done when the board feels the person purchasing is of questionable character (such as a suspected drug dealer) or will not be able to pay the monthly maintenance fee.

Co-op: The board can turn down a buyer for any reason without giving an explanation. The only exceptions are those based on discrimination. But experts said that proving that a turn-down was based on discrimination is difficult. The board makes its decision behind closed doors and doesn't have to reveal to anyone why the prospective buyer was rejected. Government officials, however, in some states that have co-ops have been paying closer attention to complaints lodged by qualified minority buyers who have been turned down.

HOA: Units can be sold whenever and to whomever the owner wants.

Making Changes to Your Unit

Condo: Owners can do what they want to the interior, but the board may restrict what can be done to the exterior. For example, the board may say no decks are allowed or that all units must be painted the same color or use the same type of window design. This is all being done, in theory, to maintain property values.

Co-op: Any interior remodeling must usually be approved by the board. Some co-op boards don't require approval if only minor work is being done, such as replacing kitchen cabinets. But almost every co-op will require approval when walls are being taking taken down or pipes being moved. If the board doesn't like what's being done, it can turn the design down, provided it's not on unreasonable grounds. For example, if board members believe that relocating kitchen plumbing will result in leaks to the units below, the remodeling project will be rejected. Likewise, the board can restrict what a shareholder may do to the exterior of the unit, such as by not allowing an existing deck to be enclosed or a new one to be built.

HOA: Owners can do what they want to the interiors, but may find restrictions as to what they can do to the exterior.

Other Restrictions

Condo: There are usually few other restrictions, although the condo board may impose some house rules such as hours that loud music may be played in the unit. All rules and restrictions are found in the association's bylaws or offering plan.

Co-op: The co-op board can impose any restrictions it sees fit, from not allowing pets to requiring that front doors be painted a certain color. Many highrise co-ops often require that a certain percentage of the floors in the unit be carpeted to keep noise levels down. This is the most restrictive form of ownership, with rules found in the proprietary lease.

HOA: There are usually few restrictions. Any that have been implemented will be in the association's bylaws.

Buying Into Each

Condo: Your ability to buy into a condo development will depend solely on your finances, with the one exception being the condo board's right of first refusal. A board can turn you down, although experts agree this seldom happens because most associations don't have the money to purchase units. If the unit is in a brand-new condominium development, then there is no board to contend with because you are buying directly from the builder (called the sponsor). The board begins to form as more people move in.

Co-op: To buy into an existing co-op, you will have to supply any and all financial records required by the co-op board. This can include everything from W-2 forms to past federal and state income tax returns. Because of the recession, boards are paying even closer attention to a person's ability to pay not only the mortgage on the unit, but also the monthy maintenance charge. You will also have to be interviewed by the board.

Some co-ops require that buyers pay for a certain percentage of the unit (or shares) in cash. For example, some buildings in New York City require cash payment of anywhere from 50 to 100 percent of the unit or shares; little or no mortgage is allowed.

After going through the interview and scrutinization, you can be turned down by the board for any reason. The one exception is in a new co-op, where you purchase your shares or unit directly from the developer (or sponsor) with no board approval necessary. You can then join the board and be one of the people setting the initial rules future owners will have to follow (there will, however, already be some rules built into the offering plan by the developer).

When going for a mortgage, or shareholder's loan, as financing on a co-op is sometimes called, you may find that the interest rate on these loans will be anywhere from 1/4 to 1/2 percent higher than mortgages for a condo or a single-family home.

HOA: It's as simple to buy into one of these as a single-family home.

Which Is the Best Form of Ownership for You as a First-Time Buyer?

Condo: If you want the freedom to sell your unit whenever you want, but want someone to maintain the outside of your unit, then stick with a condo, advise experts such as attorney Jeffrey C. Daniels, a partner with the law firm of Daniels & Daniels.

Co-op: If there's a great concern on your part about controlling who lives in your complex or building, a co-op is for you, said attorney Stuart Saft, a partner with the law firm Wolf Haldenstein Adler Freeman & Herz. But be aware that because the co-op can turn your buyer down when you go to sell your shares at a future date, this could delay your sale. Another problem co-op buyers are finding, especially in the New York City metropolitan area, is that a lot of rental buildings that were converted into co-ops are having financial difficulties. Some sponsors have not been able to pay the monthly maintenance on the unsold units they still hold and have been foreclosed upon by lenders. Before buying a co-op, have a lawyer examine the financials of the building to make sure it is financially sound—for example, that it has a large enough reserve fund to pay for any needed capital improvements. As the economy picks up, the financial difficulties experienced by shaky co-ops should improve. But regardless of the economy, it's best to check the financials. One other reason some people don't feel comfortable in a co-op is the many rules placed on the building or complex by the board. "If you don't want the co-op board to run your life," Saft said, "you'll probably be happier in a condo."

HOA: Because the freedoms of an HOA are similar to those of a condo, reasons for owning one are the same.

Single-Family Home: Perhaps the greatest freedoms of all are with owning a single-family home. You can sell, rent, renovate and do whatever you want whenever you want. The only drawback is that you must maintain both the interior and exterior of the home yourself. However, some experts point out that for what some associations levy each month in the way of maintenance fees, you can hire a gardener to cut your lawn and employ someone in the winter to shovel your snow. One thing single-family homes don't have are community rooms, swimming pools and clubhouses to socialize in. Most condos and some co-ops offer these amenities.

Price

The initial price for a co-op will probably be lower than for a single-family home, HOA or condo because of the underlying mortgage the co-op building carries. But the co-op's underlying mortgage will result in a higher monthly maintenance fee. Thus your combined monthly costs for maintenance and your own mortgage could be as high as, or perhaps higher than, the costs of a condo or single-family home having an initially higher asking price.

THE NEED TO BE REALISTIC

Now, while you're trying to decide which type of ownership is right as your first home purchase, one other thing you'll need to determine is what the home should contain to satisfy your own personal lifestyle.

Despite recent price declines in most parts of the country, "it takes a lot of money to buy a home today," said Linda Albo, owner of her own real estate firm. "Prices are higher than what your mom and dad paid. You need to be realistic about your expectations."

Likewise, said Bob Herrick, owner of three real estate offices, this first home shouldn't be viewed as your final residence or even your dream home. Look at it as an escalator that is going to take you up to the next floor or home as your family grows and you move up the job ladder. You'll want certain things to be in this first home, he said, "but your expectation level has to be in line with your pocketbook." True, your dollar will buy more today than it would have three years ago, thanks to lower home prices and more favorable interest rates, but you still have to be realistic in your expectations.

As was stated in Chapter 2, before going out to shop, determine first how much home you can afford to buy.

Knowing what your budget ceiling is means that, if you're like most first-time buyers, you will probably have to compromise on certain features and some of your dreams in order to purchase a home, Albo said. But, she added, to be somewhat happy with the home you do buy, some of your dreams and needs have to be realized.

To figure out what you must have and what you can do without in this first home, said broker Bonnie Lazar, "you have to start with priorities." Make a list, she said, putting the things that you really need or want at the top and then juggling the list around so that the least important things are at the bottom. Then, as you shop for your home, you can compare what the property has with what's on your list. If the home lacks certain things and you have to make compromises, those compromises should be made based on the items at the bottom of your list and not at the top. This list is similar to the one you make when determining the neighborhood you want to live in.

Using a Camcorder While Shopping

Before getting into how to formulate your list of needs, one tip passed on by some brokers is that when going shopping, you'll be seeing a lot of different homes. Some buyers, said Dennis Brown, owner of his own real estate firm, "are now bringing along camcorders. It's a great way of keeping track of all the homes that you'll be viewing." Without a camcorder, buyers often begin mixing the dining room they saw in one home with the living room they saw in another.

Brokers have long used still pictures to help refresh buyers' memories of what they've seen. But a still photo, Brown said, doesn't give the same flavor of the home as a video does. A camcorder captures the room flow and the home's atmosphere better. The broker can also be standing before the camera, pointing out the important features that the home contains. But remember, before using a camcorder, to ask for permission from the broker and seller. Linda Albo remembers being in the midst of showing a home to a gentleman when all of a sudden he pulled a camcorder from out of his briefcase and began taping the house. "It upset the homeowner tremendously," she said. The seller was concerned about whether this tape was really going to be used for comparing homes or as the basis for a robbery. The feeling was that the tape might be recording the valuables in the home and ways of getting into the residence, rather than the room dimensions and atmosphere of each room, Albo said.

When used with permission, camcorders can be a valuable homebuying tool. Some brokers around the country, said George A. Jacob, manager of a Schlott Realtors office, now keep a camcorder in their office and make it available to buyers as they set out to inspect properties. And even when a seller doesn't allow a camcorder to be used on initial viewings of the home, once a contract of sale is signed, the homeowner usually allows videotaping to aid the buyer in deciding how to decorate or remodel each room in the home he or she has committed to purchase, Albo said.

If a camcorder is not used while shopping, or is not allowed, to help keep track of the homes you see, request a still photo or floor plan from the broker. If neither of these is available, make notes about the house based on your checklist.

The Checklist

Which brings us back to what should be on that checklist you'll be using when homeshopping.

Below are a number of things that brokers said buyers consider and often request in a home. Look it over. Also examine your own lifestyle, jotting down things you may want that aren't listed below. After you have a list of must-haves, go back and rewrite them on another piece of paper in their order of importance to you. This will result in a final checklist emphasizing what your first home should have. Items to consider include:

- Type of home—Do I need one level (perhaps because of personal handicaps or illness), or are several levels O.K.?

- Do any of the bedrooms have to be on the main level (sometimes necessary if an older person will be living with you)?

- Size of home—How many square feet do I really need? (When deciding this, remember that in colder climates, you will have to pay to heat these areas and in warmer climates, to pay to air condition this space).

- Number of bedrooms.

- Number of bathrooms—Do I really need a bathroom off the master bedroom?

- Kitchen—Does it need a dishwasher? Should it have an eating area?

- Dining room—Do I really need a separate, formal dining area or can it be part of the kitchen or living room?

- Living room—How big does it need to be?

- Family room or den—How often will I really use this?

- Room for home office—Do I do enough work at home to warrant having a separate area for this? If you do, then this could also be a tax write-off. Check with your accountant, because during the first quarter of 1993, the IRS placed stricter rules on home office deductions.

- Porch—How important is it to have one, and should it be in the back or front of the home? Should it be open or screened in?

- Garage—Do I need one, and for how many cars? Is it O.K. if it's a separate building, or does it need to be attached to the house?

- Backyard—How big an area does it need to be? Should it be fenced in because I have a pet? Should it have an area where I can have a vegetable or flower garden? Should it have a minimal amount of grass because I don't want to spend a lot of time on lawncutting?

- Front yard—How big an area does it need to be?

- Closets—How many do I really need? Will I need a big one in the master bedroom? Do I need a separate one for linens?

- Basement—Do I need this extra space, and does it have to be finished when I buy the home or can it wait until after I move in and have the money? Does the basement have to contain a spot for a work area and tool storage because I plan to do a lot of renovation of the home myself?

- Attic—Is this space necessary and, if so, how large should it be? Should it be just big enough for storage, or do I want an attic that can be expanded and finished in case I decide I need additional room down the road?

- Cable TV—Does the home have to be in an area that can be hooked up to a local cable company?

- Recreational facilities—If I'm looking to buy a condo, co-op or HOA, what recreational facilities do I need, such as a pool, tennis court or exercise room?

- Parking—If this is a condo, co-op or HOA, how many parking spots do I need for myself and the rest of my family?

- Other services—Does the condo or co-op come with a doorman or concierge? Do I need one? Is there an elevator, or is the building a walkup? Is there a laundry room, or can I have a washer and dryer in the apartment?

One last thing to consider when buying a home is what it should contain to help it resell quickly later on. Chapter 14 examines the items that make one home worth more than another and what buyers look for when purchasing a home. You might also want to keep these tips in mind before going out to home shop.

Chapter 5

BARGAIN ALTERNATIVES FOR CASH-TIGHT HOMEBUYERS

Before going out to home shop, every first-time buyer starts out with a particular type of residence in mind—a dream property—that he or she would like to live in. But, as was mentioned before, finding that dream property and staying within budget is often difficult to accomplish.

When the real estate market is soft, as it was recently in many parts of the country and still is in others, home prices either stabilize, after escalating yearly, or begin to fall. This makes it possible for a buyer to get more house than when the market was hot and in the seller's favor. A dream property (or something almost like it) becomes more attainable.

If an area's real estate market becomes really depressed, as happened in Texas in the early eighties and the Northeast in the early nineties, then even more home can be bought for the dollar. But while a severely depressed economy might sound like the perfect thing for helping you to get your first home, one thing you have to analyze is how secure your own job is. If you see a chance of your position or department being phased out, you may want to delay making a major purchase like that of a home, even if prices are declining.

However, if the market is hot, as it is in a few parts of the country, prices will keep climbing, putting a further strain on your budget. For example, prices actually rose 18.3 percent in the first quarter of 1993 over the year before in Oklahoma City and 26.1 percent in Richland, Washington, in the same period.

Whether the market is hot or cold, there are some strategies that a buyer can use to help stretch his or her home purchasing dollar, ranging from estate sales to auctions to looking in neighborhoods that had been neglected but are coming back. The strategies discussed here can be followed by anyone and, in keeping with the promise in this book's introduction, are not plans that have been executed successfully by one person, never to be duplicated easily by anyone else. The pros and cons of each will be discussed.

BUYING IN GENTRIFIED NEIGHBORHOODS

Over the course of any city or town's life, there are certain neighborhoods that everyone wants to live in and other areas that were once desirable, but have since fallen by the wayside. But neglected neighborhoods often come back, said broker Bonnie Lazar. These are often areas that have aged. The population grew old and didn't make any improvements to their homes while businesses started moving out, she explained.

They are also areas, other brokers pointed out, where the population base has changed—those homeowners with money fled, leaving lower-income families behind. Slowly, the area deteriorated as crime rates increased. Or sometimes the area has turned from being heavily residential to mostly industrial.

But slowly a number of these areas around the country are coming back. (At the same time, remember, some good neighborhoods are on the brink of decay.) The trick in getting a good buy, brokers said, is to purchase a home in an area just as it's starting to turn around. By doing this, as the neighborhood improves, property prices will appreciate, often faster than the appreciation rate of homes in the better areas of the city or town.

Determining Whether a Neighborhood Is Sliding Or Coming Back

How can you tell whether a neighborhood is decaying or starting to come back? For one thing, "look at the pride of owner-ship and see if the homes in the neighborhood are being fixed up," said Bob Herrick. As you ride around, do you see people putting on new roofs and siding? Are some owners building extensions? Are the front lawns neatly cut and shrubs well maintained? All are signs of people taking pride in their homes, he said.

In addition, Lazar said, look at the makeup of the neighbor-hood. Walk the streets and take notice of who is walking in and out of the homes. Are there more young people coming into the area? Do you see more swing sets in the backyards and kids playing in the street? Younger people means new blood coming into the area. These buyers often come in with plans of fixing their homes up and making changes. While there's nothing wrong with older people living in a neighborhood, this population segment is often set in its ways and less inclined to invest money in the updating of homes that helps increase a whole community's property values.

Also, look around to see if new homes are being built, devel-opers said. This shows a commitment on the part of both builders and lenders to the area—not promised dollars of someday improv-ing the area, but a real, current investment.

Likewise, Herrick said, look at what the government munici-pality is spending in the community. Is it putting in new streets, fixing up sidewalks and trying to beautify the downtown district? Is there a new library, bus station, office building or some other government project going up or planned for the area? You can find out about planned projects by asking a broker or going to the area's village or town hall. Reading back issues of the local paper is another good way to find out what's planned for the neighbor-hood. Check at the local library for these.

Another thing to do, Lazar said, is walk the main business streets of the community. An area in decline will usually be filled with boarded-up stores and businesses that are dying. An area coming back will have new stores and other commercial ventures opening. In addition, the existing stores will be fixing their interiors, sprucing up their facades and making other improvements to attract customers and keep up with the changing area. You should also look at the merchandise being sold in the local stores. This will give you some idea of the income levels of the people both living in and moving into the area, Lazar added. Another thing to do is visit the school, even if you don't have children, and ask the principal, a teacher or some other administrator whether the enrollment is increasing or decreasing. If the enrollment is on the rise, this is another sign that new families are moving into the area.

Making the Most of Gentrification

To obtain your best bargain and build up equity in a property faster, you want to buy a home just as a neighborhood is turning around, experts said. The nearer the neighborhood is to its "decay period," the lower sales prices will be. As new homes go up, businesses improve and the area straightens itself out, your own property's value will appreciate. But, by the same token, buying this way is somewhat of a gamble, experts added. While the first in will get the best prices, they may have to put up with the problems the neighborhood encountered during its decay period. Crime rates may be high; stores may not be the best; municipal services may be spotty. The schools may not have the greatest reputation. However, you can be part of the change, helping shape it and bring it about.

SWEAT EQUITY

In real estate parlance they're called "handyman specials." But in the eyes of many first-time buyers strapped for cash, they're known as affordable housing.

A "handyman special" is a house that needs some work. What has to be done can be anything from the installation of a new roof to practically tearing the entire home down.

One thing engineer Warren Cronacher, president of Tauscher Cronacher, recommended is never buying a home whose basic structure isn't sound. If the foundation is cracked or not in good shape, getting it back into solid condition can be either impossible or extremely expensive, making the low price of the home no bargain at all, he said. Bringing an engineer or home inspector in BEFORE signing the contract of sale and purchasing the property can help you evaluate the soundness of the home and save you from making a costly mistake.

Brokers will tell you that your fastest appreciation will be found in a home that needs work in a neighborhood that's just starting to turn around. But one of the big problems with buying a fixer-upper is that for it to be a bargain, you have to do much of the work yourself. Often, bringing in a contractor will push the overall acquisition cost of the home to a level that your budget just can't afford.

How Handy Are You?

Before taking on a home fixer-upper, ask yourself (and truthfully answer), "How handy am I?"

"The biggest problem for do-it-yourselfers," said Doug Griffin, president of Griffin Construction, "is not knowing how good or bad their knowledge is." While Griffin admitted, "there's nothing secretive in what I do," it takes practice. Much can be learned by buying a book, such as one on carpentry, and reading up on the subject. If you can relate to what's being said, then you can do it, he added. Griffin recalled finishing the attic in the home he grew up in when he was 14. "I got a book from Sear's, read it and even did the wiring myself. It was a matter of translating what I read into ability."

But some people, he added, don't have the ability. Unfortunately, they don't realize this until they've bought the home. They close on the property, start their first project and then find they can't do anything.

Time. The other problem with fixing up an old, decaying home is finding the time to accomplish all that has to be done.

Tom and Michaela Taylor estimated that doing the work themselves on the 90-year-old home they purchased saved them at least 50 percent over hiring a contractor. Doing this labor enabled them to buy a home in an area they might not otherwise have been able to afford. But it also meant giving up weekends, nights, vacations and every free minute they could find in order to work on the home. Pride and exhaustion are the twin cousins of doing any labor yourself. It took the couple four years to complete the project. And in their eyes, there are still minor things to be done, even though they've completed the floors, windows, kitchen, bathroom and every other major element of the home that originally was in poor shape.

While the Taylors finished their project, Carlos Naudon and Susan Steingass, who bought their home in 1977, are still sitting with an unfinished kitchen, bedroom and other parts of a brownstone they had intended to fix up but still haven't had the time to complete. The married couple had the best of intentions to do everything themselves. They had the ability, and what they have completed is beautiful. But both put long hours in their respective businesses five to six days a week. On top of that, a first child was born, and then a second.

"It requires a lot of vigilance if you want to bring a home back to what it was," Susan said. When they saw the amount of time that remodeling was taking them, the couple at one point tried to act as their own general contractor and bring in people to do work as needed. But that also took a lot of time. They had to find and interview workers and contractors who would meet the high standards they had set.

Time also had to be spent staying home, letting people in and supervising their work, Carlos said. In addition, they had to sign a contract pretty far ahead, telling each contractor what they wanted him to do. "But that's not our style," he noted. The couple likes to change ideas as they go along, something you can't do with hired laborers unless you are there every minute to watch what they've done. And making a change often throws off the timing of when the next workers have to be brought in, something you can't do when laborers are contracted for and available on only certain dates.

At the moment, the couple is still doing some of the work themselves, while bringing in contractors as needed.

A Sweat Equity Success

While Susan and Carlos still live in a home in need of many improvements, Kevin and Sandy Zeluck are an example of what you can do if you have both the ability and time. In a two-and-a-half-year period they went from living in a rental apartment to fixing up two homes, selling them and finally buying a third fixer-upper in an area filled with million-dollar properties. They accomplished this, Sandy said, "by buying the dogs on the block."

"We definitely knew we wanted land in a prime location," Kevin said. They also knew the neighborhood they wanted the home to be in. But like most young, first-time buyers, a home in that area was out of their reach. So what they did, each time they traded up, was go into a good neighborhood and buy the home that needed the greatest amount of work.

"I shopped the market like you do a blouse," Sandy said, trying to find high-quality merchandise marked down to the lowest price. Added Kevin, "it was a real scare, the first time (we did this), going from a $350-a-month apartment to a $66,000 home having a 14.75 percent mortgage that was costing us $1,200 a month."

They got their first home by scraping together $20,000 in savings and money borrowed from their respective families. In the initial home, and in each successive property, they acted as their own contractors. Some of the jobs were subcontracted out, while they handled other projects themselves. They invested about $20,000 in the first home, doing only the things that would help improve the property's resale, such as putting in a new kitchen, new bath and skylights (see Chapter 14 for what affects the price of a home most). Just as one fixer-upper was being finished, Sandy would have another in a slightly better neighborhood lined up.

Their second home cost $255,000 and sold for $420,000 after 17 months of ownership. The next was a $400,000 fixer-upper in their dream neighborhood that would have cost $800,000 to $1 million had it been in mint condition, Kevin said.

Keep in mind that what helped this couple trade up the way they did was buying at a time when the market in their area was hot and real estate prices were appreciating rapidly, sometimes by 20 to 30 percent in one year. To move up today the way the Zelucks did in many areas of the country is a lot harder, brokers pointed out. In many markets, home prices have actually declined since the late eighties and are still declining in some parts of the country. If the Zelucks had started this in an area with dropping prices, the improvements they made would have still increased the value of the home from the wreck they originally bought, but it's hard to say how much of a profit they would have made. And brokers, such as Lee Testa, owner of his own real estate office, pointed out that going from a rental to a million-dollar home in 3.5 years today is pretty close to impossible in most markets.

However, there are still areas of the country where home prices are escalating, and if you know your market and analyze each move right, it is possible to trade up the way the Zelucks did.

ESTATE SALES

If sweat equity doesn't appeal to you, another bargain alternative you might want to try is estate sales. But be forewarned: estate sales don't always yield the bargains everyone thinks they do, brokers and other real estate experts said. These properties, left to family members, friends and others, and often sold by the estate's executor or heirs, can sometimes turn into complicated headaches.

In most of the estate sales that Jack Murphy, former owner/broker of Century 21 Petry Real Estate, gets, the home is placed on the market because children inheriting the property already own a home. They are more interested in the cash that can be derived from selling the property, he said, than the property itself. The biggest problem in this type of deal, Murphy added, is getting the heirs to agree on a single price.

Noted Barbara Frechter, owner/broker of Glen Jay Realty Inc., her firm picks up many estate sales because it does appraisals for executors. In the course of the heirs selling the property, she said, "we're constantly hearing arguments." The squabbles are over price, whether or not to leave a dining room or some other piece of furniture in the home and whether to hold out for a higher price or to go after a fast sale."

The hardest thing from the broker's point of view, Murphy said, "is convincing the heirs to operate on the same frequency." This becomes a problem for the buyer as well, because instead of dealing with one seller, he or she is actually dealing with several.

What the broker has to do, according to Murphy, is get one family member to act as spokesperson. For example, if five heirs have to agree on price, it may be easier to get each owner to come down $2,000 than to try to convince a single seller to come down $10,000.

Things To Be Wary of with Estate Sales

One thing a buyer should be sure of in an estate sale is that he or she is dealing with the person who legally has the right to sell the property, said attorney C. Jaye Berger. She's seen cases where a buyer thought he had cemented a great deal with a friend of the family only to learn that the person didn't have the authority to sell the property.

To be certain a buyer is dealing with an authorized individual, the seller should be able to produce what are called "letters testamentary," Berger said. This is the official court document stating that a person is the appointed executor of the estate.

The buyer should also take out title insurance, she added, to protect against unclear title. There have been instances where an heir has sold a home, the buyer has moved in and sometime later, another person comes by, asking, "What are you doing living in my house?" Unknown heirs have been known to pop up and complicate matters.

As for getting a bargain, it's going to depend on the circumstances of both the heirs and the estate. The objective of the estate's executor is to obtain the highest price for any property sold, Berger said. The executor will get the home appraised, list it with a broker and listen to as many offers as possible, said William Lippman, a partner with the law firm of Kronish, Lieb, Weiner & Hellman. The executor doesn't want an heir challenging the sale in court, claiming the executor didn't fulfill his or her fiduciary duty. As long as the executor acted in a responsible manner, even if the home is sold for below-market value, no one can question what he or she has done, Lippman said.

The Best Bargains with Estate Sales

The best estate sale bargains come from heirs living out of state who find having property so far from their own home a headache and want to get rid of it, Murphy said. These sellers are the most flexible in negotiating price. Likewise, Frechter said, heirs who have had the property on the market for a long time, like any other seller, are more willing to come down in price, especially if the home has a mortgage on it and is costing the heirs money.

If the inherited home is in poor shape, a good deal might also be had, Lippman said, because most estates are reluctant to spend money fixing up a property it's trying to dispose of. However, if the property is a co-op apartment, a lowball price might be thwarted by the building's board of directors, Berger said. In an effort to protect the resale value of the building's units, the board might reject a buyer offering a price far below market value.

Bargains can also be gotten from estates that are cash poor but asset rich. It's the estate that must pay federal and any state inheritance taxes, and not the individuals receiving the assets, explained Alan E. Weiner, a partner in the accounting firm of Holtz Rubenstein & Co. At this writing, estates valued below $600,000 pay no federal tax. Above that amount, the estate pays a graduated tax ranging from 18 percent to 55 percent.

If the deceased left little or no cash and taxes must be paid, a buyer might find an heir more desperate to sell, Lippman said. One caveat for the buyer here is to make sure that all estate taxes have been paid, he noted. If they haven't, the home could wind up with a lien on it until inheritance taxes are settled.

Sometimes the real estate is auctioned off by the estate, Frechter added. However, she has seldom seen a bargain here. Usually, many potential buyers show up and, caught in the frenzy of the auction, the property is bid up to market value.

Buyers seeking estate sale property can check with local brokers and attorneys (who sometimes act as the selling agent). Real estate classifieds also carry ads for homes being sold through an estate.

GOVERNMENT FORECLOSURES

Not every FHA (Federal Housing Administration) loan or other mortgage that is backed by the federal government works out. Sometimes a homeowner loses his or her job, the family's financial status changes and the home is lost.

When a home is foreclosed on, the government then tries to sell it, like any lender, to recover as much of the mortgage money still outstanding. "We get calls from people who want to buy these foreclosures all the time," said Gerard Troha, district manager for Continental Capitol. "People feel that they're getting a good buy."

The homes are usually advertised in a local paper and are sold to the highest bidder. Sealed bids must be sent to the nearest office of the U.S. Department of Housing & Urban Development, or HUD, which oversees the bidding. Earnest money—a certain percentage of the bid price (usually ranging from 5 to 10 percent)—must be included with the bid. It must be in the form of a certified cashier's check or money order made payable to HUD.

The problem with these homes, Troha said, is that they are not usually good buys. The homes are often in need of repair and in terrible shape. They are sealed up, and buyers can't inspect the interior of what they are getting. "Purchasers are bidding and buying blindly," Troha noted. He recalled one home where the former owners had taken everything from piping and fixtures to even the boiler.

The other drawback of buying a government foreclosure is that the home can't be financed. Most lenders, including the FHA, won't make a loan on these properties, Troha said. If you come up with the winning bid, you have 30 days to come up with the rest of the purchase price in cash. Getting this money is not contingent on being approved for a mortgage, the way it is with any other home sale, Troha noted. Once your bid is accepted, if you can't produce the remaining cash, you lose the earnest money you sent in. Another problem, pointed out by an attorney, is that sometimes you may find the home is still occupied by the former owners. The new buyer then has to go through an eviction process, which could take months.

There have been numerous books written by people on how to make money buying government foreclosures, Troha said. They contend that such properties can be bought for a little money, fixed up and then sold at a tremendous profit. But some of these homes are not in the best of neighborhoods, and the cost of fixing them up can be tremendous. The people making money on these foreclosures, notes Troha, are those writing the books on them.

The better way to buy property like this is to approach an owner in financial difficulty before the home has actually been foreclosed on. How to do this is described below.

Resolution Trust Corporation

Commonly known as the RTC, the Resolution Trust Corporation is the government agency assigned to selling assets of failed savings and loans, including many foreclosed properties.

Homebuyers assume that everything the RTC is selling will be a bargain, but once again, buyer beware. Know the prices of homes in the surrounding area. Unlike the FHA or VA, which are only interested in acquiring the mortgage amount outstanding, the RTC is trying to get as near market value as possible on the homes it holds to minimize the S&L bailout cost to taxpayers, real estate attorneys said. It has certain rules it must abide by when marketing properties, such as that, by law, it can't accept an offer of less than 95 percent of the market value of a building in certain areas of the country such as Arkansas, Colorado and New Mexico. These rules, however, are sometimes changed in an area depending on how much unsold property the RTC is holding.

In Texas, Louisiana and several other states, RTC homes are eligible with below-market financing through the state's housing authority (see Chapter 8 for details). But again, experts warned, like many foreclosed properties, RTC homes have often been abused by the previous owners and are in poor condition.

Rules accompanying RTC properties are constantly changing. To order an RTC catalogue listing residential parcels around the country, call 800-431-0600. There is a charge. A cheaper way of seeing the latest catalog is to go to the nearest federal government depository library. The location of the library in your area can also be gotten by calling the above 800 number.

The number of homes under the RTC's jurisdiction is constantly changing, depending on how many S&L branches have been closed in an area. There may not be homes available in every area of the country all the time. And as the economy improves, the number of properties the RTC deals with is certain to drop.

Buying Lender Foreclosures at Auction

It's not only the FHA that finds itself holding homes on which a homeowner suddenly can't make the payments. Lenders of conventional loans find themselves in the same situation, especially when there's a dip in the area or nation's economy.

In 1992, 971,517 bankruptcy petitions were filed nationwide, according to the American Bankruptcy Institute. That's the highest number ever in the United States, and indications are that the figure for 1993 could be just as high. With bankruptcy, many homes enter foreclosure.

At a bank foreclosure auction, explained real estate attorney Craig D. Robins, a referee is hired by the lender to get the highest bid possible so that the lender will recover all the money he or she has laid out for the mortgage.

A notice of foreclosure is placed in local papers announcing when and where the auction is, Robins said. Buyers can then check the house out, but they probably won't be able to see the interior. After all, the current owners are not holding open houses on a home that's about to be taken away from them.

The auction is then held. But, said Barbara Frechter, owner of Glen Jay Realty, she has seldom seen a bidder getting a bargain. Caught up in the frenzy of the whole proceedings, people end up bidding the property up fairly close to or even above market value.

In addition, professionals attend these auctions, Robins noted. They know what surrounding homes in the area are going for, something you should find out before attending an auction. The professionals then begin bidding on the property along with everyone else. But as soon as it rises above the point of what they think it's worth, the pros drop out. Besides these speculators, Robins said, you will often find the lender holding the mortgage bidding on the property. As strange as that may seem, financial institutions do this, he said, because they don't want the mortgage to show up as a loss on their books. State and federal regulators are closely monitoring lenders now and the fewer nonperforming loans (as they're called) that are on a bank's books, the better. So the lender will bid on the home, even going slightly above its fair market value. If the lender is the winning bidder, it can then pay the mortgage back through the proceeds (wiping a potential nonperforming loan off its books). The home is then sold through a broker for as much as he or she can get. Any loss taken, Robins said, shows up somewhere else on the lender's ledger.

Bargains can be gotten if you know what you're doing, said Melissa S. Kollen, author of *Buying Real Estate Foreclosures*. But too often, people bid on a home without doing their homework, such as first finding out if the home's title is clear.

Before attending a foreclosure auction, Robins said:

- Examine the property.
- Research the title.
- Find out what surrounding homes have recently sold for.
- Place a cap on your bidding and stick to it.

If you are seriously considering purchasing a foreclosure, do additional research into how an auction is conducted, how the property must be paid for and how to determine if the home is worth bidding on. But be aware, this is not the best route for first-time buyers unless they fully understand the procedure.

Buying REOs. Those wanting to buy a foreclosed home, but looking to eliminate some of the risks and problems encountered with purchasing at an auction, should consider buying bank-owned properties. Known as REOs (real estate owned) or OREs (owned real estate), these are foreclosed properties which, at an auction, failed to attract the minimum bid the lender was seeking. A few REOs are obtained when homeowners, in order to avoid foreclosure, turn over their deed to the lender with the agreement that no other payments or debt obligations be required.

"REOs are a great opportunity for newcomers to foreclosures," Kollen said. A person makes an offer on an REO and if the lender accepts, it's a done deal.

While a person will pay more for an REO than the property would have gone for at auction, prices still average about 30 percent below market value, Kollen said. In addition, some—but not all—of the risks and problems encountered with auctions are removed.

Auctions require handing over 10 percent of your winning bid right after the auctioneer yells "sold," Kollen said. You have 30 days to come up with the rest—often too short a time to secure a mortgage—or lose the property and down payment. With an REO, many lenders not only give financing to creditworthy buyers, but often waive some closing costs. One national lender said it gives up to 80 percent financing with a one-year adjustable mortgage and 75 percent with fixed-rate loans on REOs.

At an auction, Kollen added, properties have to be bought as-is. But with REOs, some lenders make repairs. They may paint the interior, replace the heating system or do other things that they believe will help them get more for the property.

One risk REO buyers still take is ending up with a property that has a rental tenant or the original owner still living in it. It can take months to go through eviction proceedings before the local sheriff removes the inhabitants.

Kollen, who works with investors and also consults with people looking to buy their first foreclosure, said that lenders do a lot of negotiating on REO prices. "These are nonperforming assets that are sitting ducks," she added, subject to vandalism. Lenders have to continue paying real estate taxes while collecting nothing on the outstanding mortgage balance, so they are anxious to get rid of these homes.

Prices will vary depending on whether the buyer is making an all-cash offer or looking for financing. The price will also be negotiated downward if the purchaser declines repair work that the lender was willing to make.

REOs are often advertised in newspaper real estate sections. The lenders try to be discreet, Kollen said, by not listing the lending institution's name (no one likes to advertise they have bad loans). REOs are also found by calling lenders and asking for a list of their foreclosed properties. Some lenders charge for their lists.

Once you have a list and find something that interests you, either an employee of the lender or an outside real estate broker will show the property and handle offers. If the house is vacant, or the current resident is agreeable, interiors can be inspected.

Buying Troubled Properties Before They're Fore-closed On. According to Troha, another way to get a good deal on a home on which the mortgage payments are not being met is by trying to get to the financially strapped homeowner before the lender has foreclosed on the property. The advantage is that you can inspect the interior of the home and make an offer, as you would on any other property, based on what shape the residence is in.

Another plus is that you can then apply for a regular mortgage and purchase the home the way you would any resale. There's no need to submit a bid along with 10 percent of the purchase price that you won't get back if you can't secure financing, Troha said.

Noted other brokers, bargains can be gotten because the owner, desperate, realizes that at a foreclosure auction he or she has lost the home and whatever the highest bidder comes in with is what the lender will use to pay off the existing mortgage. If the bid price doesn't cover the full mortgage, the homeowner will have to make up the difference out of his or her own pocket. A foreclosed owner also winds up not being able to get any credit for at least six years, pointed out Patricia A. Rouse, formerly a sales manager for the Lend-Mor Corporation.

If the home is sold before the foreclosure, the sale proceeds like any other. The homeowner keeps all of the money received and then uses that to pay off the loan. A buyer, in trying to get a lower price, can bargain with the homeowner, pointing out that he or she will pay more than any auction will yield that person, while also keeping the homeowner from ruining his or her credit rating, Robins said.

These about-to-be-foreclosed-on properties can be found by looking through either the real estate section of newspapers (sellers sometimes play up that they're about to be foreclosed on in classified ads) or by scanning the legal notices for pending foreclosures (also found in a paper's classifieds). A ledger in the county clerk's office will also list properties that have a Notice of Pendency of Action posted on them (meaning the lender is trying to foreclose). This is the first step in the foreclosure process. If you jot down the index number of the case and look up the file, you can get the name and address of the owner.

Attorneys such as Joseph Covello advised driving by the property to see what it looks like. If it interests you, contact the owner by mail. In your letter, be sympathetic to his or her situation as you state you are interested in buying the home. Ask whether you could meet to discuss details.

AUCTIONS AS A MARKETING TOOL

Currently popping up around the country is another type of auction used to sell residential property, especially townhomes, condos and co-ops. These auctions are not selling foreclosed real estate, but homes in sound financial shape.

"Auctions are now another method of selling property," said Elizabeth Meyer, vice president of Properties At Auction. Instead of letting units stay on the market indefinitely, an auction brings buyers and sellers together, disposing of the property in just a couple of hours, she said.

Some units are sold absolute—meaning the highest bid is taken, no matter how high or low it turns out to be. The majority of units, however, are sold with the seller having usually 48 hours to accept or reject the winning bid, explained Jim Byczek with Sheldon Good & Company, a Chicago-based auction company operating throughout the country. Experts said that savings on original selling prices can be substantial. For example, 20 brand-new condominium units in Hackensack, New Jersey, were recently sold for prices ranging from $36,000 to $133,000. The original selling prices were $110,000 to $236,000, said Steven Good, president of Sheldon Good & Company.

Marketing properties via auctions has been a practice for years around the world, said Bonnie Barkley, vice president of Merrill Lynch Realty's auction division. The trend reached Australia 15 years ago, she noted. Today more than half the property exchanging hands in that country is sold via auctions.

What the developer loses by accepting lower bid prices is made up by quickly eliminating carrying costs, said Aaron Smiles, president of First Continental Realty. In a single afternoon, the builder can be rid of all his unsold units, he noted.

To bid, buyers are required to register in advance and leave a certified or cashier's check for a predetermined amount at the door when attending the auction. This is returned if nothing is bought and is used as a down payment if a property is won, Byczek said. Sometimes, builders have arranged for lenders to be at the auction to offer loans at attractive mortgage rates so that everything can be taken care of at the auction. Should you bid on a property and not be able to get financing, you could lose your deposit.

The nice thing about this type of auction is that you can inspect the exact unit you want to bid on prior to the event, Meyer said. But brokers and other experts offer these caveats:

- Inspect the unit before buying.

- Don't get caught up in the bidding frenzy. Determine what that unit is worth to you (basing it on the selling price of similar units in the area); then stop bidding.

MOVING A HOME

Moving a home from one location to another may not seem like a bargain alternative, but under the right circumstances, it can actually save you tens of thousands of dollars.

Take Fred and Bonnie D'Acierno, who were living in a 600-square-foot one-bedroom summer cottage that they owned, but needed more space after their daughter was born. With the high price of housing in their area, they couldn't afford to trade up. Then they heard about a two-story, 1,800-square-foot home, 2.7 miles from their present property, that could be theirs for only $15,000. The only hitch was that they had to pay to have the home moved off the existing site. The D'Aciernos knocked down their present home, built a new foundation, and had the second home moved and placed onto it.

The cost for moving a home will vary around the country. But a 1,000-square-foot ranch can be moved for about $6,000, said Stan Kazel, president of Dawn House Movers. Others estimated simple moves in the $10,000 range. There will be other costs as well, including having to pay to have utility and phone lines removed along the route if the home being moved can't clear these as it makes its journey, said Emmett Drake, owner of Emmett Drake & Sons Inc., a home moving company.

The cost of the home itself will vary. Moving company presidents said that there have been cases where owners have given homes away if the new owner agreed to pay the moving costs. For the present owner, this can save thousands of dollars in demolition expenses (or even on having to pay to move the home).

There are a variety of reasons why owners want existing homes moved from their property, said William Hewlett, vice president of Kennelly House Moving. Perhaps the zoning in the area has changed and the new owner can build a commercial building where the old home now sits. Or perhaps the property owner wants to build a new, bigger home on the current site.

The Nuts and Bolts of Moving a Home

To have a home moved, you have to first, of course, have a piece of property to put it on. In some areas of the country, this can be a major stumbling block because the price of land can be prohibitive or the land can even be hard to find. A foundation plus sewer, water and electric lines leading to the home then have to be paid for. However, acquiring a home this way can save a considerable amount of money over conventional methods.

Before any move is done, said Curt Davis, president of Davis Brothers Engineer Corp, another house-moving firm, you should figure out the route with the least number of obstacles. Also budget in a little bit more money in case problems are encountered along the way, he said.

While this method may not be good for someone trying to find affordable housing in downtown Boston or Chicago, it is a strategy that many suburban and rural first-time buyers should check out.

Part Two

FINANCING YOUR HOME

Chapter 6

WHERE TO GET A MORTGAGE

One of the initial questions first-time buyers ask when beginning the home buying process is, "How am I going to pay for this piece of property?" The answer is with a mortgage.

A mortgage is made for a specified period of time, called the term. The lender makes some of his or her money by charging fees for certain things connected with the loan, but most of the "profit" comes from charging interest on the money being lent.

The loan is paid back monthly, as a combination of principal (the money you borrowed) and interest. Although there are bi-weekly mortgages, with a payment made every two weeks, they are not popular among budget-conscious first-time buyers.

Before considering specific types of mortgages, one thing that should be kept in mind is that while a mortgage payment in some types of loans may be the same every month, year after year, the mix of interest and principal is not. In the early years of any type of home mortgage, said Paul Havemann, vice president of the mortgage research firm HSH Associates, a borrower is paying nearly all interest. This is because the average American moves every seven years. When you move, you must pay off your present mortgage before you can take out another on a new home. If you borrowed $50,000, after seven years you may have paid just a few hundred dollars in principal; the remainder of each payment will have gone to interest. This is a way a lender maximizes the return on the money he or she is lending you, Havemann said.

A DIFFERENT WORLD

The lending industry has changed since the time your parents went to buy their first home. Where once buyers took out a mortgage at their neighborhood savings and loans—the same place they used to keep their savings account—today there are a variety of places a person can turn to, Havemann said. Credit unions make mortgages, as do lending divisions of large corporations such as General Motors and Prudential. Likewise, pointed out Stanley Greenstein, executive vice president of the Mortgage Clearing House, where your parents had only fixed rate mortgages, with 30 years being the most popular term, now there are hundreds of different products.

Old Reliable: The Fixed-Rate Loan

Fixed-rate loans are just as the name implies: mortgages that come with a set rate of interest for the life of the loan. Experts say the advantage of this mortgage for borrowers is that home purchasers know exactly what their payment will be every month for the duration of the loan. And if interest rates drop, your loan rate still remains the same.

However, you can refinance the loan, that is, have the mortgage rewritten at the current lower rate. The general rule of thumb is that by the time you pay closing costs and any other fees associated with refinancing, this strategy pays only if the difference between the old and new rate is 2 percentage points or more, said numerous mortgage officers. However, if the term is shortened when the loan is refinanced, the 2 percent rule doesn't always apply. The reason: a shorter term means you're paying less interest over the life of the loan. If you plan to stay in your home for a long period of time, then you'll recover your closing costs and it may be worthwhile to refinance with only a 1 percent difference.

Adjustable Rate Mortgages

In 1982, a new product was introduced to the market that changed the face of mortgage lending, Havemann said—the adjustable rate mortgage, or ARM. "It was the ARM that opened a whole new world of mortgage options," he explained.

Originally ARMs were designed to aid ailing savings and loan institutions. After interest rates were deregulated at the beginning of the eighties, lenders found their portfolios bloated with low-interest, fixed-rate mortgages. The ARM was introduced to shift some of the risk of rising rates back to borrowers.

Whereas a fixed-rate mortgage has the same interest rate for the life of the loan, the interest on an ARM can change, explained Edward B. Kramer, a senior vice president with the Dime Savings Bank. Depending on the lending institution, the ARM can change every month, six months, year, two years, or more. The most common ARM, said a spokesperson for the Mortgage Bankers Association, adjusts every year.

To figure out what the ARM will adjust to, you have to find out to which index the loan is pegged. Many ARMs are geared towards the prime rate. You'll see the ARM's interest rate listed sometimes as "prime plus two." This means that if the current prime rate, which is listed in the business section of many newspapers, is 10 percent, then the ARM's interest rate will be 12 percent (the prime plus 2 percent).

Noted Kramer, the index to which the ARM is pegged is important for the borrower to know because some indexes move up or down faster than others. The reason a borrower should be concerned about the ARM's index is because in a one-year adjustable, for example, the interest rate can rise or fall by a maximum of 2 percentage points. (Some ARMs limit the rise or fall in any one year to 1.5 percent or 1 percent, although a 2-percent increase is the most common.)

Now, you may be thinking, "If interest rates rise to 21 percent, as they did back in the mid-eighties, I can be paying a fortune for my loan." But, as Havemann pointed out, ARMs usually come with a lifetime cap in addition to the yearly one. This is spelled out in the commitment letter (explained later), as well as in the final mortgage contract you sign at closing. For example, the cap may be 6 points, meaning that the rate can never rise any higher than 6 percentage points above your initial interest rate over the life of the loan. Every lending institution sets its own cap, so it's wise to ask each what its ARM's cap is as you shop around for your mortgage.

One advantage of ARMs over fixed-rate loans is that they usually start at a lower rate of interest. Borrowers who couldn't qualify for a fixed-rate mortgage at 9 percent, for example, could try to qualify for a lower-rate ARM at 5 percent. However, lenders were finding that when rates rose, some borrowers were unable to meet their monthly mortgage as the payment adjusted upwards. So in 1992, the Federal National Mortgage Association, one of the biggest purchasers of loans on the secondary market, said it would continue buying adjustable mortgages from lenders only if borrowers were qualified at 7 percent, even if the initial rate was lower. They did this in response to rates that began to fall in the early 90's. In addition, borrowers now have to qualify at the adjustable's second-year rate when:

- The adjustable mortgage has a 2 percent annual adjustment cap.

- The term is longer than 15 years.

- Less than 25 percent is put down.

When the above criteria exist, borrowers who find an adjustable for 6 percent have to qualify at 8 percent. The new guidelines apply to any adjustable mortgage and are permanent. Borrowers who put 25 percent or more down only have to qualify at 7 percent, if the initial rate is below that, and not at the second-year rate.

The changes mean that buyers attracted to a 5 percent adjustable mortgage and looking to borrow $100,000 need $5,000 more in annual income, because they must qualify at 7 percent, said Stephen Sorahan, president of Sterling Mortgage Corp., a mortgage broker. However, if the lender keeps the loan in its own portfolio, said Nick Rizzetta, a former vice president with Dollar Dry Dock, "the lender can be more flexible."

ARM Teaser Rates. The borrower should be on the look-out for teaser rates, warned Al Sorrentino, a vice president with Citibank. These are artificially low introductory rates to entice you to take out one lender's loan instead of another's.

If the actual ARM rate is 10 percent, the lender may offer a teaser rate of 7.9 percent. Sounds good. But Sorrentino warned that the lender makes up for this lower rate with either higher origination fees or a slightly higher true interest rate that must be paid over the life of the loan. For this reason, you should be aware of a loan's APR—which will be explained shortly.

Of course, even if the teaser rate is 3 percent, you'll still have to qualify at 7 percent for the reasons explained above. The exception is if the lender keeps the loan in its own portfolio.

40-Year Loans. One recent innovation of adjustable loans is that some lenders have started offering 40-year mortgages. (There are also fixed-rate loans being offered with a 40-year term.) The Bowery Savings Bank reported that in 1988, of the $14 billion in mortgages written through the 19 states they were in, 25 percent were ARMs with 40-year terms. Said a vice president there, the reason for the popularity is that stretching the loan out results in lower monthly payments for a borrower. This is especially attractive to a first-time buyer.

However, Sorrentino pointed out that the difference in payment between a 40-year and a 30-year loan is not as great as a person thinks. A $100,000, 30-year fixed loan with a 12 percent interest rate would yield monthly payments of $1,028.62, while the same loan with a 40-year term would result in monthly payments of $1,008.50. That's a difference, he said, of only about $20 a month. "Although people are hyping the loan, the benefit to the consumer is very minor."

In addition, the amount of interest paid out over the life of a 40-year loan (fixed or adjustable) is considerably more than that for a 30-year loan. Stanley Greenstein, vice president of Mortgage

Clearing House, calculated that a borrower pays $230,167.66 in interest over the life of a 30-year fixed-rate loan of $100,000 made at 10.5 percent. Extended 10 years, the interest swells to $327,309.83, roughly 30 percent more. If this were an ARM, the interest paid could be even more if rates were on the rise, Greenstein said. It might also be less, he added, if rates were to drop and remain low. (In actuality, over 40 years, rates would more than likely rise and fall several times.)

But as mentioned before, the average person stays in his or her home seven years before moving on. Since first-time buyers are just using this initial home as a steppingstone to something else, the 40-year loan actually becomes a good deal for the short term.

After seven years on a fixed-rate loan, a person borrowing $100,000 at 10.5 percent pays $71,938 in interest, Havemann said. In that same period, that person will pay $72,967 with a 40-year fixed loan. The interest difference is about $1,000. But remember, the borrower is also making slightly smaller monthly payments with the 40-year loan. In addition, Havemann noted, the borrower can qualify with less income because of the smaller monthly payments. But if the borrower were to keep the 40-year loan for the whole term, he said, "he'd get socked."

Convertible Mortgages

Another fairly new loan product now available to buyers is the convertible mortgage. This begins as an adjustable in the early years of the loan and ends up as a fixed-rate mortgage for the duration.

For example, Sorahan explained, the loan starts out as an adjustable with an 8.5 percent rate of interest. There is a 2 percent annual cap on the loan, meaning that it can't rise by more than 2 percent in any year should interest rates climb. Over the life of the loan, there is a 6 percent cap, meaning that during the adjustable years, the loan can't rise by more than 6 percent.

The convertible feature comes in, said Camille M. Barbone, a former loan officer with Dale Mortgage Bankers, between the tenth and fiftieth months of the loan (the time span can differ depending on the lender). During that period, the borrower can elect to have the adjustable rate converted into a fixed rate of interest that will remain for the duration of the loan's term (be it 15, 20 or whatever number of years the loan term is). A fee of roughly $250 must be paid to exercise the convertible option, Barbone said.

On top of that, approximately 5/8 percent is added to whatever fixed-rate index is being used to figure the loan, Sorahan said. Most base the rate on the Fannie Mae or Freddie Mac 60-day price for fixed-rate loans. So if the current rate is 10 percent, you'd pay 10 5/8 percent for the fixed-rate part of the loan upon converting.

One disadvantage of the loan, Sorahan said, is that when you elect to change from the ARM to the fixed rate, the rate in effect on that date may not be the rate you wind up with. It can take two weeks to do all the paperwork, and the rate you receive is the rate in effect when the paperwork is completed. That rate could be higher or lower than when you elected the convertible option.

The convertible loan is good for someone who can't qualify for a fixed-rate loan from the beginning, Sorahan said. Both adjustables and convertibles start with lower rates of interest, meaning that people can qualify with less income.

But if you can qualify for a fixed-rate loan and want a fixed rate, go with that type of mortgage from the outset, Sorahan added. This way you skip having to pay the conversion fee and the 5/8 percent premium after the loan converts. And in the low-interest climate that exists as this book goes to print, starting with a fixed rate makes even more sense.

The Fannie Mae Two-Step

The two-step is a sort of cross between an ARM and a fixed-rate mortgage devised by the Federal National Mortgage Association, also known as Fannie Mae.

As a spokesperson at Fannie Mae explained, the loan is typically written for 30 years. It begins with an interest rate about one-half percent lower than that of a conventional, fixed-rate loan, where it then stays for seven years. If the homeowner doesn't move to a new home after the seventh year, he or she can continue the loan for the next 23 years at a new rate of interest, which would be 2.25 or 2.5 points higher than the rate being charged on 10-year treasury notes at the time. The new rate, however, cannot exceed the initial interest rate of the loan by more than 6 percent.

The loan is actually an ARM, Barbone said, which is adjusted once, after the first seven years. When the loan makes its adjustment after seven years, there is no refinancing charge or fee of any kind. All points and loan origination costs are paid up front, with nothing due on the second adjustment.

This loan is ideal for first-time buyers who don't expect to be in their first home for more than seven years, said Samuel K. Won, senior negotiator with Fannie Mae. And buyers seem to be responding to it, he added. Two months after its introduction in 1990, Fannie Mae did $1 billion in two-step business.

The Community Home Buyer's Program

The Community Home Buyer's Program is yet another Fannie Mae loan that will lend a borrower up to $203,200. There are income limits for qualifying for this loan, which fluctuate depending on where the home is being purchased. The minimum down payment required is 5 percent, but 2 percent can come from outside sources, such as a gift from family members or an employer. And remember those numbers talked about before: 28/36? With this loan, borrowers' housing expenses can be as high as 33 percent of income and as much as 38 percent of monthly income can go towards paying all debt, including the mortgage.

The Parent Power Program

In various parts of the country (and new areas are continuously being added) the Merrill Lynch Credit Corp, the lending arm of the well-known brokerage house, has introduced a loan requiring nothing down. To qualify, the borrower or the borrower's parents must keep securities (such as stocks or bonds) totaling roughly 40 percent of the loan amount in a Merrill Lynch account, explained Robert Cummings, a vice president with the firm. The securities can be bought and sold (with any dividends credited to the account), but they can't be withdrawn until the mortgage balance is reduced to 75 percent of its original amount.

And Still More Loan Choices

According to lenders, as home prices have increased and competition to make mortgages has grown, lenders have become more creative in shaping products to meet first-time buyers' needs. There is a wider choice of low-down-payment loans today than there has ever been before, said Carolyn Webber, vice president of Century 21 of the Northeast. In Chapter 9, variations of fixed and adjustable loans are discussed. Chapter 8 also looks at reduced rate loans offered by various states around the country, as well as government-backed loans offered by the Veterans Administration and Federal Housing Authority. A borrower should also sit down with a lender and ask whether any new programs have been introduced recently that might help his or her particular financial situation. In addition, pay attention to the real estate section of your local paper, as new programs are introduced all the time.

WHERE TO BORROW

There are three basic categories of places where you can go for your mortgage.

First, there are lending institutions, such as commercial banks and savings and loans. These usually have many branches throughout an area or even throughout the entire country. Besides making home mortgages, they also offer savings and checking accounts, as well as making numerous other types of loans such as for boats and automobiles. These lenders will either keep the loans they make in their own portfolio or sell them to the secondary market, such as to Fannie Mae and Freddie Mac. These secondary markets then repackage the loans and sell them to investors. Because the secondary market is buying the loan, Havemann said, they will set regulations or guidelines for lenders to follow. If an individual institution wants to sell to these markets, lenders must make their loans conform to these guidelines, as was explained in Chapter 2.

Mortgage Bankers

Another type of lender is a mortgage banker. These lenders are like a commercial bank, Barbone said, but unlike the traditional corner bank most people are familiar with, a mortgage banker doesn't offer savings and checking accounts. Commercial banks and savings and loans get a portion of their mortgage loan funds from deposits in these two types of accounts.

Most mortgage bankers get their funds for lending from private backers and investors, such as pension funds, Barbone said. Unlike a savings and loan or commercial bank, which has the option of keeping a loan in its own portfolio, mortgage bankers sell all their loans to the secondary market. The lending divisions of large corporations, such as General Motors and Prudential, fit into the category of mortgage bankers.

Some people, Barbone said, think a mortgage banker is more lenient in making its loans because it's selling off all the mortgages it makes. But the opposite is true, because mortgage bankers have to follow the rules and regulations of the secondary market to the letter. If they don't, explained Stephen Sorahan, a secondary-market buyer can turn around and refuse to make a loan or ask the mortgage banker to take back a loan that has already been closed.

Mortgage Brokers

A third type of mortgage vendor are mortgage brokers, who, explained Donald Henig, former president of the National Association of Mortgage Brokers, don't fund or make loans to consumers. They are middlemen, acting as liaisons between borrowers and lenders. Noted David Drucker, president of The Real Estate Funding Center, a mortgage broker, "Think of us as sort of matchmakers." Brokers, he said, can have associations with dozens of different lending institutions.

In theory, borrowers should end up with a better deal from a lender by going through a broker than they would if they walked directly into the lender's office. The broker, Henig explained, is given a wholesale rate by the lending institution in exchange for steering numerous customers in his or her direction. In return, the broker is paid a fee, which varies from broker to broker. Sometimes the fee is paid by the lending institution; more often, it is the borrower who pays it at the closing, when the home changes hands from seller to purchaser.

But borrowers may not always get a better deal by using a broker, said Stephen J. Rotella, a vice president with Chemical Bank. It will depend on how many points the broker is tacking onto the wholesale rate of the loan. One point is equal to 1 percent of the mortgage amount borrowed. These points are the fee that the broker will collect. Mortgage broker Ralph LoVuolo noted that he's seen cases where brokers are charging consumers four or five points. In this case, the consumer can do better by going directly to the lender, he said. One point is equal to 1 percent of the loan amount. Some lenders, such as mortgage banker Stanley Greenstein, don't deal with brokers in order to keep their rates as low as possible. The secret, experts said, is to shop around from lender to broker to savings and loan and see who is giving you the best deal and what services you are getting for the fees you are paying.

Even mortgage bankers, when they don't have a particular product that a borrower needs, sometimes broker the product of another lender, Barbone said. As with a mortgage broker, a fee would be paid for this service.

Which brings up one other thing to remember, Barbone added. Points paid to a broker are considered a fee and are not deductible on federal and state taxes; points paid to a mortgage banker, commercial bank or savings and loan are considered part of the closing costs and are deductible.

HOW TO PICK A LENDER

Before picking a mortgage banker, broker or any other type of lender, here are some tips offered by experts:

- Do some homework, suggested Tom Marder, former spokesman for the Mortgage Bankers Association. Learn the terminology of the industry and become aware of what's going on. To help you, this trade organization puts out a series of booklets explaining home buying and financing. Information can be obtained by writing Consumer Brochures, Mortgage Bankers Association, 1125 15th Street N.W., Washington, D.C. 20005.

- Ask for recommendations from friends and relatives, Lo Vuolo said. The lender should also be able to give a consumer several names of recently completed deals for the borrower to check as references. (Noted an attorney with the New York State Attorney General's Office, some lenders may not provide consumers with actual names but have letters on file from satisfied customers for consumers to look over.)

- Ask how long the mortgage broker or banker has been in business, LoVuolo said. Experience is a plus. It should be noted here that real estate brokers will often recommend lenders' names to buyers. However, pointed out Robert Katz, president of the Empire State Mortgage Bankers Association, be aware that some brokers are tied in with lenders who pay a commission for referring business to them. The broker is paid a fee. Katz said he had a "tremendous problem" with brokers getting a commission from both selling a home and setting up a mortgage.

  But Frank Orlandino, a partner with Eisenoff Realty, said that the broker is providing a service and arranging a loan for less than the borrower would have gotten on his own. He saw nothing wrong with this and believed that it benefited many consumers.

  However, in an early 1990 survey commissioned by the Mortgage Bankers Association of America, research found that more than half of the homebuyers who asked their real estate broker for help in finding a lender were given the name of only a single mortgage-making institution. The survey also found that borrowers using this advice ended up paying higher rates of interest for their mortgages than those who found a lender through other channels.

The Department of Housing and Urban Development issued new guidelines in December 1992 for when a real estate broker could charge a buyer a fee for helping find a loan. Regulations require that the broker use a computer loan origination system that has the loan programs of several lenders on it so that buyers have a better shot at getting the best loan. Should you use a real estate broker to help secure a loan? The best advice is to see what program such brokers can offer while you shop other lenders on your own. Then pick the loan that has the best rate and lowest closing costs.

- If you're thinking of using a mortgage broker, inquire which specific lenders the broker does business with, advised Melissa Cohn, chairwoman of Manhattan Mortgage Company. The more lenders a broker represents, the more choices he or she can offer to you.

- When a rate is quoted, find out if it can be locked in and for how long, Henig recommended. If a rate is locked in at application, for example, this means that the quoted rate won't change when you go to close several weeks or months later, even if interest rates have risen.

- Visit the banker or broker's office rather than using the convenience of a mortgage officer coming to your home or place of business, suggested Howard Newman, an attorney who helps mortgage bankers and brokers comply with lending laws. "There's no better way of getting a true sense of character." You can see whether the lender is operating from an office that looks businesslike and permanent, as opposed to a temporary office in a storefront that may not be there in a few months. Some brokers and bankers have even been known to operate from nothing more than a pay phone and the back of a car.

- Check to see whether the mortgage broker or banker is licensed in states requiring licensing. Licensed bankers and brokers must follow certain regulations. Commercial banks and savings and loans will also be chartered either by the federal government or a particular state.

- Check to see whether the mortgage banker or mortgage broker is a member of a state or national association, such as, in the case of brokers, The National Association of Mortgage Brokers. These trade groups have codes of ethics that members are required to follow. The associations also police those in their industry who operate outside both the association's code and the law, Newman said. Quality lenders don't want to suffer credibility because of the unscrupulous actions of a few bad apples in their industry.

- When being offered a loan by a mortgage broker, find out which lending institution the mortgage will be made from, Cohn said. Many brokers don't want to reveal the lender's name. Having this information, however, allows you to contact the lender yourself to see if the rate you are getting through the broker is a better one than you would have gotten going directly to the lender itself.

- Let your attorney look over any loan commitment before signing it, Newman said. Both mortgage bankers and brokers will give consumers advice, such as which loan is right for that particular borrower. And much of that advice will be good, Newman said. But this information should never be the only professional advice you receive. Have your attorney, who is working on your behalf, go over everything to make sure there are no hidden charges or conditions with the deal being offered.

- Never sign any blank applications. Make sure everything is filled in.

- Don't rely on oral promises. If it's not in writing, be wary of it, Cohn advised.

- Make sure you understand all terms and conditions of the contract. Again, this is why you should show the lending agreement to your attorney. You don't want to sign something you don't understand that may require you to pay an extra $50,000, for example, if you want to pay off the loan early.

WHAT A LOAN WILL COST

Before you apply for any loan, you should shop around, Havemann said, because lenders' interest rates, closing costs and application fees are not all the same. It's like shopping for a chicken: one supermarket may be charging 98 cents a pound while another is charging 79 cents. In addition, money borrowed at a quoted rate of 5 percent could actually be costing you 12 percent, with fees and closing costs.

Most lenders charge an application fee when applying for the loan. It can be $150, $200, or whatever. The setting of application fees is a matter of bank policy, according to the Comptroller of Currency, which regulates federally chartered banks. And although no numbers are kept, "99 percent of the time they're nonrefundable," said a spokesperson with that office. Application fees in state-chartered banks, as well as for mortgage bankers and brokers, are usually not set either, although if excessive fees are found and people complain to their state's banking department, these practices are often looked into. Most banking departments (or whoever's lending the state agency is overseeing) are looking to see that reasonable fees are being charged.

In addition to the application fee, when applying for the loan, you will most likely be charged for a credit check and an appraisal of the property. In some states, such as New York, only the true cost of the credit check and appraisal can be passed on to the borrower. Experts advised checking with your own state's banking department to see what its policy is. An application fee is charged because, as one lender explained, with people comparing loans all over the place, if no application fee were charged, "we'd go through all this work, time and expense and the borrower would say no to the loan and we'd be out of luck."

Junk Fees

For the most part, lenders' application fees are reasonable. But some lenders have been getting creative with fees, warned attorney Howard Newman. Some lenders will entice borrowers with a low application fee. They later make up for this by charging "junk fees" that show up somewhere else as part of the closing costs.

Closing costs are fees and charges tacked onto the mortgage over and beyond the interest rate being quoted. They usually run between 6 and 8 percent of the mortgage amount being borrowed. Closing costs include attorney fees, title insurance and points. One point is equal to 1 percent of the mortgage amount borrowed and must be paid upfront at the closing. Only with FHA loans (explained in Chapter 8) can points be financed along with the rest of the mortgage. A complete list of closing costs is detailed in Chapter 15.

Junk fees came about because of the cut-throat competition created by the huge number of lenders competing for mortgage business around the country, Paul Havemann explained. Consumers care mostly about rates and points and, when shopping around, that's what people compare, he said. A low application fee might also be quoted and what was once part of that fee thrown into closing cost fees. (When business is slow, however, lenders seem to eliminate a number of these junk fees and closing costs to make their loans more attractive and competitive. A number of states have also been cracking down on what these fees are called and what can be charged upfront.)

A favorite fee of Havemann's is the "document preparation fee." This fee can cost as much as several hundred dollars, he said, and is for nothing more than a secretary typing up the loan's paperwork.

Donald Henig, past president of the National Association of Mortgage Brokers, has seen lenders charge $25 for a flood certification, where an independent agency checks to see if a property is in a flood zone. The cost to the lender for this is roughly half that amount.

RESPA to the Rescue. Borrowers are not without protection from being misled about all the fees charged by lenders. Under a federal law known as the Real Estate Settlement Procedures Act of 1974 (or RESPA), a lender must send out a good-faith estimate within 72 hours of receiving a consumer's application fee, Newman said. This lists all the costs and fees connected with the loan. But, Newman added, by the time borrowers are in possession of this piece of paper, they have already paid their nonrefundable application fee.

How else can you tell what closing costs will be BEFORE making the application? Ask what the loan's APR (annual percentage rate) is.

Every loan, when advertised, carries two rates of interest, with the first number usually lower than the second. The ad may read "fixed rate loans 10%," followed by "APR 11.5%." The APR, Newman said, is the true cost of the loan including all closing costs. When shopping around and comparing loans, the APR is what should be compared, not just the interest rate and number of points charged. The APR includes the points and junk fees. Noted Havemann, because too many people don't check the APR, lenders can legally quote a lower interest rate while making extra money on a loan by charging all these junk fees and tacking them onto the closing costs.

Beware of Points

One thing that should be noted here is that all APRs include the cost of points, which is good. But the cost of points is calculated over the life of the loan. The tricky part here is that points are paid upfront (usually at the closing). Should you sell your home before the mortgage term is up, the APR of a loan with points is actually much higher than is listed on the APR in the ad.

An article by real estate columnist Kenneth Harney pointed out how a 30-year fixed-rate loan at 9.75 percent with three points (two paid by the buyer and one by the seller) had an APR of 10.1 percent. If the home were sold after two years, the APR would really be 11.5 percent, meaning you were paying more in the way of interest for your loan than the original APR indicated. If the home had to be sold within the first six months, the APR would actually be 22.3 percent.

When considering whether to pick a mortgage with a slightly lower interest rate and points or a slightly higher interest rate without points, try to calculate how long you plan to stay in the home, experts said. The longer you own the home, the less those points end up costing you and the closer to the true APR the interest rate will be. The reason for this is that the true cost of the points gets stretched out over a longer period. But if, like most first-time buyers, you move up to another home within seven years, then a no-points loan may be less costly for you. The only true way to compare which is the better value is to sit down with your accountant comparing the interest rates, points and time you believe you'll own this first home.

Ask for Closing Costs in Advance

Of course, the more closing costs you have to pay when getting your loan, the more money you'll need upfront to close on the home.

Before filling out any mortgage application forms (and paying any application fees to a lender), ask for a list of closing costs, advised Norman Wellen, president of the Professional Mortgage Banker's Corp. If the lender refuses to give you these costs ahead of time, said Wellen, "I'd be cautious and wonder why."

Newman also suggested asking the lender whether there are any other fees that are not reflected in the closing costs or application fee. "Then read everything and if you see something you don't understand—ask!" Havemann said. To which he added, you should also find out if some of the costs can be reduced.

Trimming Closing Costs. When Havemann was getting his own loan to buy his first home, he saw a charge for title insurance that was higher than what was normally charged. He asked whether the title company being used could be switched to another firm that he knew charged less. The lender did. While you may not be able to spot these higher costs yourself, your attorney may be able to help you.

Another bone of contention with Havemann and others is the borrower paying for the bank's attorney. That attorney is looking out for the bank's interest, Havemann said. Why should the borrower have to pay this cost? Sometimes, you may get lucky and be able to eliminate or reduce this fee. But as one lender said, the bank attorney is a cost of doing business and if it disappears as a fee in one place, it will just show up somewhere else, perhaps in added points or a slightly higher interest rate. However, if you already have the interest, points and other closing costs in writing, adding a new fee will be hard.

Other fees that lenders around the country have attached to closing costs are charges for special service fees and warehousing fees. Warehousing fees cover the difference between what a lender must pay for the money he is borrowing to make a loan and the rate he is charging the customer versus what he gets for the money when the loan is sold on the secondary market.

Havemann's advice is to go over all the fees and then, if you see something that bothers you, "yell a lot. Sometimes you can get rid of a fee and sometimes you can't." But remember, once you sign the application, you are agreeing to the fees.

Also keep in mind, Stanley Greenstein reiterated, "the only common basis that all loans can be compared on is the APR." Only by comparing the APR of loans can you compare the true costs of each and find out which is the best deal.

And when shopping for a mortgage, Havemann repeated, don't sign anything until you understand the terms, payments and what everything means. Then have your attorney look it all over.

OTHER QUESTIONS TO ASK

Besides asking about a loan's APR, there are other questions to put before a lender when inquiring about a loan, including:

- Will I need private mortgage insurance? Most loans with a down payment of less than 20 percent require this. It's a protection for the lender in case you default on the loan, but a cost YOU pay, as mentioned in an earlier chapter.

- Is the loan assumable? That is, can the loan be passed on to a future buyer of your home? When interest rates are up, and you hold a mortgage with a lower rate of interest, this becomes a great selling feature. According to lenders, fewer conventional loans come with the assumability feature. FHA and VA loans still have this, although the new borrower must be approved by the institution.

- If the loan is assumable, is there a fee for transferring it from one party to another? In addition, will the rate of interest, upon transferring it, remain the same?

- At closing, are there any escrow accounts that you will have to put money into? Usually there will be, said Jeffrey C. Daniels, a partner in the law firm of Daniels & Daniels, for such things as property taxes. Added to the principal and interest of each monthly mortgage payment will be 1/12 of your yearly property taxes. Lenders require that government municipalities send all tax bills directly to them instead of to the homeowner. (Some lenders do allow the borrower to pay his or her own property taxes. Instead of paying taxes on an installment plan over the year, the borrower has to come up with a lump sum either half-yearly or yearly, depending on the municipality.) The lender acquires the money to pay these bills from you through a yearly escrow account. This means that monthly mortgage payments will always be higher than

mortgage rate books show (because your payment includes 1/12 of the yearly escrow account used to pay for
taxes, home insurance and any other items).

COMMITMENTS

When you file your application, the lender will ask you to
supply a number of things, including:

- a copy of the contract of sale showing the purchase price,
- W-2 forms,
- one, or possibly two, years' worth of federal tax returns,
- your place of employment, work history and references,
- checking and savings account numbers,
- a list of any other assets you may own, such as stocks or bonds,
- the names and addresses of any other creditors to whom you owe money.

If the loan officer doesn't specify what items to bring, the
borrower should ask prior to showing up to fill out the application,
said Charles Sewright, executive vice president for mortgage lending with Anchor Savings Bank. Each missing piece of information
requires the lender to go back to the borrower, wasting time.

People with special circumstances may need additional paperwork. For example, a divorced person may have to produce his or
her divorce decree. When filling out the application, be honest,
even if you missed a few months' work and fell behind on your
bills, said mortgage broker Carl L. Johnson, Jr. These things eventually come out when the lender does a full credit check.

After all the necessary information is obtained by the lender,
the borrower will receive a commitment letter, Becker said, stating
the loan amount, loan term, interest rate, monthly payments, any
late charges and where the loan closing will be. There will also be

a commitment expiration date, meaning that the rate of interest the borrower has been guaranteed will be good only until this stated day. An extension will often be granted, Becker said, but the lender may charge an additional fee. The rate could also be higher. Both of these items will be spelled out in the commitment letter.

Cash Required at Commitment

At the time of the commitment you will be required to send a nonrefundable check, Becker said. In Lend-Mor's case, the amount required is 1 percent of the loan. Some lenders require more, others less. A borrower should ask what this fee will be prior to making an application. If you do not close on the home for any reason, you lose this money, Becker pointed out.

Conditional Commitments

Sometimes the commitment will carry conditions, said attorney Jeffrey Daniels. This is called a conditional commitment. For first-time buyers coming from a rental, there will usually be no problem with this because many of the conditions often have to do with proving the sale of a previous home. However, if there are any conditions placed on the commitment, each will have to be met before the loan can close.

As previously mentioned, the loan comes with a rate that is locked in for a certain period of time. As attorney C. Jaye Berger pointed out, this becomes critical if a closing date has to be put off. Should there be complications with fulfilling the commitment, or should the seller keep delaying the closing for one reason or another (perhaps because his next home is not ready on time), then you may wind up losing the rate of interest promised. If rates are on the rise, you wind up paying a higher mortgage rate than you originally expected.

If the delay is on the part of the seller, and you do have to pay a higher rate of interest, some sort of penalty can be worked out between the buyer and seller, Berger said. But such a contingency should be put into the contract of sale, illustrating another reason to have a good attorney.

SHORT APPRAISALS

One other problem that a buyer may face, especially in an area where home prices are dropping (and that happened in many areas during the early part of this decade), is that the appraised value of the home doesn't agree with what you, the buyer, have promised to purchase the property for, Daniels said.

For example, if you have agreed to pay $100,000 for a two-bedroom condo, but the appraisal comes back showing that the unit is worth only $90,000, this will affect the amount of money you can borrow from the bank, Daniels said. Lenders give money based only on a certain loan-to-value ratio, usually 80 percent. This means that the lender will make a mortgage for no more than 80 percent of what the home's appraised value is. Lenders do this to protect themselves in case they have to foreclose on the loan. The lender wants to make sure that if the home has to be sold (because you've stopped making payments), it can still get back what has been lent, Daniels explained.

If the appraisal comes back lower than the price you've agreed upon, you either have to renegotiate the selling price, the attorney said, or come up with more cash because the mortgage will no longer cover the full amount of the selling price. (You could also try first asking the bank to make another appraisal or pay to have an outside appraiser come in.)

As prices of homes began dropping in various parts of the country at the start of this decade they have proven to be both a bane and a boom for some buyers. Lower prices have made some homes more affordable for purchasers shut out of the market before. But falling prices have also made appraisals harder to calculate. With many appraisers acting conservatively, said John Monaco, a mortgage broker, the property values they are coming up with are falling short of what some people are agreeing to pay—hence short appraisals and buyers not getting the mortgages they need.

Many buyers can cover a few thousand dollars, Monaco said. But if the difference between the purchase price and the appraised price is $50,000, then the purchaser—especially the first-time purchaser who is strapped for cash—has a real problem.

What a short appraisal also does to buyers, Monaco said, is cause them to question whether the price they have agreed to pay is actually too much. If this does happen to you, experts said it's a good way of reopening negotiations with the seller and asking him or her to cut his or her price further. If the seller refuses, then you will either have to accept the original purchase price and find the additional funds that the lender will now not give you or continue looking at more homes.

Which all goes to prove that even when prices are dropping (which is supposed to be good news for buyers), there's always some wrinkle to complicate an already convoluted process even further.

Chapter 7

GETTING OVER
THE DOWN-PAYMENT
HURDLE

Without a doubt, the most difficult hurdle a first-time buyer has to overcome when purchasing a home is putting together a down payment. Because a lender wants a borrower to have a stake in the house he or she is buying, banks require that a certain percentage of the home's purchase price be put down, upfront, at the time of closing.

The theory behind this is that the more money and equity a person has invested in a home, the less likely the purchaser will be to walk away from the property should he or she run into some kind of financial bind. Likewise, the down payment is further protection that the lender will get his or her mortgage money back should the purchaser default on the loan. Home values sometimes decline, as many markets around the country witnessed during the beginning of this decade. A lender making a 100 percent, or even a 90 percent, loan on a home's purchase price could find himself not being able to get back the mortgage money he lent should he have to foreclose. This happened in Texas during the early 1980's and occurred recently to lenders throughout the Northeast when home prices declined in value.

That's a brief explanation of why a lender requires a down payment. Coming up with the money needed for the down payment, however, isn't usually as simple as the explanation. Observed Keith Asdourian, vice president of Realty World Worth, "most first-time buyers are coming in by the skin of their teeth." It's taking longer to put together the down payment, and many people are buying with barely enough savings and income left over to make ends meet.

HOW MUCH OF A DOWN PAYMENT YOU'LL NEED

Depending on the lender, down payments on conventional loans can range anywhere from 5 to 20 percent of the home's purchase price. You can, of course, put down more to reduce your monthly mortgage payments. Lenders won't complain about that. But the actual dollar figure you'll need for the down payment will depend on the area of the country you're buying your home in. Obviously, the higher the home's price, the more up-front cash you'll need.

In a high housing-cost area where, according to the National Association of Realtors, the median resale price for an existing home was $382,000 in the first quarter of 1992, a 20 percent down payment means you would have to come up with $74,400! Even for the average American home, which was hovering at around $103,000 at that same point in time, you'll need $20,600.

To help keep costs down, first-time buyers will want to seek out homes as far below the median price of the area as they can. They will also want to try to find lenders offering the best mortgage terms with the lowest down-payment requirements.

Aside from state- and government-backed loans, such as FHA and VA loans (which will be discussed in the next chapter and can be gotten with practically nothing to 5 percent down), the minimum down payment requested by many lenders for most conventional loans is now 5 percent. But according to Camille M. Barbone, a loan officer formerly with Dale Mortgage Bankers, lenders are making fewer 5-percent-down loans these days because of a tightening in the credit markets, the failure of many savings-and-loan associations over the past few years and the number of bad loans that wound up on lenders' books during the recession. This can, of course, change at any time for better or for worse. In fact, with the addition of Fannie Mae's Community Home Buyer's program in 1992 allowing 5 percent down, things improved for borrowers. But overall, to get a 5 percent loan, Barbone said, "you have to have incredible A-number-one, crystalline credit along with a specific amount of savings that will help you float the loan should you find yourself out of work." Most people should probably figure on getting a 10-percent-down conventional loan, she said.

WHERE DO YOU FIND A DOWN PAYMENT?

So how do you come up with the thousands of dollars that you're going to need for this down payment?

"If there were any magic answers, I could probably increase my sales phenomenally," said James J. Burke, an associate broker with RE/MAX Realtors. "But there are no magic answers." For many people, the down payment will come from good old scrimping and saving, he added.

Burke has seen a number of first-time buyers remaining with their parents at home for longer periods of time while squirreling away the money they would have shelled out in rent to a landlord. At the same time, these hopeful potential buyers are passing on nights out on the town, foregoing vacations and putting off purchasing new cars. Some are even taking on second jobs, he pointed out. Burke knows from experience what young buyers are going through in putting together a down payment because, a few years ago, he did a number of these things himself while trying to buy his own first home. At that point in his life, he was a financial planner and not a real estate broker.

Backing up Burke's observations about the sacrificing and difficulties in putting a down payment together are people like Margaret Metayer, a single nurse whose housebuying experience was detailed in Chapter 1. She got the $22,000 down payment for her $110,000 home by saving for three years while she took on evening and weekend private nursing jobs. Vacations, eating out, going to the movies, buying new fall and summer wardrobes and lots of other frills were all cut out, she said. She really watched her expenses. In the end, Metayer did achieve her goal, with the entire down payment coming from money she had saved on her own.

But Barbone has observed that, especially in high-cost housing areas like Los Angeles, the New York metropolitan area and Honolulu, those who use only savings to come up with a down payment tend to be couples in their late 20s and early 30s with both partners working. They also appear to have been saving for a number of years, she said, to put that stake together.

High home prices discourage some buyers, said Asdourian. Young couples start with the best of intentions to save for that new home, but after a year or two, they find they still can't buy anything. Instead of stories of how these people scrimped and saved, he said, "I hear more stories of how we tried, but couldn't put it together."

But experts say, as do the people in the first chapter of this book and other first-time buyers all across the country, that if a person is really willing to make the necessary sacrifices, both a down payment and a home can be obtained. And with prices having come down around the country, that means that less of a down payment has to be saved to obtain a home.

"GIL" Financing

Because a growing number of young couples are having trouble saving up the money needed for a down payment, many first-time buyers turn to what Burke calls "GIL Financing," or Good In-Law Financing. Noted Barbone, "Mom and dad are probably the biggest source of down payments."

Currently, each parent can give a child up to $10,000 a year without having to pay any gift tax, said Eric J. Engelhardt, head of his own accounting and financial services firm. That works out to be $20,000 a year from one set of parents. Two sets of parents could gift a couple $40,000. Since tax laws are constantly changing, it's wise to ask your accountant if gift ceilings have been raised or lowered.

Wealthier parents may want to shower their children with a larger gift, paying the IRS the necessary gift tax, but, in these cases, borrowers will run into another problem with their lenders. With a 10-percent-down loan, no more than half of the down payment can come from a gift, said Stephen Sorahan, president of Sterling Mortgage Corporation, a mortgage broker. Five percent of the money has to come from the borrower. This is a guideline set down by the secondary market, which, as has been mentioned before, buys the loans that many lenders make.

One exception is Fannie Mae's Community Home Buyer's Program, detailed in the previous chapter, that permits 2 percent of the 5 percent down payment to come from outside sources such as a parent or employer. The reason for requiring that 2 or 5 percent come from the borrower, Sorahan explained, is that the lender wants to see that a person is capable of saving money on his or her own. For mortgages with down payments over 10 percent, a larger percentage of the money can come from a gift, he said. For example, with a 25-percent-down loan, 20 percent can be a gift while 5 percent must come from the borrower. On 5-percent-down loans, with the exception of the Community Home Buyer's program, ALL of the money for the down payment must come from the borrower. No doubt other programs will surface as the months progress.

Accepting Larger Gifts from Parents. O.K., you say, "we'll take the larger gift from mom and dad, but not tell the lender. We'll say that we saved up all the cash ourselves."

Good theory! But according to Troha, the gift money has to be documented. The parents have to show the lender their savings passbook or transaction slip from the sale of stock or any other documentation that proves where the money was obtained. In addition, the child will have to show his or her own savings passbook documenting the date the money was put in. The lender, Troha explained, wants to be able to trace the trail of the gifted money from the parent right into the child's savings account.

In addition, Sorahan said, according to secondary market regulations, the person gifting money to a borrower has to be a blood relative—a father, mother, aunt, uncle, brother or some other blood relation. A friend giving you money is a grey area and could be challenged. Likewise, the money can't be a gift from the seller. The Community Home Buyer's Program does permit employers and friends to gift money.

Gift money is strictly monitored, Sorahan said, because a lender doesn't want to see a drug dealer, for example, pulling money from out of his mattress, placing it in his savings account and saying that it was a gift from a good friend.

If the purchaser of a lender's loan on the secondary market is not happy with the lender's documentation, that loan buyer could turn around and force the lender, who made the mortgage, to repurchase it. Improper documentation is the number-one reason that loans are repurchased, Sorahan added.

Other Reasons Checks on Gifted Money Are Made. Lenders, Sorahan said, usually go back and check three months' worth of a borrower's bank statements. If a large sum of cash shows up for which the borrower can't document the source, then the lender will refuse to make the loan.

Because of the uncertainty in the industry today, not only is the lender looking closer at the loan, Sorahan added, but so is the secondary market and the private mortgage insurance firm that is insuring the loan when less than 20 percent is put down.

Lenders carefully document the flow of money into a borrower's checking and saving's accounts because, in some instances, borrowers try to pull a fast one and come up with the missing down-payment funds by borrowing the money, Troha said. They may take a loan out against their credit cards. But a lender doesn't want to see any of the down payment borrowed, he said, because that's going to affect a person's ability to repay the mortgage.

As noted in Chapter 6, many lenders use a 28/36 formula that takes into account how much debt you have. If you suddenly borrow money for the down payment, you are throwing this whole formula off and you no longer have the same debt profile that the lender approved, Troha explained. This affects the amount of mortgage money that the lender feels you can borrow and comfortably repay.

"If someone is trying to pull a fast one, then it's probably a deal that shouldn't be done," Sorahan said. In the end, the borrower's failure to repay the mortgage will not only hurt the lender, but also the buyer. The purchaser can lose his house and have his credit rating ruined for years to come.

One Way Around the Gifting Limitations. According to Sorahan and other lenders, it is permissible to get down-payment money by borrowing against a secured asset, such as a car. But that liability has to be figured into the 28/36 debt ratio. Lenders are very careful in tracing the source of a down payment, Sorahan said, because "there's a lot of hocus pocus that goes on with down payments." A lender wants to be sure the down payment is not borrowed, overgifted or gotten through nefarious means.

Should a lender not sell its loans to the secondary market, Sorahan added, then it can set whatever rules it wants with regard to down payments. A bigger percentage of this money may be allowed to be a gift. But many lenders, even those who keep the loans in their own portfolios, follow secondary market regulations, he pointed out, just in case they may want to sell the loan at a later date.

However, some real estate experts say there is a legal way for a parent to make a large gift and have it look as if it belongs to the first-time buyer. If mom and dad want to give you a large gift that works out to be more than half of your 10 percent down payment, Asdourian said, have them make the gift more than three months before the lender starts investigating your checking and savings accounts. For example, eight months before you go home shopping, transfer the money into your savings account.

Some lenders believe that while such a practice is perfectly legal, if everyone started doing it, guidelines would be changed. Those that buy loans might start requiring that lenders investigate eight months' or a year's worth of transactions in a buyer's savings and checking accounts.

More Sources for Down-Payment Money

Another source of down-payment money, Barbone said, is an unexpected cash windfall, something lenders won't question. "Frequently, I hear things like 'I was in a car accident and accumulated money' or 'my grandmother died and left me some money,'" she said. Newlyweds often put together down payments from cash wedding gifts they've gotten.

For Joseph Petrillo and his sister Frances, two recent first-time buyers, a down payment was gotten from their parents, who refinanced their present home. Having bought the property many years ago, Petrillo's parents had a lot of equity built up in the home. His parents pulled out enough money for him and his sister to make a down payment on their own home. "We're a reasonably close family," Joseph Petrillo said. "We all try to help each other achieve their goals."

If mom and dad don't have money to gift to you, or a lottery jackpot isn't in your future, then you might try getting some money for your down payment by selling some of your assets, Burke said. When he was buying his first home, he not only sold some stock, but a red sports car that he had saved up for over a number of years. "I loved that car," Burke recalled. He and his then wife had put together all the cash they could for a down payment, but were still short money to buy the first home they wanted. He ended up selling the car, much to his wife's surprise, because she knew how hard he had saved for it and what it meant to him. "But I wanted a house," he said. And when you sit down to decide whether or not to sell an asset you value, the decision "comes down to how much you want a house."

Barbone has also seen buyers cashing certificates of deposit that still have a few years to go before maturity and paying the early withdrawal penalties just to put together a down payment. But once again, she pointed out, if you cash in a CD, the lender will want verification of where this sudden burst of money into your savings account came from.

Help from Employers

Sometimes, help can be gotten from an employer, Asdourian said. Especially on transfers from a less expensive housing area to a more costly one, employers will kick in money towards the buying of a home.

But once again the lender is going to look at this money, Troha said. The money coming from an employer can't be a loan that you have to pay back. That will affect the mortgage that you're getting (remember 28/36?). The money also can't be a gift for a down payment, because the secondary market limits gifts to blood relatives. There are exceptions to this, however, such as the Community Home Buyer's Program. What employers can do, Sorahan said, is allocate money to pay for a real estate broker's commission. Noted Troha, an employee can also give you a $5,000 bonus that you can use for anything you want when buying the house. The money can be designated for help with closing costs.

DON'T FORGET THOSE CLOSING COSTS WHEN SAVING FOR A HOME

Closing costs will be discussed in detail in Chapter 15. But for now, this expense is something you should keep in the back of your mind while putting together your stake for your home.

Noted Barbone, "A lot of people in the banking industry play down closing costs because it's a deterrent to sales." But the reality is that closing costs can run between 6 and 8 percent of the mortgage amount being borrowed.

A couple buying a $100,000 home with 10 percent down struggles to put together the $10,000 down payment, Barbone explained. "They have no idea that they then need another $8,000 for closing costs." All of a sudden, the home that seemed like it was close to becoming a reality is now $8,000 further out of reach, she said.

But while a seller can't give you money towards the down payment of a home, the seller can help with the closing costs, Troha said. Lending rules allow a seller to contribute up to 6 percent of the purchase price of a home to closing costs when a 10 percent down payment is being made by the purchaser. The amount of closing costs that can be given by the seller increases to 9 percent if the buyer is putting 25 percent down. "This is a good way for cash poor borrowers to buy a home," Troha said. If the seller kicks in money for closing costs, then more of the buyer's savings can be used towards the down payment.

With a buyer saving 5 percent for a down payment, a parent kicking in 5 percent and the seller giving you 6 percent for closing costs, a home becomes a little easier to obtain, Troha said. And, of course, an employer can also designate money for closing costs, making it that much easier.

SHOPPING CAREFULLY FOR A LOAN

Depending on how competitive your local market is, if you shop well, you may be able to find a mortgage without any closing costs, Engelhardt advised. This will help reduce a buyer's up-front costs, he added. A lender is especially likely to offer this type of deal in a competitive market.

But experts pointed out that the interest rate on the mortgage should be compared along with the closing costs. Sometimes you could end up paying a higher rate of interest for the privilege of not paying any closing costs. However, if up-front money is your problem and you can meet the payments of a slightly higher interest rate, this may be the wiser way to go.

MORE DOWN-PAYMENT HELP

Another source of down payments, Engelhardt said, is borrowing from a 401(k) savings plan. But getting money from this source has to be structured correctly, he warned. In the eyes of the Internal Revenue Service, the tapping of this money has to be viewed as a loan and not an early withdrawal or distribution of income. If the IRS doesn't view this as a loan, there are tax penalties to be reckoned with. Before going this route, check with your accountant, Engelhardt advised.

There has also been talk of allowing first-time buyers to borrow from their Individual Retirement Accounts, better known as IRAs. But while many keep lobbying Congress to allow this, as of this writing, nothing has been done.

Builder Incentives When Buying New

When shopping for a newly constructed home (or a condo or co-op converted from an existing rental building), sometimes you can find a builder who is offering incentives to purchase, especially in areas where the market is slow. These incentives often include no or low down-payment financing, Barbone said. The builder works out a deal with a lender to offer reduced rate financing, or financing with little or no down payment, as an incentive to get people to buy at his development as opposed to somewhere else, she explained.

The builder sometimes offers these incentives, Barbone said, because he realizes the reason people aren't buying is not because the home's price is too high, but because the first-time buyer market he is aiming for can't come up with the necessary down payment. The purchasers have the income to make the monthly mortgage, but they're cash poor and don't have the money for the up-front costs. Instead of reducing the home's selling price, the builder makes a price cut through financing incentives, Barbone said. Some builders will also pick up any closing costs connected with the mortgage.

But many experts warned buyers to check all incentives out carefully. Some offer no-down-payment loans, but with an interest rate that rises after two or three years. Monthly mortgage payments can wind up costing you a lot more than you anticipated as the years go on. You should always have an attorney check any offer out and be sure that you fully understand what it means.

No-Down-Payment Loans from Sellers

Some have asked, "What about getting a no-down-payment loan from a desperate seller?" You see ads on TV all the time about people who made millions buying real estate with no money down of their own. But Burke said you see no-down deals mostly when the market is rising. Many of the ads on TV, he said, suggest that you can get a desperate seller to give you a no-down deal because he really has to sell his or her home. The theory is good, but Burke has found that sellers who are desperate to leave town for one reason or another usually don't want to have any ties left to the place they are moving from. If they make a loan to a buyer and that purchaser defaults, then the seller has to come back looking for his or her money. In Burke's experience, most sellers who are relocating don't want to get involved with this type of loan.

So what about getting a no-down-payment loan from a desperate seller who is unloading his home because he's in some kind of financial bind and can't afford to keep the house? In most of these cases, the seller needs all the cash he can get his hands on to pay off the existing mortgage, said Burke, who saw sellers like this when he was a financial planner. Cash-poor, most of these sellers can't afford to give you a no-down deal, he pointed out. They need all the money they can get from the sale of the property.

In cases where sellers can make a mortgage because they don't really need the money from one home to buy another, as is the case with a retiring couple moving from one area of the country to another, it's the seller's attorney who nixes the deal, Burke said. The reasoning is that the buyer may turn out to be a deadbeat and then the seller will have to go through all sorts of legal maneuvering, including foreclosure, to get his or her money back. But sometimes, these deals do get made and the seller will agree to play banker (Chapter 9 deals with this in greater detail).

Creative Down Payments

Buyers feeling cash poor and not having the money for a down payment, but still hungry for property, may want to consider purchasing a home using a contract for deed sale. Also known as an installment land sale, land contract for deed or contract of sale, a contract for deed sale requires little or no money down. Payments of principal plus interest are made over a specified period of time with the seller retaining title on the property until the last payment is made.

To buy a home this way, you need a seller who once again doesn't need the money from the home to buy another. But there are advantages to persuade a seller to go along with this type of deal, said Ray Connor, a broker and owner of The Housing Exchange.

In exchange for no money down, you can agree to a slightly higher rate of interest than the person would get if he or she put the money into a savings account in a bank, Connor said. In addition, the seller pays less in federal taxes with this type of sale. "If the property is sold outright," Connor noted, "whatever profits he makes, the seller pays in capital gains taxes in one year." However, with a land contract sale, the gain can be spread out over a number of years. The interest that the seller collects on the mortgage does have to be reported as income, Connor explained.

There is a risk for the buyer, however, with a land contract sale, said real estate attorney Ronald J. Schwartz. If the buyer defaults on the loan, the seller is entitled to keep all or part of the money already paid (depending on how the contract is worded). The buyer then ends up with nothing, Schwartz explained.

Another problem is that since the seller is retaining title until the last payment is made, a buyer never knows if that title is clear, Schwartz added. A final check on a title is usually done the day before closing in a conventional deal. With a land contract for sale deal, what was clear title when you went into the agreement 15 years ago could wind up with numerous liens against it when you take it over, meaning you will have to clear those judgments up before you can sell the property. "These deals really are filled with too many risks," Schwartz said.

But Connor, who bought an office building this way, said that you can protect yourself if you record the installment contract with the local county clerk's office, noting, "Now you have legal recourse and can prove that the property is part of a land contract for deed sale." The buyer should also have an attorney draw up the contract with all the pitfalls spelled out, such as requiring a reasonable period of time to make a payment if it's late. In addition, the buyer should ask to be notified if a payment is not received, just in case a check is lost in the mail.

The title should also be kept with a third party, Connor said. This way, if the seller dies, the heirs know that the property is involved in a contract for land sale. "With the right precautions, this a good deal for both sides to get into," Connor maintained.

Contract Vendee

An even riskier method of coming up with a down payment, Burke said, is with a contract vendee. For this to work, you need to find a person who is selling a home for less than its actual or appraised value, such as sometimes happens with an estate sale.

For example, Burke was involved in a deal where the owners wanted anything over $100,000 for a home that was appraised for $130,000. Burke's client offered $105,000 for the home, but with the proviso that he could sell his right to buy the property to someone else before the closing. If another buyer was not found by Burke's client prior to the closing, then the gentleman would buy the property himself. The seller agreed. The buyer then went out and found someone willing to purchase the home for $130,000. At the closing, the seller and the two buyers were all present. The seller received his $105,000, while the second buyer received the home. The first buyer (Burke's client) made a $25,000 profit on a piece of property he never really owned. The gentleman took that money and used it as a down payment on another residence that he planned to live in, Burke explained.

While a contract vendee is a quick way to make money for a down payment, "this is not for the average person," Burke pointed out. Should you not be able to find a buyer willing to pay a higher price than you've committed to pay within the period between signing the contract of sale and the closing (usually about three months), then you will wind up having to buy that home yourself. If you do attempt this, Burke added, it helps to have a good broker working with you who can help locate both a suitable property (with a seller willing to do a contract vendee) and another buyer.

The Parent as Banker

One other method for a no-down-payment loan is through a wealthy parent, Eric Engelhardt said. He had a client, for example, who made a $300,000 loan to his son. The offspring then went out and bought a home for cash.

For the son, there were far fewer closing costs than he would have encountered with a traditional lender. In addition, the parent required no down payment on the loan. The parent also gave the son an attractive, below-market interest rate.

The actual loan was a five-year mortgage with a balloon payment due at the end of the fifth year, Engelhardt went on the explain. This meant that, at the end of the fifth year, the borrower (the man's son) would have to find a traditional lender to refinance the property so the son could repay his father.

"Of course, not everyone has parents who can do this," Engelhardt admitted. But the father realized that his son was cash poor, yet had the income to make the monthly payments on a $300,000 mortgage. Once the son built up some equity in the home, and was also making more money as he moved up in his job, a traditional lender would easily write a loan for him, Engel-hardt said.

Saving, Scrimping and Gifts

Both Burke's contract vendee tactic and Engelhardt's wealthy parent example are novel ideas for overcoming the down-payment hassle. The trouble is, these ideas are not for the average person.

For most first-time buyers, a down payment will most likely be achieved by scrimping, saving and probably a gift from a relative, Asdourian said. "There's just not a lot of innovative ways out there to get a down payment," he noted.

While Barbone has seen people trying all sorts of things to get a down payment—ranging from selling assets (which is fine) to taking out credit card loans (which is forbidden), her best advice for obtaining one is to "work your butt off and save." If the motivation for a home is strong enough and a person or young couple is willing to make some sacrifices, both brokers and lenders agreed that while it may be rough, a down payment can be put together and home ownership achieved.

Chapter 8

GOVERNMENT HELP

In seeking financing for a first home, many people go off to their local lender trying to find the mortgage with the best interest rate and term. But before going after a conventional loan, experts recommend first checking whether you qualify for any state or federal government-backed loan programs. As you'll see, many come with below-market rates of interest while others require less in the way of a down payment. Your qualification for these loans, however, often depends on limits on income and how much the new home or resale can cost.

FHA LOANS

During the last decade, Federal Housing Administration guaranteed loans, which were once sought after by most first-time buyers, have lost some of their luster. One of the prime reasons, said John P. Cullen, a retired partner of Saxon Equities, which makes such loans, is that home prices in many high-cost areas, such as the Northeast and California, began rising 20 to 30 percent a year. FHA loan guarantee ceilings of $101,250 didn't cover many of the properties in those areas, he said.

In addition, "conventional loan rates used to be much higher than FHA," Cullen noted. But about six or seven years ago, conventional rates became more competitive. The result was that the number of FHA loans made in some areas of the country dropped to nearly zero.

However, in the last few years the FHA has been positioning itself for a comeback. According to Martin Sckalor, director of the housing development division at the FHA, mortgage ceilings have been raised since early 1990 in high-cost areas around the country and problems that lenders had with administering these loans have been ironed out. "We think the changes will make a dramatic impact," he said.

The Pros and Cons of FHA Mortgages

Cullen pointed out some of the advantages of FHA loans over conventional mortgages, which include the allowance of putting as little as 3 percent down, the ability to include closing costs in the financing and letting borrowers qualify using a greater percentage of their income for housing.

Noted Cullen, FHA loan rates are not set by the government. While the FHA guarantees these loans, lenders fund them. Closing costs vary and rates fluctuate with the market.

Some lenders and real estate brokers often steer buyers away from FHA mortgages because they believe there's a lot of extra paperwork involved and that it takes a long time to get a commitment. But that's a misconception based on experiences from a decade or more ago, Sckalor said. Things have speeded up considerably.

Cullen said lenders can now take an FHA application to commitment in only three weeks and possibly less if income and credit checks come back promptly. "It isn't like it used to be," he said.

With its direct endorsement program, a lender can now do everything from credit checks to appraisals, Sckalor said. John Petrillo, who recently closed on his first home using an FHA mortgage, said that it took him less than a month to go from application to commitment.

FHA Misconceptions. Three misconceptions that borrowers have about FHA loans is that there are income, age and home sale price limits. The fact is, there are no limitations on any of these three items. An FHA loan is limited in high-cost areas of the country to $151,725 as of January 1993. But if more money is put down, a home costing more than the limit can be purchased. (Loan limits are lower in parts of the country with lower housing prices. Check with a local lender for FHA limits.)

Other things to remember with FHA loans include that:

- Mortgages can be adjustable or 30-year fixed, with the latter being the preferred.

- FHA loans can be used to finance condos and new construction, but not co-ops.

- The loans are assumable. However, where assumability was previously automatic, Sckalor said, now a credit check has to be done and the buyer approved before the loan is passed along by the seller. It was found some people were abusing the assumability feature, passing loans on to unqualified people.

- The seller doesn't have to pay the points on the loan (as once was the case). Today, Sckalor said, this is negotiable. One point is equal to one percent of the mortgage amount borrowed.

- FHA loans can be made with approximately 5 percent down, Sckalor said, with the first $25,000 requiring only 3 percent down, 5 percent down on amounts up to $124,875 and 10 percent for the remainder up to $151,725 (in high-cost areas). Noted Cullen, a one-half percent fee of the borrowed amount must be paid for an insurance premium. This protects the FHA in case the borrower defaults on the loan. However, both this fee and all closing costs can be financed as part of the loan. This means that someone borrowing $150,000 can buy a home with an FHA loan involving up-front expenses of just $4,500. One negative, said Scott Lanoff, manager of

131

GMAC Mortgage Corp., is that conventional loans may still carry a slightly lower rate of interest than FHA loans. Joseph Petrillo, however, said that he found his FHA rate was about 1 percent lower than other lenders were quoting him for conventional mortgages. Since loan rates are constantly changing, it pays to shop around. However, remember that most conventional loans will not have many of the features that an FHA loan has, which can be a big asset for a first-time buyer.

More Pros and Cons of FHA Loans. American Savings Bank no longer makes FHA loans. Said Thomas Szczepaniak, a vice president with the bank, first-time buyers can do better with some state-backed loans. He did admit, however, that FHA guidelines are more flexible than either some state or conventional loans. While most conventional loans require that no more than 28 percent of a borrower's monthly gross income go towards mortgage payments, real estate taxes and homeowners insurance and no more than 36 percent of monthly gross income go towards debt, the FHA's limits are 29/41, Skalor said. Noted Troha, there is even flexibility with this: Some loans have been made allowing 35 percent of a person's monthly gross income to go towards housing.

"FHA loans let a lot of our buyers qualify for homes who couldn't qualify with a conventional mortgage," said broker Bob Herrick. Someone who had a bankruptcy two or more years ago and has established credit in three places—such as a credit card or car loan—can qualify for an FHA loan, Cullen said. Few conventional loans would be written on so current a bankruptcy.

Some critics say FHA appraisals come out lower than those done for conventional mortgages. "Not true," responded Cullen. His staff appraiser comes up with realistic values no lower than those obtained for a conventional loan.

Other Reasons Why the Number of FHA Loans Being Made Has Slipped in Some Areas

Said Bob Herrick, "A lot of brokers are losing sales left and right because they don't understand FHA." But some brokers, like Frank Fava, owner/broker of Huntington Squire Real Estate, said that agents don't push FHA loans because home prices in their areas are much higher than current price-range limitations. For a first-time buyer who needs to finance as much as he can, if homes in an area are going for $200,000, then $151,725, the ceiling set for high-cost areas around the country in January 1993, won't be enough.

Even more FHA business could be done if mortgage brokers were allowed to both originate and process the loans, said Donald Henig, former president of the National Association of Mortgage Brokers. Mortgage Brokers originated over $100 billion in mortgages nationwide in 1989, he said.

But mortgage brokers can't originate or process FHA loans, Sckalor said, "because they are not approved as FHA lenders." They can, however, steer borrowers to a lender doing FHA loans.

Which leads to the point that it is not the Federal Housing Administration, overseeing the program, that is making the loans. It is local mortgage bankers and savings-and-loan institutions. The FHA is guaranteeing that the loan will be paid back. Many lenders are qualified to make FHA loans, Sckalor said. However, some that are qualified have not been offering them. To find out which lenders are making FHA loans in your area, contact nearby lenders or call your local FHA office for a list of participating financial institutions.

Many lenders, such as Cullen, believe that if FHA limits were raised higher, FHA business would increase even more. Ceilings do change and they are different in some areas of the country, depending on what housing prices are in a particular locality. To find out current ceilings for your community, contact a participating FHA lender.

VA LOANS

Introduced in 1944 to help returning GIs from World War II purchase homes with no money down, the Veteran's Administration, or VA, loan has been helping homebuyers, especially first-time home purchasers, ever since.

However, in some higher-priced areas of the country, VA loans became less in demand in the eighties as home prices rose. Buyers turned to other loans because sellers balked at having to pay any points connected with the loan (as the VA required), and lenders and real estate brokers complained about the additional weeks it took to close a deal using a VA loan. But interest in these loans is on the rise again, thanks to sweeping changes instituted by the VA on November 1, 1992. "These are the biggest changes since the inception of the VA loan," said Gerard J. Prizeman, head of the VA's loan program for the eastern two-thirds of New York State. Changes include:

- Approximately 500,000 more Americans nationwide are eligible for the loan, with the inclusion of National Guard members and reservists with six years of service and still serving, as well as those honorably discharged. Previously eligible for the loan:

  - Vets honorably discharged who had 90 days of war-time service in WWII, Korea, Vietnam or the Persian Gulf.

  - Any person in the armed forces who put in 24 months of peacetime service.

  - Persons who were injured while serving and then discharged no matter how long they were in.

  - Spouses of vets who died and remain unmarried.

- The interest rate will no longer be set by the Secretary of Veteran's Affairs in Washington, DC, but fluctuate with market conditions, as do other loan rates. This makes the rate more competitive.

- Along with the fixed-rate loan, an adjustable mortgage is now available as part of a three-year experiment, which could be extended after 1995. The ARM can't go up or down more than 1 percent in any year and has a 5 percent lifetime cap.

- Sellers are no longer required to pay points. They can be negotiated as part of the deal. "This was the biggest negative people saw with a VA loan," Prizeman said.

  "The VA is finally joining the real world," Herrick said. While it's good that the VA watches after a veteran's interests, some past policies—such as the seller having to pay points—were too protective and sometimes resulted in vets taking another type of loan.

VA loans require no down payment. However, a funding fee of 1.25 percent of the loan balance must be paid when nothing is put down. The fee drops to .75 percent when between 5 and 10 percent is put down and .50 percent when 10 percent or more is put down.

Other Benefits of a VA Loan

- There are no income maximums for borrowers. As long as the vet can meet the loan's monthly payments, he or she will qualify for the loan.

- The loan is good for homes up to $184,000. A more expensive home can be purchased if the vet pays the difference as a down payment.

- After a VA loan is repaid, another can be taken out. This is called restoration of entitlement. All veterans now receive an entitlement of $36,000.

- Up to 41 percent of a vet's monthly income can go towards paying debt, including the mortgage.

- Like the FHA, the VA is not making the mortgage, but guaranteeing each loan for up to $36,000. If a veteran defaults, and the house must be sold, the VA reimburses the lender the difference between the mortgage and the unrecovered amount after the sale, up to $36,000. For this reason, no private mortgage insurance is needed with a VA mortgage, as it is with conventional loans when less than 20 percent is put down.

- If a vet does default, the lender must notify the VA 90 days after this occurs. The VA then tries to help the vet keep the home, looking at ways the vet can become current with payments.

- If a vet can't stay current with payments, the VA will help the owner sell the house.

- If the vet is foreclosed on, but the mortgage balance exceeds what's recovered in a sale, the VA will pay the difference. The vet will not be obligated to repay the VA.

- The VA will take over a mortgage if a vet is having problems paying a loan because a job was lost and the vet's new job pays less. The vet can stay in the home, making payments directly to the VA, which can lower the interest rate up to 3 percent. The VA can also extend the loan's term to 30 years.

- VA loans can be used for single-family homes and condos. Co-ops are not eligible because they are not real property.

- The loan is assumable even to a non-vet. However, the VA or an automatic lender must approve the transfer.

- Both VA and conventional loans can be refinanced with a VA loan. Closing costs can be factored into the mortgage as long as the total loan is not more than 90 percent of the home's current appraised value.

Some Past VA Loan Negatives

One reason lenders and real estate sales people shied away from recommending VA mortgages, said broker Frank Orlandino, a partner in Eisenoff Realty, is that it used to take four to six months to get these loans approved. However, Prizeman said, these loans can now be closed within 45 days or less. There will still be delays, though, if there is a problem getting information, such as with a credit check.

There had also been complaints that the VA requires too many repairs be made to a home before it approves the loan. But, Prizeman said, 70 percent of all mortgages now go through with no repairs needed. The only changes required are for safety, sanitary or structural reasons. These are based on the report issued by the appraiser sent to examine whether the home is worth what the veteran is paying.

VA Guidelines. There are certain guidelines for a buyer to be approved for a VA loan, Prizeman said. His or her present debt is looked at, along with his or her ability to pay the added mortgage payments and property taxes. On a home priced $70,000 or more, a family of four must have at least $913 a month left after all expenses are paid. A single needs $401 and a couple $673. A family of three needs $810 (these figures can change as interest rates drop or rise). "But this is not fixed in stone," Prizeman said. "Guidelines are flexible." Lenders said they've seen the VA stretch its rules to help, for example, a disabled veteran qualify.

To find out more about VA mortgages as well as the lenders in your area offering these loans, contact your local Veterans Administration office.

STATE HELP

Another place to turn to for obtaining help in buying your first home is the housing finance authority in the state where you reside. Throughout the nation, each state offers at least one program that makes low-cost financing available as well as, sometimes, below-market-rate housing.

One thing to keep in mind is that unlike conventional mortgages, most of these programs have family income limits and often ceiling prices on homes that can be purchased. Within a particular state, income limits and home ceiling prices may differ depending on what part of the state you live in. In high cost-of-living areas, such as major cities, the ceilings and limits are often higher than for the rest of the state. Additionally, depending on a state's fiscal condition, programs can be added, dropped or changed. It pays to call your local housing finance authority for the latest information.

On the next page are some of the programs offered by states around the nation at the time this book was being put together. Not every program that a state was offering at that time is listed. In the case of below-market mortgages, interest rates are not quoted because these fluctuate like any other mortgage rate. Likewise, home ceiling prices and income limits differ around the state and change from time to time. Phone numbers and addresses are given so that you can contact your state housing finance authority for specifics, updates and the names of the lenders in your area participating in the programs. Remember, on low-interest mortgages, in the majority of cases, the state is not making the loan, but guaranteeing it. The loan is actually being made by an established lender.

ALABAMA

Alabama Housing Finance Authority
P.O. Box 230909
Montgomery, AL 36123-0909
Phone: 1-800-325-AHFA

PROGRAM: SINGLE-FAMILY MORTGAGE REVENUE BOND PROGRAM. This offers below-interest mortgages on 30-year fixed-rate FHA or VA guaranteed loans. There are income limits that differ around the state. Mortgages will be made only on single-family homes, fee simple townhomes, condominiums and permanently affixed mobile homes and manufactured housing. There are ceiling prices on the homes eligible for these loans.

PROGRAM: MORTGAGE CREDIT CERTIFICATES (MCC). The MCC reduces the amount of federal income tax paid, giving the buyer more available income to qualify for, and pay off, his or her monthly mortgage payments. The buyer receives a tax credit equal to 20 percent of the annual interest paid on the mortgage loan. This is a dollar-for-dollar reduction on any federal tax liability. The remaining 80 percent of the buyer's mortgage interest qualifies as an itemized tax deduction.
   There are income limits for eligibility in this program, and it is open only to people who have not had an ownership interest in a principal residence at any time during the three years prior to obtaining financing.

PROGRAM: HOMESTEAD EXEMPTIONS AND ALLOW-ANCES. Alabama offers homestead exemptions from county ad valorem (or property) taxes, excluding school taxes, up to a certain dollar amount.

ALASKA

Alaska Housing Finance Corporation
520 East 34th Avenue
Anchorage, AK 99503
Phone: (907)561-1900

PROGRAM: BELOW-MARKET LOANS. These rates fluctuate with the market and have a minimum down payment of 10 percent (unless used with a VA or FHA loan, where down payment requirements are lower). There are income limits differing throughout the state, as well as ceiling prices for homes. These 30-year fixed-rate loans can be used on single-family dwellings, condominium units and certain types of mobile homes.

PROGRAM: SECOND-MORTGAGE LOAN PURCHASE PROGRAM. After buying a home, if it needs work, Alaska offers below-market second mortgages that can be used on projects that improve the basic livability or energy efficiency of the dwelling, including completions or additions. There are loan limits. Mobile homes are not eligible.

ARIZONA

Arizona Department of Commerce
State Capitol
1700 West Washington
Phoenix, AZ 85007
Phone: (602)542-5371

PROGRAM: MORTGAGE REVENUE BOND PROGRAM.
Low-interest mortgages are available in all areas except
the city of Phoenix and Pima County. The loan is a
30-year, fixed-rate VA or FHA loan, with applicants meeting the usual qualifications for these types of mortgages
(these are listed earlier in this chapter). There are income
limits based on the area of the state in which the buyer
lives. The loans may be used only on single-family homes,
condominiums, townhouses and manufactured homes.

ARKANSAS

Arkansas Development Finance Authority
P.O. Box 8023
Little Rock, AR 72203
Phone: (501)682-5900

PROGRAM: SINGLE-FAMILY RESIDENTIAL HOUSING PROGRAMS. Low-interest mortgages are made through participating lending institutions. There are purchase price limits and borrower income limits based on the county in which the purchaser resides.

CALIFORNIA

California Housing Finance Agency
1121 L Street
7th Floor
Sacramento, CA 95814-3974
Phone: (916)322-3991
or
California Housing Finance Agency
5711 Slauson Avenue
Culver City, CA 90230
Phone: (213)736-2355

PROGRAM: CHAF RESALE PROGRAM. Offers below-market, fixed-rate mortgages to first-time buyers whose incomes and home sale prices do not exceed established limits.

PROGRAM: SELF-HELP HOUSING. Nonprofit developers acquire land, provide building plans and select eligible families to participate in the program. Self-help borrowers, who receive below-market mortgages on the finished home, must be first-time buyers and meet income and underwriting requirements. Home-building families are organized into labor-sharing groups and, under the direct supervision of the technical staff of the nonprofit corporation, work as a group to construct their own homes. Typically, families devote 30 to 40 hours per week for seven to nine months constructing the residences. In most cases, foundations, plumbing and other technical work is subcontracted out.

PROGRAM: HOME PURCHASE ASSISTANCE PROGRAM. This program assists qualified lower-income first-time buyers by providing funds through a deferred-payment second loan. The second mortgage reduces the principal and interest payments on the first mortgage and/or pays all or a portion of the loan's closing costs. Borrowers' incomes must not exceed established limits and must also meet other requirements.

PROGRAM: MATCHING DOWN-PAYMENT PROGRAM. The program assists lower-income homebuyers by providing funds through a deferred second loan to pay closing costs and/or reduce the monthly principal and interest payments on the first mortgage. The borrower does not have a monthly payment on the second loan, which carries a low simple interest rate. The interest is due and payable at the time the home is sold or refinanced. The program matches the dollar amount of the borrower's down payment, up to a maximum of $5,000. There are income limitations, and borrowers must meet all other FHA loan underwriting standards.

COLORADO

Colorado Housing and Finance Authority
Home Ownership Division
1981 Blake Street
Denver, CO 80202-1272
Phone: (303)297-2432

PROGRAM: TRANSITIONAL HOUSING PROGRAM. Eligible buyers can take mobile homes and move them to permanent sites (with foundations). Improvements are then made on the homes, such as the construction of extensions and garages. Below-market financing is available to help with improvements. Buyers can then take the equity built up in the home to trade up to something else.

CONNECTICUT

Connecticut Housing Finance Authority
40 Cold Spring Road
Rocky Hill, CT 06067-4005
Phone: (203)721-9501

PROGRAM: HOME MORTGAGE LOANS. The program offers mortgages at interest rates lower than those generally available from other sources. These are fixed-rate loans on homes that meet applicable sales price limits in different areas of the state. Borrowers' incomes must also be within set limits. Condominiums can be financed if the CHFA has approved the unit.

PROGRAM: DOWNPAYMENT ASSISTANCE PROGRAM. This is a low-interest loan for individuals who don't have a down payment to acquire a home. This loan can be used only in conjunction with a CHFA first mortgage and may cover up to 25 percent of the purchase price for a period of 30 years. The applicant's income must be within the limits set by the CHFA.

DELAWARE

Delaware State Housing Authority
18 The Green
P.O. Box 1401
Dover, DE 19903
Phone: (302)736-4263
or
Elbert N. Carvel State Building
820 North French Street
Wilmington, DE 19801
Phone: (302)571-3720

PROGRAM: HOME OWNERSHIP MORTGAGE PRO-GRAM. Below-market mortgages are made available to first-time buyers who have not owned a principal residence in the past three years and who meet income and sales-price limits. There are different interest rates based on household income. A mobile home on rented land or on a temporary foundation does not count as previous homeownership.

PROGRAM: SECOND MORTGAGE ASSISTANCE LOAN. Borrowers with the lowest qualifying household incomes, whose first mortgages are financed through the DSHA, can also qualify for a second mortgage to help with down-payment and closing costs in excess of $1,000. The borrower must put up the first $1,000. The second mortgage will be a lien against the property and must be paid in full, along with accrued interest, when the home is sold or refinanced.

FLORIDA

Florida Housing Finance Agency
2740 Centerview Drive
Suite 300
Tallahassee, FL 32399-2100
Phone: (904)488-4197

PROGRAM: HOME OWNERSHIP REVENUE BOND PRO-GRAM. Below-market, 30-year fixed rate VA and FHA loans are available. A borrower's income and a home's purchase price must not exceed limits that vary through-out the state.

PROGRAM: DOWNPAYMENT ASSISTANCE. For lower-income homebuyers, zero-interest second mortgage loans are available that can be applied toward closing costs, the down payment and the reduction of the first mortgage amount, which must be gotten through the FHFA.

PROGRAM: HUD REPO PROPERTIES. These are prop-erties that were originally financed with FHA mortgage money and have been repossessed by the Department of Housing and Urban Development (HUD). First-time buy-ers can make a bid and, if theirs is the winner, the FHFA mortgage can be used to finance the property. These properties are not available at all times.

GEORGIA

Georgia Residential Finance Authority
60 Executive Parkway South
Suite 250
Atlanta, GA 30329
Phone: (404)320-4840

PROGRAM: SINGLE FAMILY HOMEOWNERSHIP LOAN PROGRAM. This provides below-market interest rate mortgages to first-time homebuyers through participating lenders. Income and home prices must not exceed established ceilings.

PROGRAM: MORTGAGE CREDIT CERTIFICATE (MCC) PROGRAM. This allows for the reduction of a homebuyer's tax liability on a dollar-for-dollar basis. The specific amount of the credit depends on how much interest is paid on a mortgage loan obtained from the GRFA. MCCs are available to homebuyers who meet household income and home purchase-price limits.

PROGRAM: GEORGIA HOMESTEADING PROGRAM. The GRFA buys HUD-foreclosed homes and then sells them for $1 to qualified low-income families selected in a drawing. The new owners must agree to live in the home for a minimum of five years and do whatever work is necessary to bring the house up to standard building-code conditions. This program is available in only a limited number of Georgia communities.

HAWAII

For low-interest mortgage information, contact:
Housing Finance and Development Corporation
Seven Waterfront Plaza
Suite 300
500 Ala Moana Boulevard
Honolulu, HI 96813
Phone: Participating lenders

For homesteading information, contact:
Department of Hawaiian Home Lands
P.O. Box 1879
Honolulu, HI 96805
Phone: 1-800-GOV-4644

PROGRAM: HULA MAE PROGRAM. Below-market mortgages are offered through participating lenders. Borrowers' incomes must be below certain levels, depending on where they live in the state. The homes being purchased must not exceed posted ceilings. Eligible are single-family residences, condos and townhomes. Leasehold properties are eligible if the remaining term of the lease is 35 years or more.

PROGRAM: HAWAIIAN HOMES PROGRAM. Approximately 200,000 acres are available in this program on the islands of Oahu, Hawaii, Kauai, Maui and Molokai. Applicants may apply for only one residence homestead lease on one of the five islands. There is currently a waiting list. Applicants must be "native Hawaiians," defined as having not less than one-half Hawaiian ancestry. The program was set up to enable native Hawaiians to recapture possession and control of some of the public lands of Hawaii as homesteads and to encourage their rehabilitation.

IDAHO

Idaho Housing Agency
760 West Myrtle Street
Boise, ID 83702-7671
Phone: (208)336-0440

PROGRAM: SINGLE FAMILY MORTGAGE LOAN PRO-GRAM. Provides reduced-interest-rate mortgage loans through participating lenders on homes not exceeding ceiling levels, which differ throughout the state. There are also borrower income limits.

PROGRAM: MORTGAGE CREDIT CERTIFICATES. MCC reduces the amount of federal income tax a first-time buyer pays, giving him or her more available income to qualify for a mortgage and assisting with house payments. The amount of the credit cannot be more than a person's annual federal income-tax liability. These are available to home buyers who meet IHA-established household income and home purchase price limits and who are eligible under federal regulations. The MCC will be in effect for the life of the mortgage, as long as the home remains the person's principal residence.

PROGRAM: URBAN HOMESTEAD PROGRAM. Currently available only in the city of Boise, vacant homes in need of repair are purchased by the local housing agency. These are transferred to homesteaders who pay a minimal amount in closing costs and then agree to repair the home (bringing them up to city building codes) and reside in it for at least five years. There are income limits. Call (208)384-4272 for information on this program only.

ILLINOIS

Illinois Housing Development Authority
401 North Michigan Avenue
Suite 900
Chicago, IL 60611
Phone: (312)836-5200

PROGRAM: FIRST-TIME BUYER PROGRAM. Below-market home mortgages are available to buyers whose household income is within specified ceilings. Homes, which can be single-family, condos or townhomes, must not cost more than established limits. The home must be occupied as a principal residence within 60 days of closing.

PROGRAM: HOME OWNERSHIP MADE EASY (H.O.M.E.). Endorsed by the Illinois State Treasurer, the purpose of H.O.M.E. is to help first-time buyers put aside funds for a down payment. Enrolling in the H.O.M.E. program requires an initial deposit of $250 or more. Thereafter, the person must make deposits at least twice a year and stay enrolled in the program for at least three years. Competitive interest, which is exempt from all state income tax, is paid on the account. After a home has been purchased, the real estate transfer tax (about 1 percent of the home's total cost) is reimbursed to the buyer. Participants also receive priority consideration in the First-Time Buyer Program. The hotline number for H.O.M.E. information is 1-800-535-1164.

INDIANA

Indiana Housing Finance Authority
1 North Capitol Avenue
#515
Indianapolis, IN 46204
Phone: (317)232-7777

PROGRAM: SINGLE-FAMILY MORTGAGE REVENUE BOND PROGRAM. Reduced-interest loans are made by participating lenders to borrowers meeting established income ceilings. Homes must also not cost more than established levels and must be occupied within 60 days of closing.

PROGRAM: MORTGAGE CREDIT CERTIFICATES (MCC). At least 25 percent of the interest paid on a mortgage can be applied to a dollar-for-dollar reduction on any federal tax liability helping a buyer have a better chance at affording a home. The MCC is in effect the life of the mortgage.

IOWA

Iowa Finance Authority
200 E. Grand
Suite 222
Des Moines, IA 50309
Phone: (515)281-4058

PROGRAM: SINGLE-FAMILY MORTGAGE LOAN PRO-GRAM. This provides qualified buyers a mortgage at a low interest rate on either a new or existing home falling below purchase-price limits. All loans are fixed rate.

PROGRAM: CLOSING COST ASSISTANCE. Borrowers qualifying for the above program but having an income below 65 percent of the area median (on households consisting of one or two people) are also eligible for closing cost assistance. This is limited to a certain percentage of the mortgage.

PROGRAM: MORTGAGE CREDIT CERTIFICATES (MCC). This allows the new homeowner to take an annual federal tax credit of up to 25 percent of the interest paid annually on a mortgage loan. Borrowers' incomes must be below the maximum guidelines, and the homes must fall at or below the listed purchase-price limits.

KANSAS

No information available.

KENTUCKY

Kentucky Housing Corporation
1231 Louisville Road
Frankfort, KY 40601
Phone: (502)564-7630

PROGRAM: CLUSTER LOAN PROGRAM. This provides below-market-interest mortgages to qualified buyers of new homes in older, distressed urban neighborhoods. The homes must qualify for VA or FHA mortgage insurance and borrowers must meet eligibility requirements with regard to income and credit worthiness.

PROGRAM: THREE HOME PURCHASE OPTIONS. Depending on income and need, the KHC offers three different options for below-market-rate mortgages at a fixed rate of interest for 30 years. Loan sizes and incomes vary around the state.

LOUISIANA

Louisiana Housing Finance Agency
P.O. Box 94455
Baton Rouge, LA 70804
Phone: 504-925-1767

PROGRAM: SINGLE-FAMILY MORTGAGE PROGRAM. Thirty-year, fixed-rate below-market mortgages are available to people whose incomes qualify and who are buying homes falling within certain price ceilings, both of which differ from parish to parish.

PROGRAM: RESOLUTION TRUST PROGRAM. Below-market-interest mortgages are available to qualifying first-time buyers who purchase properties held by the RTC. Homes are purchased through participating brokers.

MAINE

Maine State Housing Authority
295 Water Street
P.O. Box 2669
Augusta, ME 04338-2669
Phone: 1-800-454-4668

> *PROGRAM: MSHA HOME START LOANS.* This is several programs rolled into one that helps qualified first-time buyers obtain below-market mortgage money for not only purchasing a home, but also making improvements to it. There are ceilings on both home prices and purchasers' income levels, as well as the buyers' net worth. In addition, some buyers may qualify for help in financing closing costs. Loans are made by participating lenders throughout the state.

MARYLAND

Maryland Department of Housing & Community Development
45 Calvert Street
Annapolis, MD 21401
Phone: (301)974-3821

*PROGRAM: MARYLAND HOME FINANCING PRO-
GRAM—HOME PURCHASE (MHFP).* This program enables people with incomes below 55 percent of the state
median to purchase a first home at below-market, fixed
interest rates for 30-year terms through private lending
institutions. There are home purchase ceilings.

*PROGRAM: SETTLEMENT EXPENSE LOAN PROGRAM
(SELP).* SELP helps buyers who have insufficient assets
to pay for all reasonable closing costs. Buyers must meet
income limits and home purchase price ceilings, must
not have owned any other residential real estate for at
least three years prior to closing on the SELP loan and
must have a commitment for a first mortgage on the
property from a lender.

*PROGRAM: MARYLAND HOUSING REHABILITATION
PROGRAM—SINGLE-FAMILY (MHRP SF).* This program was set up to help preserve and improve existing
small residential properties and bring them up to applicable building codes and standards. Interest rates for
these loans are below conventional rates and are determined by the homeowner's income, which cannot exceed set limits.

MASSACHUSETTS

Massachusetts Housing Finance Agency
50 Milk Street
Boston, MA 02109
Phone: (617)451-3480

PROGRAM: HOME MORTGAGE LOAN PROGRAM. These are below-market rate loans for buyers with qualifying incomes on homes that don't exceed established ceilings. The loans are processed and made through participating lenders.

PROGRAM: HOMEOWNERSHIP OPPORTUNITY PROGRAM (HOP). HOP is based upon a partnership that uses state, local and private-sector resources to provide affordable homes and low-cost mortgages to income-eligible first-time buyers. In any HOP development, at least 30 percent of the newly constructed units must fall within what is defined as the affordable category.

MICHIGAN

Michigan State Housing Development Authority
Plaza One
Fourth Floor
401 South Washington Square
P.O. Box 30044
Lansing, MI 48909
Phone: 1-800-327-9158

PROGRAM: SINGLE-FAMILY PROGRAM. First-time buyers meeting income requirements can apply for 30-year, fixed-rate loans at below-market interest rates. Homes that meet set maximum purchase prices can be new or resales and be single-family homes, townhouses or condos as well as manufactured or mobile homes that are affixed to permanent foundations. Applications are made to participating lenders with MSHDA purchasing the loans.

PROGRAM: MICHIGAN MORTGAGE CREDIT CERTIFI-CATE PROGRAMS. Operating separately from the above program, MCC provides buyers with a federal income tax credit of up to 20 percent of the interest paid on a mortgage loan obtained from a private-sector lender. This credit comes directly from the taxes owed the federal government by the homebuyer. There is a maximum sales price for the home, as well as income ceilings for the borrower.

MINNESOTA

Minnesota Housing Finance Agency
400 Sibley Street
Suite 300
St. Paul, MN 55101
Phone: (612)297-3127

PROGRAM: MINNESOTA MORTGAGE PROGRAM. This program provides below-market-interest first mortgages for low- and moderate-income first-time buyers. To qualify, buyers must not have owned a home during the past three years, intend to occupy the home as their principal residence and have an income at or below the prescribed limits. There are also maximum home purchase prices for both new and existing residences located throughout the state.

PROGRAM: HOMEOWNERSHIP ASSISTANCE FUND (HAF). HAF provides monthly payment and down-payment assistance to borrowers with more modest incomes purchasing their first home through the program described above. HAF assistance is provided through an interest-free second mortgage repaid on a graduated basis. Buyers may apply for this when applying for the above program.

PROGRAM: URBAN AND RURAL HOMESTEADING. Grants are awarded to organizations who acquire single-family residences that are vacant, condemned or abandoned. The group must then rehabilitate the properties and sell them to first-time homebuyers. Only a limited number of homes are available.

MISSISSIPPI

No information available.

MISSOURI

Missouri Housing Development Commission
3770 Broadway
Kansas City, MO 64111
Phone: (816)756-3790

PROGRAM: SINGLE-FAMILY PROGRAM. Funds in this program are used to provide below-market-rate mortgages for first-time buyers of new and existing single-family homes. Prospective buyers must meet certain income qualifications. There are also purchase price limitations.

PROGRAM: HOMESTEADING PROGRAM. At present, only Kansas City and St. Louis have a homestead program in operation. For details, contact the Community Development Agency in either city at The Farm and Home Building, Sixth Floor, 411 North Tenth Street, St. Louis, 63101 or City Hall, 12th and Oak, Kansas City, 64106.

MONTANA

Montana Board of Housing
2001 Eleventh Avenue
Helena, MT 59620
Phone: (406)444-3040

PROGRAM: SINGLE-FAMILY MORTGAGE PROGRAM. This offers first-time buyers a below-market mortgage. There are income and home purchase price limitations.

PROGRAM: MORTGAGE CREDIT CERTIFICATE PRO-GRAM (MCC). Buyers get federal tax credits on up to 20 percent of the mortgage interest paid annually. This credit is deducted from the federal taxes owed the government. The remainder of the mortgage interest paid can still be taken as an itemized deduction. The credit is good for the life of the mortgage. Certain annual income and home price restrictions apply.

NEBRASKA

Nebraska Investment Finance Authority
Gold's Galleria
1333 O Street
Suite 218
Lincoln, NE 68508
Phone: (402)477-4406

> *PROGRAM: SINGLE-FAMILY LOAN PROGRAM.* This offers fixed-rate, 30-year mortgages at several interest points below conventional loans. Buyers must meet income qualifications and home prices are subject to ceilings depending on what part of the state the residence is being bought in. Also available, at a slightly higher rate, is financing for two-to-four-unit dwellings of which one unit must be owner-occupied.

NEVADA

Department of Commerce
Housing Division
1050 E. William
Suite 435
Carson City, NV 89710
Phone: (702)687-4258

PROGRAM: No formal name.   The Nevada Housing Division provides below-market-rate mortgages for low- and moderate-income first-time buyers. Because only FHA- and VA-insured loans are made, income and home purchase price ceilings, as well as guidelines set by the FHA and VA, must be met.

NEW HAMPSHIRE

New Hampshire Housing Finance Authority
P.O. Box 5087
Manchester, NH 03108
Phone: 1-800-248-7887

PROGRAM: SINGLE-FAMILY PROGRAM. This provides a 30-year, fixed-rate mortgage with an interest rate below that of conventional loans. These mortgages are non-assumable and are subject to family income and home purchase price limits.

PROGRAM: LOW- AND MODERATE-INCOME HOUSING LOAN PROGRAM. Money in this program can be used to help finance a certain percentage of the home's down payment, as well some of the closing costs. Only those who qualify for the Single-Family Program can qualify for this funding. Interest rates on this loan will vary depending on a borrower's income, with all money paid back at the time of resale via a share of the home's profits. Five percent of the net profit on the home must be given back if the property is sold within five years of the initial purchase and 2.5 percent must be paid back if sold within the second five years. Nothing has to be reimbursed if the home is sold after ten years.

NEW JERSEY

New Jersey Housing & Mortgage Finance Agency
3625 Quakerbridge Road
CN 18550
Trenton, NJ 08650-2085
Phone: (609)890-8900

PROGRAM: HOME BUYERS PROGRAM. Below-market mortgage money is available to qualifying first-time home-buyers. There are income and home purchase price ceilings. All mortgages are fixed rate for up to 30 years.

PROGRAM: HOMEOWNERSHIP FOR PERFORMING EM-PLOYEES (HOPE). HOPE is an employer-assisted hous-ing program in which the employer agrees to guarantee up to 20 percent of the mortgage loan for up to five years. This enables the buyer to qualify for a home whose value is up to 20 percent greater than his or her income would normally enable the buyer to afford. The mortgages are below market rate and are subject to annual family in-come and home purchase price limitations. The down payment and closing costs are rolled into the loan, some-times resulting in 100-percent-financed mortgages. Only certain companies have signed up to be in this program, seeing it a way of retaining and attracting employees, especially in high housing-cost areas of the state.

NEW MEXICO

New Mexico Mortgage Finance Authority
P.O. Box 2047
Albuquerque, NM 87103
Phone: (505)843-6880

PROGRAM: SINGLE-FAMILY MORTGAGE PROGRAM. Below-market-rate mortgages are available to those whose incomes do not exceed certain limits, depending on the part of the state the borrower lives in. Loans are for 30 years at a fixed rate of interest. There are limits on the type and price of home that can be financed under this program.

NEW YORK

State of New York Mortgage Agency
260 Madison Avenue
New York, NY 10016
Phone:1-800-382-HOME

PROGRAM: HOMEOWNERSHIP PROGRAM. SONYMA
mortgages, as New York's below-market-rate home loans
are known, are for first-time buyers falling within certain
income limits that vary throughout the state. There is
likewise a ceiling price on the home that can be purchased. Throughout the state are what are known as
target areas, where New York has a particular interest in
encouraging investment and development. Income eligibility limits on both income and home purchase price are
higher in these target areas. Loans include the Step Mortgage Loan Program, aimed at lower-income buyers,
which has a set, below-market rate of interest for the first
five years that increases 1 percent for the remaining 25
years. Another loan program is the Low Interest Rate
Mortgage program, which has a three-year initial rate that
rises and than stays at the same level for the remaining
27 years.

NORTH CAROLINA

North Carolina Housing Finance Agency
P.O. Box 28066
Raleigh, NC 27611
Phone: (919)781-6115

PROGRAM: SINGLE-FAMILY MORTGAGE LOAN PRO-GRAM. First-time homebuyers who have not owned a home as a principal residence during the past three years are eligible for below-market-interest-rate mortgages. Borrowers' incomes and the homes being purchased must both fall within prescribed guidelines.

PROGRAM: MORTGAGE CREDIT CERTIFICATE PRO-GRAM (MCC). MCCs are credits that reduce a first-time homebuyer's federal income tax indebtedness. Buyers are allowed to take anywhere from 15 to 25 percent, depending on income, of the mortgage interest they pay in a year directly off their federal taxes. The remaining interest can be used as a normal itemized deduction.

PROGRAM: HOME OWNERSHIP CHALLENGE FUND. This is a combination of NCHFA programs designed to make housing available to first-time buyers having low incomes. The fund includes low-interest permanent financing, down-payment assistance, monthly mortgage payment subsidies and mortgage credit certificates. It is available on specific housing projects that have been built by an organization or developing firm targeting low-income buyers.

NORTH DAKOTA

North Dakota Housing Finance Agency
Box 1535
Bismarck, ND 58502
Phone: (701)224-3434

> *PROGRAM:* No specific name. Below-market mortgages are available to first-time buyers who are acceptable credit risks and meet FHA guidelines. There are both income and home purchase price ceilings. Loans are made through participating lenders.

OHIO

Ohio Housing Finance Agency
77 South High Street
26th Floor
Columbus, OH 43266-0319
Phone: (614)466-3943

> *PROGRAM: BELOW-MARKET MORTGAGES.* First-time buyers of both new and resale homes can obtain below-market mortgages if both their incomes and the home's purchase price fall below specified ceilings. There is also a two-acre limit on the amount of land that the home can sit on.

OKLAHOMA

Oklahoma Housing Finance Agency
1140 NW 63rd Street
Suite 200
Oklahoma City, OK 73126-0720
Phone: 1-800-256-1489

PROGRAM: SINGLE-FAMILY MORTGAGE REVENUE BOND PROGRAM. Loans are available to first-time buyers throughout the state meeting income limitations. Homes must also fall below certain price ceilings, with some Resolution Trust Corporation properties eligible for purchase. Buyers receive below-market, fixed-rate mortgages.

OREGON

Oregon Housing Agency
1600 State Street
Suite 100
Salem, OR 97310-0161
Phone: (503)378-4343

PROGRAM: SINGLE-FAMILY MORTGAGE PROGRAM.
This assists qualified below-median-income buyers by
making available mortgage loan funds at a fixed rate of
interest that is usually about 2 percentage points below
conventional loan rates. Buyers apply through participating lenders. Homes cannot exceed set purchase-price
limits.

PROGRAM: MORTGAGE CREDIT CERTIFICATE (MCC).
This assists qualified home buyers by entitling them to
claim a federal income tax credit equal to 20 percent of
the interest paid each year on whatever mortgage is
obtained. This helps buyers have more income to apply
towards mortgage payments.

PROGRAM: URBAN HOMESTEAD PROGRAM. The city
of Portland assists lower-income households in purchasing and rehabilitating housing that has been abandoned.
Program participants generally receive low-interest loans
to bring the home up to existing building safety codes. If
the home is lived in for five years, the person receives
title to the property. For more information about this
program only, contact Portland Development Commission, Urban Homestead Program, 1120 SW Sixth Avenue,
Portland, OR 97204 or phone (503)796-5341.

PENNSYLVANIA

Pennsylvania Housing Finance Agency
2101 North Front Street
P.O. Box 8029
Harrisburg, PA 17105
Phone: 1-800-822-1174

PROGRAM: STATEWIDE HOMEOWNERSHIP PRO-GRAM. First-time buyers meeting income and home purchase price limits having certain minimum down payments and other program fees can obtain below-market loans through participating lenders.

PROGRAM: LOWER-INCOME HOME OWNERSHIP PRO-GRAM. This program provides below-market-rate loans for buyers having lower incomes and liquid assets that do not exceed $5,000 after closing on the home.

PROGRAM: CLOSING COST ASSISTANCE PROGRAM. Buyers who qualify for the Low Income Program are also eligible for financial assistance with their closing costs. To be eligible, applicants, among other things, must not have liquid assets that exceed $1,200 after closing on the home.

RHODE ISLAND

Rhode Island Housing and Mortgage Finance Corporation
60 Eddy Street
Providence, RI 02903
Phone: (401)-751-5566

PROGRAM: FIRST HOMES MORTGAGE PROGRAM. First-time buyers can obtain mortgages at below-market rates of interest if their incomes and the homes being purchased do not exceed specified ceilings. These are 30-year-term mortgages made through participating lenders.

PROGRAM: MORTGAGE CREDIT CERTIFICATE PROGRAM (MCC). Buyers can obtain MCCs with their mortgage if they meet certain income requirements. These certificates allow a buyer to receive a tax credit against federal tax owed for up to 20 percent of the mortgage interest paid in any year. The credits are good for the life of the mortgage, but cannot exceed certain amounts.

PROGRAM: BUY-IT/FIX-IT MORTGAGE PROGRAM. First-time buyers with specified incomes can receive low-interest mortgages to cover the cost of buying an older home and making substantial needed repairs. Homes must be at least 20 years old, fall within maximum price guidelines and require repairs costing at least 25 percent of the purchase price.

SOUTH CAROLINA

South Carolina Housing Finance And Development Authority
1710 Gervais Street
Suite 300
Columbia, SC 29201
Phone: 803-734-8831

PROGRAM: HOMEOWNERSHIP MORTGAGE PUR-CHASE PROGRAM. Borrowers who are first-time buyers are eligible to receive below-market mortgages. A buyer's income must not exceed certain limits, depending on what county he or she lives in, and the home must fall below a maximum price level.

SOUTH DAKOTA

South Dakota Housing Development Authority
Post Office Box 1237
Pierre, SD 57501-1237
Phone: (605)773-3181

PROGRAM: HOMEOWNERSHIP PROGRAM. This program provides lower-interest-rate mortgages than standard conventional loans. Fixed-rate mortgages are available to borrowers whose gross annual income does not exceed a set percentage of the county or state median income (whichever is greater). The purchase price of the home also may not exceed certain limits. An executed purchase contract for an existing residence or a construction cost breakdown for a proposed new home must be presented at the time of application.

PROGRAM: LOW-INTEREST DOWN-PAYMENT PROGRAM. This program assists buyers meeting specified income limits in coming up with a down payment for a first home.

TENNESSEE

Tennessee Housing Development Agency
700 Landmark Center
401 Church Street
Nashville, TN 37219-2202
Phone: see below.

PROGRAM: HOMEOWNERSHIP PROGRAM. These loans are reserved for low- and moderate-income first-time homebuyers. There are home-purchase-price and income ceilings differing throughout the state that must be met to qualify for one of these below-market-rate mortgages. Phone (615)741-4968 for information.

PROGRAM: HOUSING OPPORTUNITIES USING STATE ENCOURAGEMENT (HOUSE). Some communities around the state are taking part in a three-year pilot program developing "buy-it-and-fix-it" programs. Eligible buyers qualify for lower-rate interest loans when they help with the rehabilitation of existing homes in need of repair. Phone (615)741-7918 for further information.

TEXAS

Texas Housing Agency
P.O. Box 13941
Capitol Station
Austin, TX 78711-3941
Phone: (512)474-2974

PROGRAM: TEXAS HOUSING AUTHORITY/RESOLU-TION TRUST CORPORATION PROGRAM. Below-market mortgages are given to qualifying first-time buyers. At this writing, all the money in the THA's budget is being allocated for the purchase of properties held by the federal government's Resolution Trust Corporation (homes that were foreclosed on). Participating lenders make the loans. The hotline number for this program is (512)478-5745.

UTAH

Utah Housing Finance Agency
177 East 100 South
Salt Lake City, UT 84111
Phone: (801)521-6950

PROGRAM: SINGLE-FAMILY MORTGAGE PROGRAM. First-time buyers who fall within the designated income limits, which vary by county, may obtain below-market-rate mortgages on homes priced up to a set level. In targeted areas, where the state is trying to encourage homeownership, purchase price ceilings are slightly higher than in nontargeted areas.

VERMONT

Vermont Housing Finance Agency
One Burlington Square
P.O. Box 408
Burlington, VT 05402-0408
Phone: see below.

PROGRAM: MORTGAGES FOR VERMONTERS (MOVE). These are 30-year, fixed-rate loans at lower interest rates than currently available with conventional mortgages. Borrowers must meet income restrictions based on size of household. The home being bought can be a resale or newly constructed, but it must not be above listed ceilings. The program also comes with other features, including an evaluation of the home's energy costs. Phone 1-800-222-VHFA for details.

PROGRAM: PERPETUALLY AFFORDABLE HOUSING PROGRAM. VHFA has targeted some mortgage funds with a lower interest rate than the current MOVE program for the purchase of homes built by developers providing homeownership opportunities that will remain affordable over the long term. Phone 1-800-287-VHFA for information on this program.

PROGRAM: RURAL VERMONT MORTGAGE. Through a joint effort with the Farmers Home Administration and VHFA, low-interest mortgage funds are available for lower-income Vermont households in rural areas. Phone 1-800-287-VHFA for details for this program only.

VIRGINIA

Virginia Housing Development Authority
601 South Belvedere Street
Richmond, VA 23220
Phone: (804)783-6705

PROGRAM: MORTGAGE LOANS FOR HOME PUR-CHASE. The goal of this program is to assist low- and moderate-income households in purchasing their first home. There is a ceiling on the purchase price of homes that may be financed using these fixed-rate 15- and 30-year mortgages. Loans are made through participating lenders.

WASHINGTON

Washington Housing Finance Commission
1111 Third Avenue
Suite 2240
Seattle, WA 98101-3202
Phone: (206)464-7139

PROGRAM: SINGLE-FAMILY HOMEOWNERSHIP PRO-GRAM. This program is designed to help first-time buyers whose incomes do not exceed set limits to purchase a home that does not cost above a certain amount, depending on the county it is located in. Mortgages are for 30 years at a fixed rate of interest that is below current conventional loan rates.

PROGRAM: MORTGAGE CREDIT CERTIFICATE PRO-GRAM (MCC). Buyers receive a credit toward any taxes owed the federal government of up to 20 percent of the annual interest paid on their real estate loan. To qualify, they must meet income and house purchase price limits.

WEST VIRGINIA

West Virginia Housing Development Fund
814 Virginia Street East
Charleston, WV 25301
Phone: (304)345-6475

PROGRAM: SINGLE-FAMILY MORTGAGE PURCHASE PROGRAM. Borrowers whose annual incomes fall below applicable limits for the county they reside in can receive below-market 25-year fixed-rate mortgages. Eligible homes may be existing or newly constructed and include condominiums, townhouses and manufactured homes, all of which must fall below certain purchase price limits.

WISCONSIN

Wisconsin Housing & Economic Development Authority
One South Pinckney Street
Suite 500
Post Office Box 1728
Madison, WI 53701-1728
Phone:1-800-362-2767

> *PROGRAM: THE HOME PROGRAM.* First-time buyers whose incomes fall within current program limits acquiring homes that do not exceed current purchase price ceilings are eligible for below-market fixed-rate mortgages. Down payments can be as low as 5 percent (provided certain credit requirements are met). This program also lets a person buy and renovate a home that's at least 20 years old and needs remodeling work equaling at least one-third of the home's original purchase price.

WYOMING

Wyoming Community Development Authority
P.O. Box 634
Casper, WY 82602
Phone: (307)266-5414

PROGRAM: SINGLE-FAMILY MORTGAGE PROGRAM. Below-market-rate loans are available to buyers of quali-fying incomes purchasing homes within the set limits.

PROGRAM: URBAN HOMESTEADING PROGRAM. This program is a modern-day version of the old Homestead Act, under which most of the western United States was settled. Today's homesteaders must agree to restore de-teriorating residences owned by the federal government. There are income ceilings. In return for receiving the home for $1, the buyer must restore and live in the residence for five consecutive years. At that time, the purchaser will receive title to the home with no further obligations to WCD.

Chapter 9

CREATIVE FINANCING

Sometimes, in order to be able to purchase a home, a buyer has to be a little creative when it comes to financing.

If you get turned down for a conventional 30-year fixed-rate mortgage, don't be discouraged, said Stanley Greenstein, vice president of the Mortgage Clearing House. One of the biggest mistakes first-time buyers makes is in thinking that if the lender turned them down for a fixed-rate loan, that's it. But, the veteran mortgage lender noted, "We have 350 to 400 different mortgage products." Each is geared to help buyers with certain deficiencies.

For example, some buyers have the income to make a certain monthly mortgage payment, but don't have enough money saved to pay the up-front costs, including the down payment and points. Other buyers have the up-front costs, but lack the income to make high monthly mortgage payments. With products ranging from buydowns to graduated payment mortgages, buyers are often surprised that although they were turned down for a fixed-rate loan, there's another mortgage instrument that may fill their needs, Greenstein said.

But if you still don't qualify for anything after going through the smorgasbord of lender's choices—or if you want to see what other options there are that might be better for you—there are some creative financing methods that are not wacky that could help you purchase a home. Within this category fall renting with the option to buy and shared equity. An explanation of some of these creative financing choices follows.

RENTING WITH THE OPTION TO BUY

As mentioned previously, one of the biggest problems first-time buyers have when purchasing a home is coming up with the down payment.

"Renting with the option to buy makes it easier for people to purchase who don't have the cash down payment up front, but have decent incomes and can pay the monthly carrying costs," said broker Amy Norman. With this method, also called lease optioning, a seller agrees to let a buyer live in the home that's up for sale for a specific period of time, with one year being the most popular term.

During that year, the buyer pays rent to the homeowner. After the twelfth month passes, the buyer can either move out of the residence, with no other financial obligations, or agree to buy the home. If the buyer exercises his buy option, a portion of the rent he has been paying during the lease is applied towards the down payment of the home. The monthly rent, the percentage of the rent to be applied to the purchase price and the selling price of the residence are all agreed upon before the buyer moves in.

Real estate attorney John P. Reali called renting with the option to buy "a much better deal for the buyer than for the seller." The seller is taking all of the risks; after a year the buyer can say "thanks a lot" and move on. The seller is then stuck coming up with another buyer and trying to sell the home again. Likewise, if home prices are appreciating, the homeowner must sell the property to the buyer for the price agreed upon when the rent-with-the-option-to-buy contract was signed, Reali said. If the home increased in price, for example, by $10,000 over the year, the seller would not get this increased price.

This is a great deal for the buyer, said developer William Schmergel, president of Schmergel Enterprises; it lets buyers "test drive the unit." They can see whether they like the house, the neighborhood and the neighbors. If they don't, then they can say good-bye without owing anything else, Schmergel said.

The buyer can also walk away from the deal if interest rates climb too high over the year and he or she finds the home isn't affordable anymore, said broker Herrick. Or, if the buyer finds that home prices have dropped considerably in the area and the contracted deal now seems high compared to asking prices in and around the area, he or she can also reject the deal and move on.

With a one-year deal, Herrick said, the buyer usually has to exercise the buy option by the ninth or tenth month. If the buyer declines to purchase, he or she can still live in the home as a renter for the rest of the year, but the seller is then free to find another buyer. The seller can also bring other buyers by to examine the unit. The current tenant, however, does have to be given advance notice that someone is coming by to inspect the property. The seller can't just walk in with someone at midnight while the tenant is asleep.

When purchasing a home this way, Reali said, "be as explicit about the buying terms as possible when formulating the contract." This avoids problems down the road. An actual contract of sale should be attached to the rental agreement specifying purchase price, what furniture will come with the house, what light fixtures are included and anything else the buyer and seller need to agree upon, Reali advised.

You'll find more sellers willing to enter into an agreement like this in areas where the housing market is slow or where a seller has already moved out of the home and into another. Said broker Lee Testa, owner of Pine Hills Property Limited, in theory, from the seller's point of view, having a tenant who has the option to buy will result in someone who will take better care of the residence because he or she has a potential financial stake in the property.

In addition, if the home is empty, Herrick said, the buyer can try and persuade a seller to enter into this type of agreement by suggesting that having a rental tenant prevents vandalism of the unoccupied property. Also play up the fact of how the seller won't have to pay the expense of heating an empty house because, as a renter, you will now foot the fuel bills.

Buyers can also convince sellers nearing the age of 55 to sell with this option because it works to their advantage as well, said Robert Bruss, a real estate investor and columnist. Suppose a seller is approaching 55 and has decided to leave his Maine home for Florida. If he sells his home outright at age 54 to move to a less expensive home, he won't be eligible for the one-time $125,000 exclusion on his federal income tax return that a seller age 55 would be. This exclusion helps bring down the taxes a seller must pay on capital gains profits when trading down from a more expensive house to a less expensive one. By leasing with the option to buy, the homeowner is actually selling the property when he turns 55, Bruss said. The option can be for one year or as long as the seller needs to reach age 55.

It should be noted that, especially when the real estate market is weak, many developers also offer buyers the rent-to-buy option. For buyers, purchasing this way lets a down payment build while they are still paying rent and even allows them to continue shopping around to see if a better deal can be obtained in the area.

SELLER FINANCING

As you scan the real estate classifieds or go home shopping with a broker, every so often you will run across the term "seller financing available." In such deals, the buyer receives a mortgage not from a traditional lender, but directly from the homeowner. The big advantage here is that the buyer can save thousands of dollars in closing costs and get terms that many banks would not offer.

"Owner financing is prevalent in stagnant markets where the seller has to do anything to sell a home," said Bruce Torrani, owner of Century 21 Fisher-Friendly. It's also obtainable from a seller who wants to dispose of a home quickly because, with no lender involved, a closing can occur in a shorter period of time.

Homeowners selling a primary residence and moving on to another home will not be able to offer this type of financing to a buyer, said mortgage broker John Monaco. Most move-up buyers need the money from the sale of their first home to buy the second. But for the person who owns more than one piece of property, such as a vacation home or a parcel of land, this type of deal is a possibility, Monaco said. Seller financing is good for a retired couple who already own a home in Florida, for example, and don't immediately need all the proceeds from the sale of their current residence in Chicago, said Frank Orlandino, a partner with Eisenoff Realty.

For the buyer, there are many advantages with a purchase money mortgage (as this type of financing is called), said real estate attorney Craig D. Robins. When the seller holds the mortgage, both he and the buyer can negotiate whatever mortgage terms and interest rate the two parties can agree upon, Monaco said. Noted Torrani, the seller is usually seeking better interest than he can get by taking the proceeds from the home's sale and investing them in a bank certificate of deposit.

One thing a buyer should point out to sellers wavering on making a purchase money mortgage is that they will eliminate the uncertainty of wondering whether they will be approved by a traditional lender for a mortgage, Robins said. With banks currently clamping down and looking closer at whom they're granting mortgages to, seller financing allows buyers who might not have obtained a mortgage to get one. The only approval needed is the seller's willingness to assume the mortgage.

The buyer might also point out the tax advantages for the seller. Yes, the buyer will have to pay any state and federal taxes on the mortgage interest received annually, said Barry Levittan, a partner with the accounting firm of Levine, Markowitz, Fein and Levittan. However, the seller will not have to pay a capital gains tax on profits in the year the home is sold, as is the case with a normal transaction. Instead, taxes on profits are paid in installments, stretching over the full term of the mortgage.

Another advantage for the buyer is considerably lower closing costs, said Curtis Luckman, president of IPC Capital Resources, a mortgage consultant. By not going through a traditional lender, the buyer doesn't have to pay a number of fees charged by most banks, including an application fee or points. Each point charged is equivalent to 1 percent of the mortgage amount borrowed. Three points on a $100,000 loan would add $3,000 to closing costs.

In addition, there is no mortgage title insurance needed, Luckman said. This is usually taken out by a lender (and paid by the borrower) to insure that the mortgage has clear title. The seller knows if his title is clear and doesn't need this. Buyers, however, should take out fee insurance to protect themselves against unclear title, Luckman advised.

In all, Luckman estimated that a buyer receiving a purchase money mortgage could save closing costs of about 5 percent of the total funds being borrowed. On a $100,000 loan, that amounts to $5,000.

The buyer WILL have to pay property taxes and insurance, instead of the bank doing this as many lenders require, Luckman said. But as a result, at the closing, the buyer won't have to put several months of property taxes and insurance payments into an escrow account with the lender. The escrow account is what the lender uses to pay these expenses as they come up throughout the year.

Because the seller realizes that a buyer's closing costs are lower, the homeowner could ask a slightly higher sales price, Torrani said. But as Luckman pointed out, the weaker the market is in the area you're buying your home in, the more leverage you will have. If homes are really moving slowly, and a property has been on the market for awhile, then the seller may not only be willing to finance the deal, but also give you a good selling price.

Another advantage a buyer should point out to a seller considering this type of financing is that a closing will occur much faster with a money purchase mortgage, Robins said. The contract of sale will have no contingency saying that the closing is subject to the buyer obtaining financing; the seller has already agreed to make the mortgage. And since the buyer doesn't have to undergo a lender's scrutiny, which seems to take forever as the bank requests just "one more piece of information," things move along a lot faster. Most closings could take place in as little as two to three weeks instead of several months, Robins estimated.

As long as the transaction is recorded with the local county clerk's office—a standard procedure among lenders—the buyer can deduct all mortgage interest costs from his or her state and federal taxes just as with any other lender-financed mortgage, Luckman said.

Sellers may ask a buyer to sign a consent form so that they can perform a credit check, Robins pointed out. It's smart for a seller to do a little homework on the buyer's finances. However, in all of the cases of seller financing Robins has been involved in, he has seen sellers doing little research on their buyers.

One of the reasons for this laxness, Robins explained, is that many sellers require a large down payment—25 percent or more—when taking back the mortgage. If the down payment is big enough, the seller usually has adequate protection that a buyer won't walk away from the home (should his or her finances get tough), resulting in a foreclosure, Torrani said.

Robins usually advises his sellers to stay away from financing both buyers with shaky credit and those who want to put nothing or very little down. Other attorneys said they advised the same thing. But again, the slower the market is, the more leverage a buyer will have over a seller, experts said.

Which leads to some of the downsides of seller financing.

While any type of term can be set, many of these deals come with balloon mortgages of five or ten years, Luckman said. This means the buyer may not get the 30-year fixed-rate mortgage that might have been available from his or her friendly local bank. When the note on such a balloon mortgage is due, the buyer will have to refinance the home to pay the seller back, Luckman said. If interest rates have risen, the buyer may not be able to make the new, higher mortgage payments. However, since several years have passed, the buyer's income has probably risen.

Another problem is that the buyer may not be able to refinance for the entire existing balance if home prices have dropped. A lender usually will grant a mortgage on only 80 percent of the home's current value. If the property was originally purchased for $100,000 (with 10 percent down), this would mean a mortgage of $90,000. If home prices had fallen 20 percent by refinancing time, the home would be worth $80,000, and 80 percent of that is $64,000. If the existing mortgage balance were above that, the buyer would have to come up with the difference out of his or her own pocket.

Because sellers always fear foreclosure with this type of deal, many attorneys require that the contract of sale spell out fees for late payments and that the buyer be liable for any attorney fees the seller might encounter should foreclosure occur, Robins said. The seller's attorney will usually draw up the contract of sale and mortgage agreement, with the buyer paying the attorney's fee, he added. However, Luckman noted, this fee will usually be far smaller than the fee a traditional lender normally charges for the bank attorney.

One other plus for the buyer is that whereas a traditional lender may immediately send out a collection letter to a buyer who is one or two payments behind on this mortgage, a seller may be more willing to work with a buyer who is experiencing a temporary cash crunch, Luckman said. A seller acting as lender doesn't have state and federal regulators watching the firm's bottom line the way a traditional lender does, he noted.

To protect their own interests, buyers should make sure their own attorneys closely review the contract of sale as well as the mortgage contract, Robins said. In addition, a buyer's attorney should check to see that there's clear title on the home, that a proper certificate of occupancy (CO) exists and that the property's survey and any other things that a local municipality requires are in order before a home changes hands.

In closings involving traditional lenders, a buyer's attorney usually isn't looking at COs and clear title too closely because he or she is relying on the bank to be the watchdog on these items, Robins said. With no lender, the buyer's attorney is the buyer's only protection.

Because of the advantages seller financing offers, even if a buyer has to put 25 percent down on the home, the deal is worth doing if structured correctly, Luckman said. Closing costs are lower and seller's are usually more flexible than a lender's on many items.

When structured correctly, these deals are really great for both parties, Luckman added.

SHARED EQUITY

Because of the high price of housing in many parts of the country, an increasing number of singles, friends, mothers and children and even pairs of married couples are buying homes together. Sometimes both parties live in the house; many times only one of the parties occupies the property even though both have put an equal amount of money up to buy the home.

Lenders said that there was no problem for borrowers wanting to get mortgage money to buy a home this way as long as loan requirements are met. The creditworthiness and incomes of both parties, whether occupying the home or not, will be investigated.

Real estate agent Ken McCord has done equity sharing as an investment. In one case, he split the cost of the home with a young married couple 50-50. His co-owners, first-time buyers, couldn't have afforded to purchase the home on their own.

The agreement that McCord and the couple drew up allowed the young marrieds to occupy the home. If either party wanted to buy the other out at some point, and become sole owner, it would be at the prevailing market value at that time. Should neither want the home and both parties agree to sell it, then any profits would be split in half. In the case of the death of either party, the half-share of the home goes to that person's heir.

"This is a good opportunity for people who might not be able to buy on their own," McCord said. "At least they own half a house now instead of having to rent." It's also profitable for the investor, who enjoys half the profits. In addition, the investor is fairly assured that the people living in the home will take care of the property, because half the money spent to buy the home, as well as half the profits that will be derived from selling the home, will go to them.

Young marrieds not able to find someone like McCord to invest with often buy a house together with other family members, said Barbara Frechter, president of Glen Jay Realty. The young couple will live on one level and the parents on another. Or the parents will just sign their name to the mortgage, agreeing to back the loan without ever living in the home, she said.

Joseph Petrillo and his sister Francis were both tired of renting separate apartments and decided to buy a home together. Their parents refinanced their own home, which had appreciated considerably in value since they bought it, and pulled enough out for their two children to have a down payment on a home of their own. Joseph and Francis then found a home they liked and used both their incomes to qualify for the mortgage. They are living in the home together and splitting all the bills.

Another common form of equity sharing are two people planning to get married buying a home together before the wedding. "We felt that rather than wasting our hard-earned dollars and putting them into someone else's pocket, we wanted to start building up equity ourselves," said Marian Clifford. "If we waited to buy a house (until after we got married) we'd be spending $700 in rent and would never have been able to do it. Instead, we decided to save money for the down payment while we were still both living at home."

When Marian and her husband, Jim, then her fiancé, had enough of a down payment, they purchased a home together. Jim then moved into the house after they closed on it. Marian continued to live at home with her parents, joining Jim three months later, after they were married.

The Cliffords had no written agreement covering their arrangement dictating how the home would be divided should their relationship fall apart. "We felt [an agreement] would have put a damper on things and we didn't feel it was necessary," Marian said.

But attorney Ronald J. Schwartz said that whether the purchasers are two engaged people or an investor and an occupant buying a home, a formal contract should be drawn up specifying how profits will be split when the home is sold, who can buy the other out and how that buyout will work. The agreement should also settle what will happen to the home if the relationship (business, friendship or otherwise) dissolves.

One casualty of equity sharing is Donna, who asked that her last name not be used. After she and her boyfriend became engaged, he suggested they buy a house together. "He knew I wanted a house, so we ended up buying one mostly with my money for the down payment—a home that I didn't particularly like," she emphasized. Both their salaries were needed to secure the mortgage. There were no contracts stipulating buyouts, who would be responsible for what costs or what would happen should one want out.

They closed on the house in October 1984, and "the problems started almost immediately," Donna said. "And it continued downhill from there. We'd fight over whether to spend $30 to get cable TV or put money into something else." The house needed work. While her fiancé paid most of the monthly bills, Donna said she was shelling out the money to remodel the bathroom, put new floors throughout the home and panel several rooms. "We were together through July 1985. Then in the beginning of August, we were living together, but not talking," she said. By October of 1985, Donna's fiancé had moved out and the marriage was off. The house was put up for sale. But because there was no formal contract, it was never made clear who would get what when the home was sold (remember, Donna had put up most of the down payment).

In some cases, said attorney Schwartz, one partner departs and the other is left behind trying to pay the mortgage and other bills on his or her own. If payments are missed, the lender then forecloses on the loan and a lot of money is lost. The person's credit rating is ruined for some time to come. But it's not just the person left behind whose credit rating is ruined. Because the second person's name is also on the mortgage agreement, that person will also be named in the foreclosure. The lender can go after all names on the mortgage and attach a judgment to any assets it can find of any or all of the parties.

Donna and her ex-boyfriend finally did come to terms. Donna said that because she sold in a rising real estate market, she ended up making a little money when the home was sold. But other buyers in similar situations have not been as lucky.

As a business venture, equity sharing is a great thing to do, Schwartz said. But when it's done by two people living together without a formal contract, it can be fraught with problems.

GRADUATED PAYMENT MORTGAGES

Graduated payment mortgages, or GPMs, are mortgages that start with a lower starting rate of interest than most adjustable mortgages, but end up with the predictability of a fixed-rate loan. Lenders say that this loan is often overlooked because most borrowers don't seem to understand it.

A GPM's interest rate can start as much as 5 percent lower than a conventional mortgage, said Paul Havemann, vice president of HSH Associates, a mortgage research firm. It then rises yearly (depending on how low a rate you start with) by 1 percent until it hits a fixed-rate level, where it remains for the life of the loan. While GPMs can be written for 30 years, most are done with 15-year terms. GPMs tend to run one-half to one full percentage point higher than conventional loans. To make up for the lower starting rate of interest, later payments are higher than they would have been all along on a standard fixed-rate mortgage, Havemann said.

Another way lenders make up for the lower initial interest rate is by requiring a subsidy or buy-down fund at the time of closing, Havemann explained. This helps the lender recover the interest he or she would have collected at the loan's regular rate.

One advantage of a GPM over an ARM is that unlike the latter, the borrower knows exactly what his or her GPM payment schedule will be for the full term of the loan, Becker said. With an ARM, the interest charged may start lower than that for a fixed-rate mortgage, but it can increase by as much as 2 percentage points a year, should rates rise. Of course, an ARM's payments can also go down by as much as 2 percentage points annually if interest rates fall.

Another advantage is that with a GPM, the lender qualifies the borrower at the lower starting interest rate instead of the higher rate to which the loan ultimately rises. This allows more people to qualify for the loan, Becker said.

Al Sorrentino, vice president of consumer real estate business management at Citibank, gave an example of how this loan works using a 15-year GPM for $100,000. The final rate is 10.75 percent, but the borrower could start the GPM with a rate as low as 5.75 percent by putting $822.40 into a subsidy fund at closing. This is used to make up the interest the lender would have gotten if the loan had started at the 10.75 percent rate.

In year one, at 5.75 percent, payments would be $830.42, Sorrentino explained—the same payment someone would make for a loan set at 5.75 percent. In year two, the rate increases to 6.75 percent with a monthly payment of $892.70. At this point, the borrower has paid only interest. In year three, the rate rises to 7.75 percent with payments of $959.65, which now include some principal. In the fourth year, the rate increases by another percent to 8.75 with payments of $1,031.62. In year five, the interest is 9.75 percent with payments of $1,108.99. In year six, the loan rises to 10.75 percent and payments of $1,192.16. In year seven, the interest rate becomes fixed, but payments rise to $1,281.57, making up for some of the principal not paid in the first two years of the loan. And in year eight, payments reach $1,309.04, where they stay until the end of the 15-year loan.

Had this $100,000 been borrowed using a conventional 15-year loan, Sorrentino said, payments would have been a constant $1,120.95 a month. Using a GPM, payments are much lower than $1,120.95 in the first five years of the loan.

The idea behind a GPM is that a first-time buyer, just starting out, would need the initial lower payments, Sorrentino explained. But as the years progressed and the borrower received promotions and pay raises, he or she could afford the higher payments.

The borrower, of course, can start a GPM at a higher rate if he or she wants, Becker said. It all depends on how much of a subsidy fee borrowers want to put up front and how low they want the initial payments to be.

But there are drawbacks to this loan, said Donald Henig, former president of the National Association of Mortgage Brokers.

One is that the mortgage payment rises by about 1 percent in each of the early years. Can someone qualifying at the lower rate be able to afford the higher payment later on without getting in over his or her head, he asked?

But, Havemann said, statistics show that the average length of time a buyer stays in a home is seven years. The buyer could use a GPM, take advantage of the lower rate, then sell the home and pay off the mortgage before ever paying the higher rate.

BUYDOWNS

What Donald Henig prefers over a GPM is a mortgage buy-down, which is somewhat similar in nature to a GPM, he said. The borrower again pays cash up front to bring the interest rate down in the initial years. The rate then rises 1 percent a year for however long the buydown is. A 3-2-1 buydown, for example, would be a 10 percent loan that starts at 8 percent in year one, rises to 9 percent in year two and tops out at 10 percent for the duration of the loan.

The advantage of the buydown over a GPM, Henig explained, is that buydowns can be gotten at the lower rates charged for conventional fixed-rate loans, as opposed to the slightly higher rates charged on GPMs. Buydowns also come with some flexibilities, he said. Instead of going up 1 percent a year, the rate can rise 1 percent every six months. This could help the borrower knock the rate down even lower for much lower up-front costs. And again, as with a GPM, Henig said, the borrower qualifies at the lower starting rate.

Buyers shopping new construction projects (as well as some condos and co-ops that have been converted from rental apartments) will also find developers offering buydown mortgages as an incentive to purchase their homes. The developer usually pays the costs connected with buying the mortgage down. The advantage for builders is that more buyers can afford to purchase their homes because of the lower starting mortgage rate.

Part Three

GOING FROM
HOUSE SHOPPING
TO HOUSE CLOSING

Chapter 10

THE BEST TIME TO BUY A HOUSE

To get a bargain on an air conditioner, the savvy shopper living in Maine or Vermont knows that the best time to purchase that unit is either pre-season or as the summer is winding down. Retailers, not wanting to keep unsold air conditioners lying around in their stockrooms all winter, will often reduce prices drastically once the season is over. Saving 30 percent or more off the list price is a matter of timing.

The same is true with real estate.

While some areas of the country run contrary to general rules (or seem to follow no rules at all), in a normal market, housing prices will usually be firmest during April and May. This is residential real estate's strongest selling period because it's when the greatest number of buyers are out shopping. Current owners with families want to close on their present homes after school lets out in June and be settled in their new residences before the next term begins in September, said real estate broker/owner Lee S. Testa. This keeps disruptions to family life at a minimum.

Likewise, retiring seniors like to be out of their present homes before the summer ends and settled in their new sun-belt located lodgings before the cold weather sets in. What the steady supply of buyers in the spring means is that sellers have more control over deals. They can turn down prices they aren't happy with, while waiting for a better deal to come along.

WINTERTIME IS BARGAIN TIME

However, from the middle of October into the following year, the tables turn. This is the period purchasers usually find their best buys, said broker Bob Herrick. As winter approaches, people tend to insulate themselves. They want to stay in their nice, warm homes and not brave the harsh elements looking for a new place to live. Fewer people venturing out means fewer buyers in the market.

Adding to the slowdown is the fact that November begins the holiday season, kicking off with Thanksgiving and lasting through Hanukkah, Christmas and the New Year, Herrick said. During this period, consumers have the holidays on their minds. Their time, as well as their money, is at a premium with gift shopping in full swing.

Usually the only people selling during this low season are those who have to (sometimes referred to as desperate sellers). These are the people who are being transferred to a new job, are in the midst of a divorce or already have a contract of sale signed for another home. The other type of seller still in the market is the one whose property was listed long before this slower selling period began but still hasn't connected with a buyer.

With fewer buyers out in the winter, Herrick said, inventory begins to build, especially in January and February, before the next surge of purchasers arrives in the spring. During this slower period, buyers have more control over prices and terms. This is the time of year first-time buyers should be out in force cementing deals.

During the winter, especially between Thanksgiving and the new year, is when sellers become more desperate and are more willing to negotiate, said Jack Dornheim, a broker representing buyers and president of North Country Associates. They don't want to have to sit with their for-sale signs perched on their lawns into the following spring, when more new product begins arriving on the market. These sellers want to be out and in their own new home come April or May, Dornheim said.

And along with resales, during this slower period new-home builders are looking to make deals because they have carrying costs and payrolls to meet. Most developers usually won't lower prices at this point because, as one prominent builder pointed out, if homes are selling for $100,000 and the developer suddenly starts charging only $90,000, he is in essence bringing down the resale value of his already sold homes. What's more likely to happen is that the developer will throw in extra appliances and carpeting, help with closing costs or offer some other incentive.

Not all brokers, however, agree with this "winter slowdown theory." Broker Bonnie Lazar recalled making a deal recently on Christmas Eve for a home that had been on the market for eight months. The seller ended up getting market value, proving, she added, "that all you need is one buyer to make a deal."

Lazar also pointed out that some brokers used to call real estate a weekend business because of open houses and most people not wanting to shop during the week. But now she finds weekdays just as busy as some weekends.

Exceptions to the Rule

Of course, even if you're a firm believer in the "strong spring, weak winter" theory, you'll always find exceptions to these rules in any area; there's nothing that says a great deal can't be found in the spring and that an inflexible seller won't refuse to lower a price in December. A smart seller, Dornheim said, "should be ready, willing and able to show his home whenever there's a live buyer around." He recalls one seller who refused to let him bring qualified purchasers to her home because it was Mother's Day. A serious seller should never pass up the opportunity to show his or her home to a buyer, he emphasized. Likewise, serious buyers should be ready to pounce whenever a great deal is available.

MARKET EXTREMES

The principles discussed above (strong spring, weak winter) hold true in most normal selling periods. But as anyone in the real estate business will tell you, this is a cyclical industry. There are years when housing is hot and homes are selling briskly even in December. Then there are times when business is so flat that even in spring, the best of homes go begging and you begin to see developers and brokers wringing their hands, throwing in the towel and leaving the business.

For the first-time buyer, hot markets are the worst time to be out looking. While it's declining interest rates that usually heat up a market (good for a buyer), that doesn't necessarily translate to your being able to afford more house. The problem is, as rates drop, buyers seem to come out of the woodwork and begin pushing housing prices up. It's your old friend supply and demand at work.

It is possible, even in a hot market, to find a desperate seller who is willing to negotiate on price and give you a good deal. But with more buyers swarming about, bargains are harder to find. Just look at what happened in the mid-eighties. After interest rates dropped from highs of 21 percent down to as low as 9 percent, home prices in areas like California and the Northeast began appreciating 20 to 30 percent a year. Real estate brokers told stories of homes being listed with them in the morning and sold by the close of business the same day. Things were so crazy, there were bidding wars in the living room of some homeowners as two buyers competed for the same property. Sometimes a homeowner would sign a contract of sale with one person, only to find a different party sitting opposite him at the closing. Because homes were appreciating so rapidly, some buyers were flipping the homes before closing—that is, they were selling the contract of sale they had received from the homeowner for a higher price than they had paid to a third party.

Back in 1986, broker Gene Francavilla told of one buyer who went to contract on a home costing $80,000. Came closing day, the homeowner found himself sitting opposite a person he had never seen before. It seems the first buyer had sold the contract of sale he had to someone else for $86,000—making a cool $6,000 profit on a home he had never even owned! This is obviously not a market for a buyer with a limited budget.

Slow and Easy

A better time for first-time buyers to be out looking is when things are slow, as is the case in many markets around the country right now. This depressed period is normally caused by a slowing of the economy, interest rates rising and homes having escalated in the past to prices higher than what most consumers' salaries can afford. As a result, prices eventually begin to cool and even start to fall.

The ideal time to buy is just as the cycle is changing from bad market to good. Prices will have dropped to their lowest because of the slow market, while interest rates will still be at good levels.

As the nineties began, homeowners in the Northeast, as well as in other parts of the country, began seeing a downturn in home prices. Values fell, partly because many buyers began sitting on the sidelines waiting for prices to hit rock bottom, said brokers and other experts. Those who were out in the market were seeking bargains. Suddenly, the rules of thumb didn't hold up. As Lee Testa noted about the summer of 1990, his business was a lot stronger in June and July (normally a slower period for him) than in April and May (normally his briskest months). Because prices were dropping in Testa's selling area, bargain hunters were out in droves seeing what they could "steal," as he put it.

As 1993 started, many markets around the country were witnessing something seldom seen before: lower home prices (from their eighties' highs) and low interest rates (imagine 30-year fixed mortgages for under 8 percent!). As was mentioned in the introduction, this combination of low rates and lower home prices during the first quarter of 1993 made homes more affordable to more first-time buyers. How long this combination will last in markets around the country is hard to say.

Timing

Of course, no one wants to buy in a market where prices are still on the way up. The ideal is to purchase just as the market has registered its last down price and the curve is starting to head up again. But hitting this period just right is difficult. As Barbara

Corcoran, president of the real estate brokerage firm The Corcoran Group, said, when the change comes, it occurs in the blink of an eye. A buyer or seller doesn't realize that the market has changed until prices begin going up again, she noted.

Wait too long, Testa said, and you not only miss the lowest price, but you also miss out on both property and mortgage-interest tax deductions on state and federal tax returns. A better tactic, he said, is to buy after prices have been declining for awhile, getting the best deal that you can, and never look back. Don't worry if the market declines another 5 or 10 percent, he said; eventually, the market will reverse itself and you'll find your property not only worth more than you paid, but appreciating a little each year. In the interim, you'll be enjoying property and mortgage tax deductions that will help make up for any lower price you might have missed out on.

VIVA LA DOWN MARKET

Sellers and real estate brokers may hate them—and few had anything kind to say of the residential real estate market found in the early part of this decade—but a down market is great for first-time buyers. It's a time for getting bargains not only on resales but new housing as well. Since developers still have to pay carrying costs on the land and homes they've built, they may try offering incentives to get buyers to purchase their product. Price reductions are now possible because values are falling everywhere and developers no longer have to worry about protecting the resale levels on their already sold units. Along with lower prices, you may also find incentives such as free basements, landscaping and other extras. Builders will also offer cheap financing. It may be for only a limited time—say three years at 8 percent before moving up to 11 percent—but it could help you get into the house.

While a limited lower rate may not seem ideal, remember that your own finances should be improving as the years go on, marketing agents point out. You'll also be moving up in salary and position at your job. Once that higher percentage on the mortgage kicks in, you can always refinance as interest rates start declining. Refinancing means trading in a higher mortgage for a lower one. But remember, because there are new closing costs involved, you'll often need a difference of at least two points to make refinancing worthwhile. (And, as one accountant pointed out, there's always the risk that when you go to refinance, interest rates will be higher than the rate you currently have. The tactic here is to just hold onto the mortgage until rates fall.)

Builder Workouts

Another phenomenon of slow markets are builder workouts, which can be a boon for buyers. What happens in a workout is that the original builder of a project begins experiencing financial problems (because of slow sales and no income) and begins to fall behind on his construction loan payments to the lender financing the project. A number of scenarios can take place, explained Michael Luskin, a partner in the law firm of Luskin & Stern. Some of the most common are:

- The lender sells the property to another developer, with the original builder now out of the picture.

- The lender brings in a new developer, paying the firm a construction fee for finishing the project and a marketing fee for selling the units. If there's a profit, the new developer may get a percentage. Once again, the original developer is out of the picture.

- The lender still has faith in the original developer and agrees to restructure the debt and work with him until the market picks up.

- The developer finds another builder and, with the lender's approval, sells the project to him.

What all this means to the buyer is that when a workout takes place, the original asking prices on the units are usually lowered to make them more appealing and saleable.

Neil Eisner, former vice president of real estate operations for The Strathmore Organization, which builds in the New York metropolitan area, gave an example of one condo development that his firm was brought in on by a lender during a workout in 1990. The condominiums that the original developer was marketing had sold for as much as $365,000 in the mid-eighties, Eisner said. But then sales stopped. The builder ran into financial problems, losing control of the project, and the lender eventually brought in Strathmore, paying it a fee to finish the development and market the units. When sales resumed in the fall of 1990, prices began at $175,000 and topped off at $250,000—$115,000 less than the original asking prices.

While a buyer can get a great deal with a workout, before buying into a development, said Charles Mancini, vice president of the development firm Park Ridge Organization, a buyer should check out the reputation of the builder. Visit his past projects, he said, and see if the builder has finished the units there. Also ask people living there how the builder responded to any complaints they might have had with the homes. Actually knock on doors and interrogate those previous buyers, Mancini said.

Conversion Bargains

Besides bargains in resales and new construction, a weak market is also an excellent time to buy apartments in rental buildings that are in the process of being converted into condominiums and cooperatives by developers.

Depending on state laws, a sponsor—the owner of the building doing the conversion—will have only a certain period of time to sell a designated amount of units to have his or her property declared a condo or co-op. In New York, for example, sponsors have one year to sell 15 percent of their units. If a sponsor fails to sell the set amount, the building remains a rental.

"In a weaker market, the convertor needs you and therefore is willing to deal," said Barbara Schwarz, president of Mega Associates Limited, a firm that markets converted rental apartments. In strong markets, buyers are plentiful and a sponsor can easily reach the needed number of sales to turn his or her building into a condo or co-op, she said. But in slower periods, finding buyers is harder. As a result, Schwarz said, sponsors are willing to make all sorts of deals.

And even after the building has converted, in any market—but especially a slower one—the sponsor will still be looking for purchasers to buy the units he or she still owns. This is so the sponsor won't have to continue paying the monthly maintenance costs on the units he or she still possesses, said Stuart Saft, a partner with the law firm of Wolf Haldenstein Adler Freeman & Herz.

In each of these situations, Schwarz said, the sponsor will offer discounts on price, pay maintenance costs for a number of months and even offer cheaper financing than what is currently available at local lenders. Other sponsors will sell apartments with no money down or lend you the down payment at zero percent interest for a few years, pointed out Barbara Ford, vice president of Phase II Lifestyles Unlimited Inc., another marketing company of converted condos and co-ops.

But before buying in any of these converted buildings, have your attorney look over the project's financials. That is, make sure the building has a large enough reserve fund to do any upcoming capital improvements. Also make sure that the current sponsor is up-to-date on paying all fees and maintenance charges to the condo or co-op's board of directors. In the early nineties, many sponsors of converted buildings in the Northeast, especially New York and New Jersey, were foreclosed on by the lenders financing the projects. Some buildings are still trying to work out their financial messes. If you're looking into purchasing one of these units, use a lawyer who specializes in sales made in condo and co-op complexes.

THE GEOGRAPHIC DIFFERENCE

It should be noted at this point that interest rates can be low and residential real estate sales humming along throughout the country while certain parts of the nation still suffer through a weak housing market. In the mid-eighties, when housing prices were going through the roof across the nation, some areas, such as Texas, were experiencing a depressed market. Oil prices had dropped, and the Lone Star State's economy was in a tailspin. Foreclosures were rampant and housing prices dropped.

Condo prices likewise plummeted in Florida during this same period, the result of overbuilding. People who bought condos in Florida in 1980 saw their units worth about 30 percent less seven years later, said Michael Pappas, a regional vice president of a real estate firm in Dade County. Likewise, in some geographic areas, the brisk spring and slow winter rule that holds true for most other areas of the country will be contrary in certain states. And within those states, you can find contradictions not only by area, but by the type of real estate being sold.

For example, the biggest buying time for a single-family house on the east coast of Florida is spring and early summer, said Mike Owen, president of the Mike Owen Company, who noted, "The sales volume is a little less in the winter with people willing to haggle a little more on price."

However, the opposite is true for condos. In this segment of the market, August to fall is weaker. There are more people visiting and living in Florida between December and April, so the pool of potential buyers is greater.

On Florida's Gulf Coast, broker Patrick Luken said prices for both condos and single-family homes are cheapest during the dog days of summer. During July and August, locals are on vacation and few northerners, who are among the big buyers of Florida condos, are visiting. "Sellers become anxious, with most wanting to be out by fall and settled into their new homes before the new school year," Luken said.

In the town of Palm Beach, however, which attracts a more affluent buyer, a manager for Merrill Lynch Realty said that some feel the summer is a better time to buy. Most people residing in Palm Beach are away during the warmer months, so sellers tend to bargain more during this period. Similarly, if your first home is going to be in ski country, buying at the height of the ski season will result in more people looking and sellers having to negotiate less on price.

And don't forget, while the rest of the country is in a slump, the opposite may be happening in several areas. In 1988, for example, the average price of a home was declining in the Northeast while most of California was still appreciating at double digits. In the first quarter of 1990, according to the National Association of Realtors, home prices dropped 11 percent from the previous year in New Haven, Connecticut, while in that same time span prices rose 14.3 percent in Peoria, Illinois.

In the first quarter of 1993, however, while some housing markets have already started to recover, many areas in California are still in a slump. Home prices fell 1.5 percent in the first quarter of 1993 in Los Angeles, while they appreciated 12 percent in Waterloo, Iowa.

STRATEGIES FOR A DISTRESSED ECONOMY

If you live in an area with a depressed economy, or where home prices have just started to drop, it may be smart to buy. You'll be able to get a lot more home for your money before prices start bouncing back again. However, if you're not planning to stay in the area for a long time, or if you think your own job may be on the endangered list, then avoid buying. According to *Money* magazine, it takes three years of annual appreciation of more than 3 percent on a home just to cover a real estate broker's commission and a mortgage's closing costs. If you plan to move soon, and the economy remains stagnant, you may not see any appreciation to clear a profit.

According to Warren Weinstock, a partner with the accounting firm of Paneth, Haber & Zimmerman, if you plan to be in an area for less than two years, it pays to rent rather than buy. You won't be able to recoup closing costs even if prices stay the same.

Added Charles J. Urstadt, president of HRE Properties, a real estate investment trust, if you live in an area where home prices are dropping and you plan to be there for a number of years, your strategy should be to both rent and buy. You should remain in your rental unit while continuing to accumulate funds. During this period, you should also be out shopping the market. If you find a good deal, don't worry about whether prices have completely bottomed out, he said. Close on the home if you can afford to buy it and it appears to be at or below market value. Eventually, Urstadt added, prices will turn around and rise above what you paid.

You can wait out a down market for the lowest possible price, added Joel L. Burzin, a partner with the accounting firm of Grant Thortan, but by the time you realize the bottom is past, prices could be back to where they were when you started watching them drop.

There is one caution to remember when buying in a down economy. If the economy is poor and you do buy and then find you have to sell because of a job change, it may be difficult to find a buyer, Burzin said. Job stability and location is something to investigate before taking on a home purchase. In the worse-case scenario, he added, you stay in an area, buy a home and then find that your job is suddenly gone. You could be stuck with a house impossible to sell and whose payments you can no longer afford.

What these experts are trying to point out is that while a depressed economy will bring lower housing prices and greater opportunities for first-time buyers, there's also a down side. In some cases, renting can actually be wiser than buying for a period of time. If apartment rentals are low and interest on savings is high, you may be better off investing the money you would have spent on a house and putting it into a certificate of deposit. As market conditions change, you can consider buying while prices are starting to climb but before they've peaked at new heights.

If you find yourself in a shaky economic area, check with an accountant to see whether renting might not make more sense for you. Have your accountant compare mortgage writeoffs on taxes vs. investing in a CD and paying rent, Weinstock advised.

There's just one other factor to consider here: the emotional element. While a house may not make sense as an investment, some people ignore all the math and go out and buy something anyway. It's the American dream to have seven rooms, a big backyard and a front lawn. Whether you listen to your heart or your calculator, the choice is ultimately going to have to be yours.

But when you have a down economy, your heart may say "buy," and later you can find yourself in dire economic straits. You may lose a job, leading you to fall behind on mortgage payments. Fall too far behind and foreclosure could take place. Before buying anything in a down economy, proceed with caution.

DETERMINING THE MARKET

Of course, deciding what you're going to do will be partly based on what the market is like in the area you're looking to buy in. And the best way to determine current market conditions and where they are headed in the future is by staying informed.

Read the real estate or business sections of your local newspapers, as well as magazines. Watch what TV news broadcasts and others are reporting. Because housing affects so many people, it is an industry closely watched and reported on by the media.

Also look at interest rates. Noted Bonnie Lazar, the lower interest rates are, the faster homes usually move. Part of the reason for this is that the lower interest rates go, the greater the pool of buyers that can afford to purchase a home.

Lee Testa finds that what often heats up a sluggish housing market is the forecast of higher rates. Everyone wants to beat paying more for their monthly mortgage payments, so they rush out and buy. With more buyers, sellers are then in control of the market.

When interest rates do begin to climb, especially past 10.5 percent, there's a good chance things will slow down. The 10 percent level is some kind of psychological level for a lot of buyers, said Melissa Cohn, chairman of the Manhattan Mortgage Company.

More than any other factor, it's interest rates that act as the barometer for how healthy the housing market will be. Again, the higher monthly payments go, the fewer people that can afford to buy, Lazar said. But the economy and the market can play havoc with this rule as well. In the summer of 1990, Testa said, interest rates were around 10 percent, home prices in the Northeast were dropping, and still the market remained slow. It was a buyer's market. And when rates dropped further in early 1993 (30-year fixed rates were below 8 percent), home sales were still slower than most experts thought they'd be in many areas. Noted Lazar, the more stories that appear in the media highlighting bad economic news, the more hesitant buyers become. A psychological factor once again comes into play, she said. People may not actually be making less money or facing the threat of a layoff, but if the media continually point to negatives in the economy, people get nervous and ultimately feel less prosperous than they actually are. This results in putting off the purchase of a new home.

But, of course, the more people that hesitate, the better for you, the first-time buyer. With no home of your own to sell, you become a prize that most sellers are willing to have. They know that if you decide to buy, there's no unloading of a current home that can get in the way and halt their sale.

The Drive-Around Test

To find out how a certain area that you want to buy a home in is doing, periodically drive through the area. If the number of "for sale" signs seems to be mushrooming, this could indicate that the resale housing stock is growing faster than homes are being absorbed by buyers. This indicates a slowdown. It also means that a buyer will have more negotiating power, said Jack Dornheim.

Your local Multiple Listing Service tracks the number of resales on the market each month. The number of listings is usually reported in your local paper, especially when the market is starting to change, experts said. Pay attention to these figures. The more homes up for sale and the longer they sit on the market, the more willing a seller will be to negotiate the asking price.

Chapter 11

DO YOU NEED
A BROKER?

J ohn and Jamie Carp had just been shown a home they liked by the broker they were using.

"So what's the asking price?" John asked the broker.

"$110,000," he answered.

"Make an offer of $90,000," John replied. "But between you and me, if the seller won't take that, we'd probably be willing to go up as high as a $110,000."

While the above conversation has been invented, the contents of the dialogue are probably heard by brokers all around the country every day.

The problem occurring here is that, while John and Jamie have started their negotiations with a low offer, they've practically insured that they will pay, not $90,000 for the home, but $110,000 because of what they've told the broker. Why?

According to New York State's Secretary of State, Gail S. Shaffer, who oversees laws regulating brokers throughout New York, while the buyer thinks that the broker wearing the red or gold jacket is a friend helping him or her as much as possible, that broker's fiduciary duty is actually to the seller. It's the seller who has a contract with the broker and for whom the broker is working. The broker's sole purpose is to get as much for the home as he or she can for the seller he or she is representing.

And if you say that you didn't realize that a broker is working for the seller, you're not alone. In a 1983 report done by the

Federal Trade Commission, 71 percent of the buyers surveyed believed that their friendly local broker was working for them, Shaffer pointed out.

When you, as a buyer, say to the broker, "We really would pay $20,000 more if we had to," it's that broker's legal responsibility to report back to the seller, "Don't accept the first offer. I know, for a fact, that this buyer is willing to pay $20,000 more," said real estate attorney John Nappi.

By the same token, it is against the broker's fiduciary duty, according to the National Association of Realtors, to tell a buyer, "I'm pretty sure the seller will come down $8,000 in price." Again, everything a broker says and does should be solely for the purpose of helping his or her client—the seller.

BEWARE A BROKER'S ADVICE

"I'm not saying that brokers are disreputable," said attorney John Nappi. They can be the source of a lot of good advice and information. In fact, many buyers have praised the help and guidance that brokers have given them while feeling their way through the home-buying maze. But, what a buyer shouldn't do is rely purely on the information a broker is giving him. Because a broker's allegiance is to the seller, there is a chance that while the advice he or she is offering you is accurate, it may not be in the buyer's best interest, but rather just the quickest way of getting something done so that a sale can be consummated. Remember, the broker doesn't get paid until the home has actually closed.

For example, a broker may give you advice on mortgages, Nappi said. But it may not be the best mortgage for you or the one available at the best rate. The mortgage being suggested may just be the one that the broker can help get you the quickest (or perhaps one he or she gets a commission on from a lender).

A good broker should suggest that a buyer check with other professionals, such as an attorney or lender, said broker Bonnie

Lazar. "Any Realtor who is a professional should go out of the way to recommend other professionals to the purchaser."

But some brokers, such as Bob Herrick, said that people like himself can be of great help to purchasers. With the aid of computers, Herrick can help a buyer figure out how much house his or her income can afford to buy. He can also supply the purchaser with a list of closing costs so the buyer knows how much to budget for this expense.

To help a buyer, however, the purchaser has to be honest with the broker. "You can't say, 'I think I'm getting $20,000 from my parents to help me with the down payment,' when you know it isn't true," Herrick said. This will just waste both your time and the broker's time. The broker will end up showing you homes that you probably won't be able to get a mortgage for.

THE DIFFERENCE BETWEEN A BROKER, A SALES ASSOCIATE, AND A REALTOR

When starting on your home-buying expedition, or even when talking to others, you will probably hear the terms broker, sales associate, and Realtor used interchangeably. There are, however, shades of difference.

According to Lazar, a former president of the Long Island Board of Realtors in New York, *Realtor* is always spelled with a capital R because the term is a registered trademark and signifies someone belonging to the local board of realtors in his or her area, as well as the state and national association.

Realtors are required to follow a code of ethics which the local, state, and national association make sure are followed. Each chapter has a grievance committee which can reprimand and take other actions against Realtors that don't live up to their printed code of ethics. In all, there are about 800,000 Realtors throughout the country.

A *broker,* Lazar said, is someone who has passed the necessary requirements to become licensed to sell real estate in his or her state. Requirements often include educational courses and an exam. Once you've become licensed and are a broker, you can then open your own place of business or real estate office. You don't have to be a Realtor to be a broker. Some brokers prefer not to be members of the national or local association of Realtors.

A *sales associate* has passed the necessary state requirements to sell real estate, but has not gone on to get the additional education or met the other requirements needed to be a broker, Lazar said. A sales associate cannot open his or her own place of business. He or she must work for a principal broker who holds the sales associate's license. If a sales associate moves on to another real estate firm, the license is then held by the new owner of the office he or she has transferred to.

DO I NEED A BROKER?

Now that you know the difference between a broker, Realtor, and sales associate, your next question is probably, "If the broker is working for the seller and owes his or her allegiance to him or her, do I really need a broker to buy a home?"

Brokers will tell you, "Yes." Sellers tend to list their homes with a broker so they don't have to be bothered by buyers contacting them directly. Some sellers don't want to have to show the home and get involved later on with the negotiations when it comes time to decide the final price the home will go for. The only way to see or purchase these homes is by going through the broker carrying the listing.

However, others will argue that if a buyer avoids a broker and purchases a home directly from a seller, he or she can save a good deal of money. The reasoning behind this is that when a broker is used, even though the seller is hiring the broker and paying the commission, it's the buyer who ultimately pays that fee. The seller, needing to clear a certain amount to buy the next house, tacks the commission onto the asking price of the home.

Vickie Metz, out to buy her first home in 1989, realized this and looked for people selling their home without the aid of a broker. When she found a home she liked, she negotiated the price downward reasoning with the seller that he didn't have to pay a 6 or 7 percent fee—the standard commission in many areas—to a broker. Therefore, she argued, the seller should come down in price by as much as the fee would have been. (Some sellers argued that they had already set their asking price with the lack of a commission to pay in mind.)

Ultimately, however, the seller Metz finally bought from did come down in price by almost the full amount of the commission that would have been paid. (There is more to the art of negotiating on price as you'll see later in Chapter 14.)

Discount Brokers

One argument that brokers give buyers for using their services is that they can save a buyer a lot of legwork. If you tell them the type of home you want, in theory, they can come up with the perfect home for you because of the inventory of homes they have listed with their agency or because they are part of a multiple listing service. A Maine buyer can actually purchase a home in Texas, by using the multiple listing service (such as *MLS*) computer in a broker's office.

But again, if you use a broker, in some way you are paying the commission being charged the seller.

One solution might be to use the services of a discount broker (where once again, you have to remember, it is the seller who is hiring the broker). Ray Connor is one such broker who charges his sellers three percent of the home's selling price plus $1,000. With the seller paying less commission, in theory, homeowners list their properties for less. The buyer, therefore, gets the use of a broker's services, but ends up paying less for a home.

Another firm, Help-U-Sell, which had 560 offices nationwide

as of June 1990, charges sellers a flat fee based on different categories of a home's selling price (for example, a property selling up to $300,000 might have a commission of $4,750—it differs from area to area). Brokers at Help-U-Sell do everything a full-service broker does, except show the home, said Kathy Mosley, regional marketing manager for the firm. She doesn't find this a negative "because most buyers want to tour properties themselves and don't want to be locked in the back seat of a broker's car." Once again, if the seller pays less in commissions, then the buyer should pay less for the home.

There also are other flat-fee brokers all around the country—some individually owned, and some operated as national chains such as Homeowners Concept—that charge one set price to the seller. You can check the Yellow Pages of your phone book to see if one of the companies mentioned here is in your area or ask friends or your attorney if they know of such a broker in your neighborhood.

Arguments Against Discount Brokers. One argument that full-commission brokers make against discount brokers is that both the buyer and seller isn't receiving the same service. Broker Albo said, "discount brokers offer discount services." They must deal in volume to make up the difference and can't devote the same amount of time to both sellers and buyers.

Connor disagrees, however, and says that he gives his sellers the same type of services any other broker does.

Another argument given is that discount brokerage firms come and go like the wind, said broker Margot Wolf. And, indeed, when the market slows in an area, you often do see discount brokers closing up shop because they depend on volume to offset the low fees they are charging.

So should you, as a buyer, buy a home from someone using a discount broker or a full service broker? Well, that's going to depend on the individual, but one thing experts recommend is that you pick a broker the way you would an attorney or anyone else whose services you employ.

HOW TO PICK A BROKER

While the seller signs a contract when hiring a broker, the buyer does not. Therefore, if he or she doesn't like the way the broker is operating, the purchaser can just move on to someone else.

Experts recommended that buyers ask friends, relatives, lenders, or their attorneys for the names of reliable brokers. Ask friends and relatives if the broker showed them exactly what they were in the market for or if the broker wasted their time showing them anything and everything. The first thing some brokers do is often show the homes they can get the biggest commissions on, Nappi said.

Diane Degl said that during her home-hunting excursions, some of the brokers she used kept showing her, and her then-fiancé, Kenneth Uher, homes that were priced more than they wanted to spend. Her solution was to thank the broker and move on to one who was more responsive to their needs.

Greg and Rosemary Bradshaw had a much better experience with the first broker they chose. They explained to the agent that they wanted a home that didn't need any work, but rather had an updated kitchen and bathroom, and new windows, plumbing and wiring. What they wanted was a home in mint condition. The first four homes their broker showed them met all of the qualifications the couple had set. In a few short weeks, they had a contract of sale on exactly the type of home they wanted.

Buyer's Brokers

Now if you want to use a broker whose sole purpose is to look after your needs, then employ a buyer's broker, a concept that is slowly spreading across the country. With such an agreement, the buyer hires and pays a broker a commission to help him or her locate a home and represent him or her in the transaction. The way the fiduciary duty of the seller's broker is to the homeowner, the buyer's broker's job is to find the type of home his or her client wants and then help the purchaser negotiate the lowest possible asking price.

Each buyer's broker works differently. Susan Bird, owner of Susan W. Bird, Inc./Buyers Co., charges a client a retainer depending on the cost of the property (it should be noted that Bird deals mostly with very expensive properties in Manhattan). If after 90 days a suitable home is not found for the buyer, the fee is returned. If a home is bought, the buyer pays half of what the selling broker's commission on the home is, with the retainer applied toward this.

Dornheim, another buyer's broker, charges one percent of the listed price plus $200 for every $1,000 he can get the listed price reduced. The fee is an incentive for him to negotiate as low an asking price as he can for his client.

However, traditional brokers said that a buyer really doesn't have to pay to hire representation of his or her own. While brokers do represent and are paid by the seller, a broker actually spends more time with the buyer, said broker Rana Rutherford. "I work with everyone's best interests. You don't get a buyer or seller to do anything he or she is not willing to do."

But this dual representation is a conflict of interest in some people's eyes, including Bird's. How can a broker employed by the seller do his or her best and get the lowest price for the buyer, if the broker's fiduciary duty is to the seller?

When a broker is hired by the buyer and works for him or her, Bird said, "There's no question in my mind that you bring about a deal that's better for the purchaser. It's a strategy based on negotiating." (And just what those tactics are that buyer's brokers use to get the price down is discussed at length in Chapter 14.)

Brokers representing purchasers said that, in many cases, what is viewed initially as an added cost by the buyer is actually absorbed by the lower asking price the agent is able to negotiate.

Another argument heard against buyer's brokers is why should a buyer pay for a service he's now getting for nothing. It's the seller who pays the traditional broker's commission. Why should a buyer add an additional cost to home buying?

But Bird argues, the buyer is already paying the commission indirectly through a higher asking price. As mentioned before, most sellers figure what they want to clear, after the home is sold, and then raise their asking price to reflect the commission. If the buyer is going to pay this fee anyway, why shouldn't a buyer get something for his or her money. Many of her clients have more than made up the commission they are paying her firm as a result of the buyer's brokers negotiating prices down for them. Her brokers' allegiance is to the buyer and getting that seller to come down as much in price as possible by giving reasons as to why a lower price is warranted.

Said Dornheim, "A broker representing the seller tries to talk the price up. I try and talk the price down." After the buyer has had a home inspection made of the property, he uses that information to help get the price down arguing that the negatives listed on the report will ultimately cost the buyer additional money to correct.

"Instead of putting a house up for sale, we're putting a buyer on the market," said broker/owner Ray Connor, who also does buyer brokering.

One other point that should be made here is that if you can't find a firm specializing in buyer brokering in your area, you can approach any broker, offering to hire him or her as your agent. Just make sure, experts said, that this broker is not also the broker for the homes they are showing you. In many areas, collecting dual commissions on a single property is against the law.

You can also ask your attorney or lender for the name of a local buyer's broker.

Being Your Own Broker

Whether you use a traditional broker, a buyer's broker, or no broker at all will depend on you.

If you do decide to bypass a broker, you're going to have to find owners who are trying to sell their homes on their own. The fastest way is to look in the real estate classifieds of your local papers. These homes are easy enough to identify because no real estate agent's name will be carried on the ad and it will usually emphasize "for sale by owner." It might also say "no brokers please." The reason for this phrase is because, besides buyers checking out "for sale by owner" listings, brokers are also hunting them down. It's their hope to find a frustrated seller who is ready to throw in the towel and list it with the broker, after unsuccessfully marketing the home on his or her own.

Another way to find homeowners selling on their own is to ride around the area you want to buy in and look for signs on the lawn, a technique Vickie Metz used. You could also ask friends and neighbors if they know of anyone selling on their own.

Once you find a home that interests you, either through an ad or by riding around, call the owner up and get some details. If it sounds like you might be interested in the property, then arrange to see it. If you decide this may be the home for you, attorneys, like Nappi, said that you will have to put a small refundable binder down while you think about getting this home. The binder should state your name and theirs, how much the binder is for, and that it is refundable after a week or some other time period specified by you and the seller. (It should be noted that in some areas of the country binders are not refundable. Check with your own attorney about the laws in your region.)

How you should negotiate on price and other terms is discussed in later chapters. But attorneys agreed that you should never sign any other agreements without first consulting your lawyer. In fact, attorneys said, you may also want to show the binder to your lawyer before signing it.

Chapter 12

INSPECTING THE HOME YOU WANT

"**P**eople who skimp on having a home inspected are being penny wise and pound foolish," said Michael Cohen, a partner with the law firm of Cohen & Warren. And yet, he sees as many buyers having inspections done as he does those passing on this service.

Once you've found the home you like, the tendency is to want to close on the deal and move in as soon as you can. But as Cohen and other experts warn, buying any home without first having it inspected could result in purchasing something that will yield headaches and problems down the road. An inspection should be done before the contract of sale is signed. You can, however, sign the contract and have your attorney write into the document that the closing is subject to a home inspection and the findings of that report.

SELF-INSPECTION VS. PROFESSIONAL INSPECTION

For the sake of economy, some buyers perform a home inspection themselves. There's nothing wrong with this tactic. However, before undertaking this task, you should ask yourself how much you really know about how a home is put together. If you understand the mechanics and can detect a bad roof vs. a new one, then save the cost of hiring a professional and by all means do the inspection yourself.

Some buyers, with little knowledge of their own, bring in a friend or relative to inspect the home being considered. Buyers reason that the friend or relative has gone through the home purchasing process before and therefore knows what to look for having lived with breakdowns and repairs over the years. But it's a mistake to rely on these non-expert reports, said Warren Cronacher, president of Tauscher Cronacher, a professional engineering firm. A relative may recognize an old heating system. But will he or she be able to detect other decaying or faulty components in the home? "Too many things can go wrong with a house that an Uncle Henry can't put a finger on."

Instead of a relative, use a professional, said Linda Albo, owner/broker of ERA Albo Agency. Despite such recommendations to her clients, she estimated only about 50 percent of the buyers she works with do a home inspection.

Beware of the "Professional" Who May Not Be

One other warning from Albo: If you do decide to bring in a "professional," be careful. Anyone can call himself a home inspector. Stay away from people in the home improvement business who do inspections as a "favor" to customers to earn a little extra money on the side.

"Anyone can hang a shingle out and say they inspect homes," confirmed Robert Dolibois, executive director of the American Society of Home Inspectors. Most are listed under "building inspectors" in the Yellow Pages. But these professionals can be anyone from a plumber to an electrician. The problem here is that an electrician may be great at detecting things wrong with a home's wiring, but will be weaker at catching things outside of his field of specialization.

Texas is the only state in the nation that currently licenses home inspectors, Dolibois added. However, Cronacher said, engineers also do home inspections and in many states, such as New York, these professionals have to be licensed.

How to Pick a Good Home Inspector

To pick a reliable inspector, Albo advised asking for recommendations from brokers, attorneys, or fellow homebuyers who were satisfied with an inspector he or she used. You should also look for someone who is connected with some type of professional association such as the American Society of Home Inspectors. These societies usually give educational seminars on the latest techniques and have a code of ethics that members must follow.

Dolibois stressed that his society's code of ethics prohibits inspectors from also doing repair work on the home being looked over. You want to make sure that the person inspecting your home isn't using this inspection as a loss leader to drum up repair work. Because home inspection is an unregulated and unlicensed business, a homebuyer has to be careful whom he or she uses.

Call several inspectors, Dolibois advised. Ask what type of report they will do for you and what it will include. Also ask if they inspect only certain parts of the building or the whole house. If you get someone with only a plumbing expertise, that inspector may give a detailed report on the bathrooms and waterpipes in the home, but perform a poor spot check on other areas. So ask what they'll inspect in advance. Also question whether or not you'll be getting a written report. This gives you something to refer back to once the inspection is completed.

Cronacher also recommended looking at the length of time the person or firm has been in business. He suggested shying away from part-time home inspectors. Those that do inspecting on the side are usually lacking in experience and can't give you as good an inspection as someone who does it each and every day.

Pick a home inspector the way you would a doctor, Dolibois

added. You are actually asking the inspector to do a physical on the home to confirm that the biggest purchase of your life thus far is in good health.

Try to Go Along on the Inspection Tour. One other important thing to inquire about is whether or not you can accompany the inspector on his or her tour of the house, Dolibois said. This is an extremely important thing to take advantage of. When you accompany the inspector, he or she can show you first hand what is found wrong both inside and outside the home. It's often a lot easier to understand a problem when it's shown to you as opposed to just reading about the defect later on in a written report. It's like seeing a video vs. a written text.

While the buyer is touring the home with the inspector, Cronacher added, the inspector can put any defaults in perspective. This prevents that missing screw you might have noticed from coming across as a major catastrophe. Likewise, a spot you noticed on the basement floor and worried about when you first looked the home over, may turn out to be only a coffee stain.

In addition, a good inspector usually has some knowledge about repairs and maintenance, Cronacher pointed out. By going along on this house tour, the inspector can tell you what repairs may be needed to correct a problem and also give you a ballpark figure of what those repairs will cost. These kinds of things may not be in the written report. Consider them bonus information, as well as a sort of mini-course in home inspection.

For example, an inspector may recommend that a power fan be installed in the attic to help reduce the home's temperature in the summer, Dolibois said. This could cost under $200 to install, but save you thousands of dollars over the years on cooling costs. In addition, the fan can also help double the lifespan of a shingle roof whose replacement costs thousands of dollars. This type of information is great to know, but is often not put into the written report.

The inspector can also tell you why some things, such as a roof, have one or maybe 10 years left to go.

Besides pointing out defects in a house, said Cohen, this inspection can be a big help in planning out your housing budget once you take possession of the property. If the inspector says you're going to need a new furnace in five years, then you can start putting money aside for this expense from the day you move in.

Another advantage in going along on the inspection, Cronacher said, is that you know about the home's condition immediately instead of having to wait for the written report to be put together and mailed out to you. This becomes a bigger plus in a really hot market when buyers are lined up to purchase properties. Time suddenly becomes a factor because, with other purchasers lurking in the wings, the seller wants you to make up your mind right away as to whether you want the home or not.

Smart Sellers Encourage Inspections

The seller's broker should actually encourage that an inspection be done (unless he or she has something to hide) because it helps set up a comfort zone for the buyer, Dolibois said. Once an inspection is performed, the purchaser will know why a bulge is in one wall and what a stain represents instead of imagining in his or her mind what type of problem these items could be.

But the main reason to do an inspection, Cohen said, "is that it helps the buyer to purchase with full and complete knowledge as to what he's getting."

After the inspection is done, Cronacher likes to sit down with the homebuyer if he's accompanied him or her on the tour, and summarize what they've seen. However, this is always done away from the seller so that the owner won't be tipped off what was found and how the buyer might use that information when negotiating on price.

The Cost of an Inspection

The cost of having an inspection done varies around the country. It's based on the size of the house and thoroughness of the inspection. Most experts estimated that a basic inspection should run between $200 and $500.

What Age Home Should Be Inspected?

Often debated is what age home should be inspected. Should buyers only have 50-year-old plus buildings looked over or should you bring in a professional to give the once over of brand new structures as well? "Every house can have a potential problem," attorney Michael Cohen said.

Warren Cronacher pointed out that his firm has looked at more than 140,000 homes over the years he's been in business and that he's found that age and the potential for problems don't always go together. You can have a three-year-old home with a major flaw, while a 100-year-old structure is in perfect shape. Likewise, a newly-built home can have wetness in the basement or be poorly constructed and not worth the money being asked. An inappropriate heating system that won't adequately keep the living and sleeping areas comfortable can be found in a home of any age.

"We're finding more of our members being asked to perform inspections on new housing," Dolibois said. The reason for this is that it's a way of settling disputes between buyers and developers of new homes. If an inspector finds a similar problem in many of the homes he's looked at in the same development, then it may be due to the manner in which the developer initially built the home.

As for resales, according to the American Society of Home Inspectors the number one problem found is overall poor maintenance. Sellers don't keep up with the preventive maintenance which preserves the cosmetic, structural, and mechanical integrity of the property. This, of course, leads to later headaches for the new owner.

Have Condos and Co-Ops Inspected As Well. "But, I'm not buying a single-family home," you're now thinking as you get ready to skip onto the next chapter. "Should I bother with an inspection?" Most definitely, Cronacher advised. Condos and co-ops should also be given the once over by a professional. The inspector should take a look at all the common areas of the building or complex to determine whether or not a major building component, such as the heating plant or roof, will soon be needed.

The buyer can then ask the building's managing agent if there is enough money in the condo or co-op's operating budget to pay for these upcoming repairs or in the reserve fund (which is earmarked for future or unexpected problems). If there isn't enough money in either of these places, the buyer may be socked with higher maintenance costs once he or she moves in, so that the condo or co-op association can pay for these items. Or the buyer (after taking over) could be hit with a special assessment levied against all the unit owners to pay for the repair.

THINGS A GOOD INSPECTOR LOOKS OVER

What should a good inspector examine when going over a house? Among the items that the American Society of Home Inspectors requires its members to examine is the type and condition of the foundation, as well as the floor and wall structure. The inspector should also examine the roof and look into attic crawl spaces noting the type of structure, installation, and ventilation the home has.

While doing a check of the home's exterior, the inspector should check the condition and type of doors and windows. He or she should also observe the exterior wall covering materials—such as brick or aluminum siding—and the condition these items are in. The inspector will also look at decks, balconies, stoops, and steps. Another thing he or she should do is to note whether or not there is any vegetation surrounding the house. He or she will examine the drainage (to see if flooding will occur after a rainstorm) and the condition of the driveway, patio, and any retaining walls located on the property.

Once he or she moves inside the home, the inspector will examine the plumbing system checking its operation, drainage, water pressure, and any possible leaks. The inspector will also look at the electrical system checking out the equipment, amperage, and voltage ratings of the service, how lighting fixtures are installed (as well as how they're operating), where switches and outlets are located, and if there are enough in each area.

He or she will then move onto the heating system and check the controls, clearance of the furnace from combustibles, and size and condition of the heating system. If the home has central air conditioning, the inspector will check ducts, air filters, and the presence of an installed cooling source in each room.

While walking around the inside of the home, he or she will also look at the condition of walls, ceilings, floor surfaces, steps, stairways, cabinets, counters, windows, doors, and anything else that may be the cause for a potential problem later on.

How the Inspector Uses the Data Collected

"Home inspection is not an exact science," Dolibois emphasized. It's going to vary from inspector to inspector. In addition, the home is being evaluated in comparison to other dwellings of that age. Many written reports rate things excellent, good, fair or poor. When the inspector checks off good, he is saying that, for example, the floors in a 50-year-old home are in good shape compared to the floors in other 50-year-old homes. When compared to the floors in a new home, however, a buyer may not find them to be as new looking or in as good condition.

THINGS INSPECTIONS DON'T REVEAL

The other thing that people should realize about inspections, Dolibois explained, is that the inspector is making observations based on what he or she can see. Because the home belongs to another person at this point in time, the inspector can't pull up carpeting or take paneling off the walls to see what's lurking underneath or behind these items.

Asked whether or not an inspector will look for building code violations, most said that they did not. This is because each community has its own codes making it hard for the inspector to keep track of. In addition, codes are continually changing in many areas, but only when a home is newly built or updated does the structure have to comply with the updated code.

As for checking for termites, radon, or asbestos, these are usually separate services not included with the home inspection unless they are visible to the inspector. Things like asbestos, Dolibois said, requires testing and takes more time than the inspector spends on this once-over of the home.

Once the inspection is made, the inspector will usually send you a written report outlining the condition of the items looked at. There also will be a spot on the report pointing out major flaws.

One thing the inspector will not do is tell you whether or not to buy the home or if the home is worth the money being asked for it. Value is an appraiser's job, Dolibois said. The inspector also won't tell you the total number of years he or she thinks the home has left. This is too hard a thing to determine. For example, a storm could come along a month after the inspection, weaken the structure, and change the home's life expectancy.

What to Do with this Report

As for what to do with this report, look at it as one more piece of information in making an intelligent decision as to whether or not a home should be purchased, Cronacher said.

While estimated life expectancies are listed for some components in the report, no one can guarantee exactly how long plumbing or a boiler will last. These are just approximations of the life left. For example, because the inspector can't rip up walls and floors, plumbing that can be seen may appear fine; however, pipes behind the wall may be in worse shape.

By the same token, experts said, buyers should realize that most resales are going to have defects of some kind. The inspection is an aid in helping the buyer pinpoint those defects that could turn into a money drain or make the property not worth buying. There is no pass or fail grade for a property, stressed engineers and home inspectors.

And while most sellers are honest, Dolibois added, some do try to play tricks when the home inspector is scheduled to come by for a visit. He recalled one seller who had put up new wall covering in the basement sometime before placing the home on the market. It wasn't until three years later that the new buyer moved in and got around to making some changes in the basement that he discovered that the wallpaper had been put up to cover fire damage.

There have been other instances where sellers have stacked heavy boxes along a wall to cover a flaw in the floor or sheetrock. "The inspector can't be moving major equipment to do his or her job," Dolibois said. Attorneys noted that depending on the severity of the problem and when it was found, it could be grounds for a suit against the seller over misrepresentation of the property— covering a defect that he or she knew existed. But it can be hard proving that the seller knowingly sold the home with a defect that was not revealed.

If a major flaw is found, Dolibois added, the buyer can use that fact to try and get the seller to either adjust his price downward or to pay to have the problem repaired. But a buyer can't turn to a seller and say, "This 17-year-old home has a 17-year-old roof, what are you going to do about it. I want compensation." A 17-year-old home is going to come with a 17-year-old roof. (For additional hints in helping you to use the inspection report to get the home price negotiated downwards, see Chapter 14.)

One Caveat about Home Inspection Reports

Herrick warns that sometimes home inspection reports scare off people from buying perfectly good homes because they aren't read correctly. Case in point was one woman buying her first home who received a report that listed a number of things wrong with the structure. Her parents looked at the house, read the report, and suggested that she not purchase the home. They declared it in terrible shape. Friends, however, were telling her that the price of the home was extremely good for the area it was in and that she should purchase the home despite what the report said.

Finally, another friend suggested the woman bring in a contractor, who that friend had used to do extensive work on his own house. "Pay the contractor to take the report and go over the house and tell you exactly how bad it is and how much money it would take to repair the structure," he told her. She thought this last piece of advice made the most sense with the cost for the contractor's time estimated to be under $100. After doing his own inspection, and referring to what the home inspector had indicated was wrong, the contractor agreed that the free-standing garage was in terrible shape and would probably have to be torn down. But as for the house, everything that was listed in the report as "fair" or "poor" could be corrected or updated for under $1,000. The woman ended up buying the home and after six months hasn't regretted the decision.

The one mistake this woman did make, however, was not to go along on the home inspection. Had she gone along, the inspector could have pointed out the flawed items and he might have even estimated how much it would have cost to correct the problems.

Parting Advice

One last bit of advice from Warren Cronacher about inspections and using them to decide whether or not to buy something: Don't buy a home with major problems. No matter what you do, you can never correct or fix a major problem and later get your money back when reselling the home.

For example, major structural problems entail big dollars to correct. But, once repaired, these are problems that future buyers can't really see the results of. You could point out to the buyer that you spent $50,000 repairing the home so that it wouldn't collapse. But most purchasers won't be impressed by this fact because they expect to be considering a home that won't collapse. This really isn't a selling feature that will support a higher asking price.

Since the idea for a first-time buyer is to use this initial home as a stepping stone to another, the less money you have to pour into correcting things that can't really be seen and won't result in a higher selling price, the better off you are. If you want to pump money into the home, Cronacher said, do it on kitchen updates and other items that will return a higher percentage of the cost when the home is sold.

Chapter 13

CHOOSING A GOOD ATTORNEY

In the course of buying your first home, you'll be working with a number of professionals ranging from bankers to brokers. But perhaps the one person you'll depend upon the most is the real estate attorney you hire to represent you at your closing and throughout the transaction. "Your attorney should be the quarterback for your home-buying venture," said Michael Cohen, a partner in the law firm of Cohen & Warren. All of the documents that you sign, as well as many of the decisions that you will have to make, should be run past him or her.

"Every attorney can do a real estate closing," added lawyer Craig D. Robins. But that doesn't mean every attorney can do it well. Many buyers, both first-time and otherwise, often turn to an attorney who has been used by the family over the years for such services as drawing up a will. Or sometimes, to save money, people turn to someone, within the family, who has a law degree, asking if he or she will handle the buyer's real estate closing. Unfortunately, Robins said, in both of the aforementioned examples, the attorney is most likely a specialist in some other field of law such as business or matrimony. While each may be brilliant in his or her own field, he or she won't know all of the little nuances of real estate law which is changing constantly.

During the course of putting a binder down, forming a contract of sale, and actually closing on the property, you can end up with all types of problems, said attorney John Nappi. If your attorney is not someone versed in real estate it could end up delaying your closing or even costing you the house.

WHEN TO HIRE AN ATTORNEY

The best time to get an attorney, Nappi said, is before you sign the binder on a home. This way, you'll have someone on your side guiding you as you go through each step. Remember, while the real estate broker can provide you with great information, the broker is an agent hired by the seller and is working for him or her. You need someone in your corner giving you advice with your interests in mind; that person is your attorney.

Some attorneys said they believed the best time for the buyer to touch base with a lawyer is when he or she first starts house hunting. Find someone you feel comfortable with and tell him or her that you are about to start shopping for a home. Then, when you find something you like and are ready to sign a binder or a contract of sale, you'll have an attorney ready to jump into action.

WHY GET AN ATTORNEY?

Now, you don't legally need an attorney in order to buy a home. You can handle everything yourself if you wish. But while there's a standard four-page contract of sale that's commonly used in most transactions, these days, few contracts go through with just those four pages, Robins said. Additions, or riders as they're called in legal parlance, are tacked on and can sometimes be longer than the contract itself.

Riders are put in to protect an attorney's client, be he or she the seller or buyer. A good lawyer will be adding riders that are best for his or her buyer's situation (perhaps you need more than the standard three months to close) while protecting the buyer from things that the seller is trying to get (for example, the seller may want the right to rent the home for another three months after closing before moving out). It all comes down to finding an attorney who knows and specializes in real estate law.

In addition, said James J. Burke, an associate broker with Schlott Realtors and former financial planner, you want an attorney who is local and familiar with the area you are buying in. While an attorney has to be licensed in the state he or she is practicing, not all areas of a state will operate the same. That is, each may have its own way of doing things based on local laws.

Choosing an Attorney by Price

One way people choose an attorney is by price and price alone. Open any newspaper and you'll see ads reading "closings done for only $199," or some other inexpensive figure. But, said attorney Jeffrey C. Daniels, a partner with Daniels & Daniels, "You get what you pay for." The service you'll receive from a discount attorney will probably be very limited. He or she may do little more than explain the contract of sale to you, show you where to sign, and then let a secretary handle the rest of the matter. The next time you'll see that attorney will be at the closing where, once again, he or she will tell you to sign some more things. You'll receive your house keys and that will be the end of the whole transaction.

People, especially first-time buyers, need someone to sit down with them and to explain how different procedures along the way will work, Cohen said. The day before a closing, Cohen actually spends time with his clients explaining to them what will happen during the frenzy of that one-hour meeting.

One trick low-priced attorneys use, Robins said, is to say that their fee covers the closing, which is usually true. However, as the days go by, they begin presenting you with additional bills such as for both writing up and looking over the contract of sale, any phone calls they have to make in connection with the closing, and for any other problems that may arise. Before you know it, you're paying as much as a good, full-priced attorney would have charged you.

Price should be one of the factors to consider when picking an attorney, said Jane Devine, Commissioner of the Suffolk County Consumer Affairs Office on Long Island, New York. "But this is one case where consumers should not look at cost alone."

Finding a Good Attorney

So how do you find a good attorney? A referral from a real estate broker was favored by Commissioner Devine. Involved with real estate transactions all the time, she felt that brokers would know who the good and bad attorneys in the area are.

But some attorneys said that using a lawyer recommended by a broker may not be a good idea. A broker only gets paid once a deal closes and the property changes hands. "The attorney may feel obligated to make sure the deal doesn't fall apart," Daniels said. The lawyer wants to be recommended again by that broker, so he or she may do whatever he or she can to keep a deal alive, even if it isn't always in the buyer's best interests.

But Devine doesn't think such a thing will happen. A broker realizes that his or her reputation is on the line. Many of the clients they get are through referrals and if people start saying, "That attorney broker X recommended was terrible; he did a couple of things to keep the deal alive which I wasn't crazy about," then the broker's reputation will be in trouble.

Likewise, "Any attorney who is ethical is working for the buyer or seller and not the broker," Burke said. While you may find one or two attorneys doing what Daniels suggested, "A good broker isn't looking to get deals done because a lawyer finagled it." Burke has recommended attorneys whom he would hire for himself. In the long run, "No one commission is worth a broker's reputation."

Using Friends' Advice and Bar Association Referral Services. If you don't want to use an attorney suggested by a broker, then ask friends for names of lawyers whom they've used and were satisfied with, said C. Jaye Berger, head of her own law firm. When collecting these names, let your friends tell you what they liked or didn't like about the attorney.

Another source is a local lawyer referral service that many bar associations around the country sponsor. Upon contacting this group, they'll ask for the field of specialization you're looking for, which in this case would be real estate. The service will then supply you with the names of several attorneys in your immediate area. But while these recommended attorneys may be in good standing with the bar, some lawyers warn that the names given to you may not always yield the best candidates for the job. According to Robins and others, any lawyer who pays a small fee can have his or her name listed with this service. Likewise, the attorneys given to you as recommendations can have anywhere from many years of experience to being fresh out of law school.

In addition, Daniels said, he's always wondered why an attorney would list his name with any referral service. Isn't that attorney able to get enough clients through recommendations? Or is the attorney so new that his or her few clients have yet to recommend him or her? Daniels, like a number of other attorneys, is very skeptical about these referral services.

Other Sources for Finding an Attorney. Another source for coming up with a reliable attorney, Berger said, is the legal referral service many unions offer their membership. These attorneys also may charge union members a lower fee than the usual going rate. The best way to find out if this service is available is to contact your union representative.

Cohen also suggested asking lenders for a recommendation.

Still other experts recommended opening the Yellow Pages and looking under "real estate attorneys." But, as some lawyers pointed out, the phone book is no better than picking representation blindly. All you are seeing in the Yellow Pages are names. There may be an accompanying ad giving some information, but these are just boasts and claims written by the attorney about himself or herself and not by a client who has used him or her. Unless you are unable to get a reliable recommendation from anyone else, most experts warned not to pick an attorney based solely on an ad in the phone book.

With Attorneys' Names in Hand, Interview Those Candidates

O.K., you've gotten a list of names from brokers, friends or your union. Now what? Call a few up and schedule an appointment to meet with each.

Devine recommended meeting with each attorney in person rather than doing an interview over the phone. You may be asked to pay for this initial consultation, but Devine feels its worth it. "Sometimes to be a smart consumer you have to invest some money." You get a better feeling for the attorney talking with him or her face-to-face.

Other real estate experts pointed out that the attorney-client relationship is a very personable one. You want someone who will not only do a good job, but who also matches your personality and who you feel comfortable working with. An in-person interview also lets you see the attorney's offices and operation. You can see if this is a huge law firm, a small intimate one, or just a store-front with the appearance that this guy could be gone by tomorrow.

During the course of this interview, Cohen said, you should ask a host of questions, including what the attorney's fee is.

The Fee

When it comes to an attorney's fee, Devine again warned that this is one place price should not be the sole determining factor. Some attorneys advertise a low price. That doesn't mean the attorney will do a poor job, but it probably means he or she deals in volume. To make up for the low cost, he or she may not be able to give you the personal attention a higher-priced attorney can.

Some attorneys will charge by the hour, others a flat fee. Some charge a percentage based on the selling price of the home. Fees for full-service attorneys can run anywhere from $500 to $1,200 and up. "But just because someone is asking a higher price, that doesn't mean you're getting a better attorney either," Robins said.

Daniels suggested that you are probably better off paying a flat fee instead of an hourly rate. When you pay by the hour, you will be less apt to call your attorney for advice. What may seem like an unimportant question, may be very important. But if you're paying by the hour, you may hesitate to ask that question to try and keep your attorney's fee down. Paying a flat rate lets you contact the attorney without worrying that every little question will run up your bill.

Burke agreed with Daniels that a set price is better than an hourly fee. However, he advised watching out for attorneys who base their flat fees on a percentage of the home's selling price. There's no more work connected with an $80,000 home than there is for one selling for a $120,000, so why pay more to close on a higher priced home?

What You Get for Your Fee. It should take a good attorney anywhere from 10 to 20 hours to do what is needed to get his or her client ready for a closing, Daniels said. Among the things the attorney will do in preparation for that day you take possession of the home are:

- Meeting with his or her client on several occasions.

- Reviewing the contract of sale and drawing up riders to protect the buyer.

- Overseeing the signing of the contract of sale (this can be in person or done by mail—a face-to-face contract signing, however, will take more time). The contract signing is when the buyer gives the seller the down payment for the home. That money is then placed into an escrow account.

- Coordinating things with the buyer's lender.

- Reviewing the lending agreement and looking over the mortgage cost estimates and conditions of the mortgage commitment.

- Ordering a title report and reviewing it.

- Attending the closing.

While there is much to do in the way of preparation, said Robins, "I've seen too many closings where all the attorney did was say sign on the dotted line. There were no explanations given." The buyer might have paid less for the attorney, but did he or she get any service for his or her money?

QUESTIONS TO ASK WHEN INTERVIEWING AN ATTORNEY

So the first question to ask an attorney when sitting down and meeting him or her for the first time is what his or her fee is and what you will be getting for that fee. In addition, Robins said, ask if the attorney will personally handle your closing or if it will be given to an associate. In a lot of firms there's an older, more experienced attorney and a younger, new associate. This is how Robins said he began his career, as the latter. The buyer should ask which of these people will be representing him or her at the closing. There is nothing wrong with the younger attorney doing the work as long as the older one is there to back him or her up.

Next ask how long the attorney feels the period between the contract of sale and closing should take, Devine said. This will give you a feeling for how soon you'll be moving into your new home. Also ask if the attorney will help arrange for a mortgage, title search, termite inspection or any other things that have to be done before the closing can take place in the area where you are buying your home.

In addition, find out the attorney's availability, Burke said. Is he or she flexible to work with you as soon as you've found the right house or is he or she so backlogged that it may be weeks before he can get to you? You want an attorney who can be available when needed, so a good deal doesn't slip away.

Two other questions to ask is what kind of experience the attorney has and what his or her fee schedule is. Some won't require you to pay anything until the closing. Others, such as Robins, say they ask for half the fee in advance and the rest at closing. Not all deals make it through from contract of sale to closing. So the next question you should ask is, how much will I have to pay should the deal fall apart? Knowing this, in advance, will help things go smoothly if something should happen later on. You should also ask if there will be any additional fees. Some attorneys said that the only extras they charge are in connection with any complications the deal may encounter such as liens against the title, meaning that the owner of the home owes money to someone who is waiting to collect once the home is sold.

"The smart consumer should ask what the fee includes and doesn't include," Robins said. Then, when you think you've found the attorney that's right for you (after doing your interviews), you should draw up a contract between the two of you that spells out the fee, the fee schedule, what the attorney will be doing for that fee, any extra charges and payments that will be due, and what the fee will be if the deal falls apart.

PROTECTING YOURSELF

So now you have an attorney. You also have a home whose price you've negotiated down to what you can afford (see Chapter 14 for negotiating tips) and want to buy. The next step is to draw up a contract of sale.

"It's the seller's attorney who usually writes the contract of sale," said broker Harriet Lion. The seller will try to make this an ironclad contract making it as difficult as possible for the buyer to get out of the deal (especially when the market is sluggish as it currently is in some areas around the country). The buyer's attorney, on the other hand, should be placing clauses in the contract that protects his or her client in case problems arise.

For example, most attorneys make a contract of sale subject

to an engineer or home inspector's report done within a certain time (usually a week) of signing the contract. But Nappi said that it's hard to word this type of clause because its subject to so many things. For example, will the buyer still go ahead with the deal if a bad roof is found, but break the contract if a poor heating system is revealed? To avoid confusion, he said, "I encourage people to get the engineer's report first, decide if they want the house, and then go to contract."

There also should be a clause in the contract saying that the deal is "subject to the buyer's ability to obtain financing." The rider will give the buyer either 30, 45, or 60 days or some other period to line up a mortgage. There will also be a clause enabling the seller to grant an extension should there be a problem with the lender. But this clause can also act as an escape for either side. Suppose the seller finds he or she has underpriced the home or has gotten a better deal after agreeing to yours. Noted Keith Asdourian, vice president of Realty World Worth, if a 30-day period was given to line up financing, on the 31st day, the seller can refuse an extension and terminate the contract.

To counteract this, Lion said, the buyer can turn around and waive the mortgage clause and agree to pay all cash. Of course, not having the money to purchase the house like this, the buyer would have to scramble to line up financing before the closing. "You should only use this tactic if you have the cash to back yourself up." If not, you might find yourself buying a home you can't afford. Or if you can secure a mortgage in time, but interest rates have been climbing since you first started shopping, you may suddenly find you can't qualify for the mortgage or you may be saddled with a higher monthly payment than you really felt comfortable with.

The financing clause, however, can also be an out for the buyer. If he or she finds a better priced home, the buyer can "play hanky panky with the mortgage," making sure it won't be approved, said Asdourian. He can, for example, delay sending in information requested by the lender. Herrick noted, "I've seen people who wanted to get out of a deal buy a car or two." With their credit overextended, the lender then rejects them.

But remember, the seller can always turn around and claim that the buyer was not making a diligent effort to obtain financing, Nappi said. The seller could then sue the buyer and if he wins, the buyer would have to purchase that house. Or, the seller could say "forget the deal" and pocket the entire down payment.

Other Items to Have Within the Contract of Sale

Contracts also should make the deal subject to a termite inspection. "If termites are found, the seller can agree to fix the problem or, if he or she wants to get out of the deal, the seller can give the buyer his or her down payment back," explained real estate attorney John P. Reali. This is the one place a seller can break the contract legally, noted Nappi. However, the buyer can protect himself or herself if his or her attorney writes into the contract that the buyer has the option of paying to fix the damage himself or herself should the seller refuse, Reali said.

The contract will also list a closing date saying "on or about" a certain day. Attorneys said that usually a month's grace or delay is acceptable from the date listed before the closing actually occurs. But should the seller have a change of heart and decide he or she doesn't want to move, he might stall the date again, hoping, Herrick said, that the buyer will just give up and look for another home. The buyer, of course, can sue the seller saying that he or she is dragging his or her feet and not living up to the contract, Reali said. But this can take six months or more to settle. Being that you're a first-time buyer, you're not faced with having to move your furniture from an old home to this new one you're trying to buy (unless, of course, you're in a rental and the lease is about to expire).

But a lawsuit can delay your looking for another home, Reali explained. Should you win the suit, you will have to buy the house. If you find something else in the meantime, you can't really purchase it because the other deal is pending placing you in a sort of "housing limbo" until everything is ironed out.

Lawsuits also cost you money, he pointed out. If the seller

starts playing games, the best thing to do is just find something else to buy—unless you really like the home and the deal is one you know you won't be able to duplicate elsewhere.

If You Really Do Change Your Mind about a Home

If there really is a change of heart about purchasing a certain home, the buyer should have his or her attorney contact the seller's lawyer. The two attorneys can then try to work out some agreement, Nappi said. Chances are the buyer will lose some of his or her down payment; however, it may be worth the loss if you don't have to purchase something you really don't want anymore.

Make Sure Contract of Sale is Subject to a Certificate of Occupancy

The contract also should state that the deal is subject to the seller's providing of a certificate of occupancy (CO), Reali said. This is important because any alterations or changes that were made to a home without a CO could be illegal in the eyes of the local municipality. For example, Reali was involved in a case where the seller had constructed a deck in the back of the house. It was nicely done and well-built. The only problem was that the seller had failed to get a CO from the local municipality before doing the project.

When it came time to sell the home, the buyer wanted the seller to produce the CO for the deck. The seller had to go back to the municipality and have the building inspector examine the work that was done a number of years prior. Upon making the inspection, it was found that the deck was built two feet over the owner's property line. Before the CO could be issued for the home, the deck had to be scaled back or removed.

The CO also is the buyer's assurance that any previous work done is up to code. You don't want to find out later that an interior wall is going to collapse because the seller redid the room himself and didn't use the right type of support beams, Reali said. Or that the seller rewired a room himself and didn't use the right type of electrical wiring. Experienced attorneys usually insist certificate of completions be shown for all alterations done on a home.

Let the Contract List All Things to Be Left in the Home

Other things the contract should include are any chandeliers, furniture, appliances, or other items not part of the structure that the seller is agreeing to leave when vacating the home. If these are not written into the contract, Reali said, then you have no way of proving that they were not left behind once you take possession of the house.

Some attorneys said that there also should be a provision written in that addresses the possibility of the seller not vacating the home immediately after closing. Sellers sometimes ask if they can remain in the home longer. This usually happens when the seller's next home is not ready on time (especially if it's new construction). According to attorneys, this issue will be addressed in the form of a rider and will state for how long the seller can remain. A certain amount of rent will also have to be paid to the buyer by the seller. This figure will also be written in, Reali said.

Never Sign Anything Without Your Attorney Reviewing It First

One last word of warning from Paul Havemann, vice president of HSH Associates, a mortgage research firm: Never sign a contract of sale before your own attorney has looked it over. You want to make sure that riders have been put in to protect you. You don't want to sign a contract that forces you to buy the home no matter what problems are found by an engineer or inspector or if you have a problem getting a mortgage.

Your attorney should also read the lending agreement for your mortgage, Havemann said. He or she can point out to you things that you may not have seen or that the lender has neglected to tell you. A lot of defaults occur because people didn't understand what they were getting into with the lending agreement. They sign because they are rushed, flustered, or confused and don't want to display their ignorance. This is the one place that it is necessary to have everything explained to you so that "You don't end up paying for it later."

HOW TO TELL IF YOUR ATTORNEY IS DOING A GOOD JOB

Once you hire an attorney, how do you know whether or not he or she is doing a good job for you? After all, you've never been through buying a home before and don't really know what your attorney should be doing between the signing of the contract of sale and the closing. There are certain signs, Daniels said, that indicate your attorney may not be on the ball. These include:

- When you have a question, does he or she return your calls or does he or she take days to get back to you? Your attorney should respond within 24 hours or have an associate call you to see what the problem is.

- Does he or she send you all copies of correspondence from the seller's attorney so you know what's happening?

- Does he or she remind you of deadlines and important dates coming up so that you can make sure you're ready for them.

- Does your attorney get in touch with you at least a few days before the closing to tell you what to bring and where to go?

If Your Attorney Is Not Doing a Good Job

Should you find that your attorney is not performing the way you had hoped, you can terminate the relationship, Berger said. Of course, the closer you are to the closing date, the harder it will be for you to come up with someone new in time. If you do have to terminate the agreement, you should only have to pay for services the attorney has already rendered.

Should a problem arise and you find that the attorney is asking too much to terminate the agreement or some other problem arises, you can file a complaint with either the bar association in your area or the government agency in your state that licenses lawyers, experts said.

The key to finding a good attorney is to do your homework ahead of time, Commissioner Devine said. Find out what he or she will do for the fee being charged and how long the whole procedure from contract of sale to closing will take. "Take the time to ask the questions before the fact. Shop for your attorney as you would for any other service so as to give yourself as much of an advantage as you can."

CHAPTER 14

NEGOTIATING THE PURCHASE PRICE

After months of looking high and low for something you both can afford and also like, you've finally found a home to purchase. Now comes the question of how much you'll pay for the property.

True, the seller has placed an asking price on the home. But that doesn't mean that's the price you will have to pay.

Think of negotiating on home prices as the equivalent of buying T-shirts in the outdoor markets of foreign countries. The more vendors that are selling shirts of a similar design (and the less busy the market is), the more likely a vendor is going to be willing to work with you on price. As you begin to walk away from that merchant's stall, after the seller has made what he or she proclaims to be the "final offer," suddenly that firm price drops by another dollar.

The same is true with real estate. The more homes there on the market, and the slower the market is, the better able buyers are to call the shots. The fewer homes there are on the market, and the more buyers there are looking, the more control the seller will have over the deal. Obviously, the trick is to be negotiating on price during a buyer's market.

A GOLDEN RULE OF HOMEBUYING

The one rule a buyer should always remember, said Jack Dornheim, owner of North Country Associates, a real estate office that represents buyers in a transaction, is that "no one should get locked into wanting any one house." If you do, he said, you could end up paying more than a residence is worth or end up purchasing a property with serious problems—such as a leaking basement.

Likewise, don't let your judgment be clouded by an urgency to move in, said buyer broker Dale Emily La Pointe. If you believe that this, and only this, is the home you must have, and that you have to get it before someone steals it from you, then again, you'll end up paying more than it's worth, she said.

Noted other brokers, whenever there are several buyers all going after the same home, it's likely that the price of that home will get pushed up past what it's really worth. The seller is now in control, and the smart buyer will drop out and let the others fight it out.

The important thing to remember, Dornheim stressed, is that the home you are zeroing in on is not the only home in the area. It may take you weeks or months to find another property you can afford or like, but it's better to move along and look at something else than to settle because some part of the deal is not right.

Figuring Value

With many areas in the nation still experiencing a slow real estate market, brokers, attorneys and other experts pointed out that agreement on the home's selling price is now *the* most important factor in any deal between a buyer and a seller. (Of course, even in a hot market price is important, but in that type of selling climate, the homeowner states the price and the buyer says yes or no. If the buyer walks away from the deal, there's usually someone else waiting in the wings to pay the seller's price. In a slow market, however, if a buyer passes on a property, the seller could be waiting months for another live prospect to come along.)

In areas where home sales are slow, sellers always come into the market believing that their home is worth more than it really is, Lazar said. And buyers go into a slow market looking for bargains, added Testa. They think that every piece of property up for sale is negotiable. But it's not, he added, if the property is priced correctly for the market.

However, buyer's brokers pointed out that all prices, even those that appear to be correct, are negotiable. The trick in coming up with a price, La Pointe said, is that the negotiation has to be fair to both parties. For that to happen, she added, preparation and research are required on both sides.

What Sellers Are Doing. Before placing their home on the market today, smart sellers are doing all the moderately inexpensive things that make a home look better, Testa said. This includes repainting the exterior and interior of the home and replacing worn carpeting. If a kitchen is in terrible shape, the owner might reface the cabinets.

Or, added Denise Quinn, manager of the real estate office Sherlock Homes, the seller might redo kitchen countertops, add new floors and fix cracked tiles in a bathroom. One thing a seller should never do, she said, is point to a leaking faucet, for example, and tell a buyer that it won't cost that much to fix the problem. A smart buyer should take the position that if it isn't going to cost much to fix, why don't you, Mr. Seller, fix it yourself, she said. A buyer should use any defects, as we'll discuss later, to negotiate the price down.

What Adds Value to a House

So what kinds of things add to the value of a home and help to increase its price?

A 1989 survey conducted by the National Association of Home Builders of 1,800 buyers from across the country who had just purchased a home found that a two-car garage was the feature deemed by 82 percent of the respondents to be the most important thing they wanted builders to include in the basic price of a new home. That was followed by 76 percent mentioning central air conditioning and 64 percent separate family rooms. (The remainder of the survey results are at the end of this chapter.)

Another survey, done in 1990 by the National Association of the Remodeling Industry, looked at home-improvement projects to see how much of the project's cost was recouped by a homeowner when the property was sold. A major kitchen remodeling job, which cost an owner on average across the nation $20,641, recouped $18,167, or 88 percent of its cost, on resale. Projects that recouped the least (coming from a survey done in 1989) included adding a swimming pool, which cost $20,692 to do, but only paid back 39 percent to the seller on resale. The reason for this, brokers said, is that many buyers find a built-in pool to be dangerous if there are young children in the family. (The complete remodeling survey is also at the end of this chapter.)

What both of these surveys indicate to a buyer is that features that were mentioned most frequently by purchasers—and home improvement projects that recouped the most on resale—will translate to properties that will fetch more if they have them. A seller having a newly refurbished kitchen and bath with a separate family room and a two-car garage is going to be able to get more for his or her home than the person having none of these. For the buyer, this means the more of these features he or she wants, the greater his or her homebuying budget will have to be.

The Pros and Cons of the Buyer Getting an Appraisal

Once a buyer zeros in on a home, he or she should begin formulating how much to offer for the property by first finding out what similar homes in the area have been selling for, Dornheim said. The buyer could hire an appraiser at this point to look the home over and suggest what it's worth. "The more ammunition you have [for backing up the offer you present]," Dornheim noted, "the better."

If an appraiser is brought in, indicate that the reason you're requesting his or her services is to purchase a home, Dornheim said. A good appraiser should come up with an accurate price (even without your stating your purpose).

Another reason an appraiser might be useful, Dornheim added, is because a lender will loan only a certain percentage of a home's value (usually 80 percent, as was discussed in Chapter 6). Knowing the appraised price will let you make a bid that will cover the mortgage amount a lender will most likely give you (plus leave you money for your down payment), without your having to come up with additional cash.

However, broker Barbara Fox, president of the Fox Residential Group, believes bringing in an appraiser at this point is a waste of money, especially in an area where home prices are dropping or rising quickly. In these markets, she said, prices are changing almost daily. Said Fox of her market when it was recently declining, "I even had a problem keeping up with current market values."

An appraiser deals with history, Fox said, and what homes sold for in the past, noting, "A broker is better at picking up the current tempo of the market." He or she can tell you if prices are still dropping or rising, or if they've reached a certain level where they're likely to remain for awhile.

When an appraiser comes up with a price, said Nick Rizzetta, a former senior vice president with Dollar Dry Dock, he or she is basing the home's value on what it could sell for in a normal selling time, usually considered between two and three months, based on what previous, similar homes in the area sold for. If prices are dropping, the appraiser plugs that information into the equation, he said.

But some in the real estate profession, such as broker Linda Albo, think that appraisers have become more conservative of late. In part, this is because of the recent crisis in the savings and loan industry, experts said, because many banks ran or continue to run into serious financial problems. After massive foreclosures in the oil belt, many lenders found they were holding homes not worth what they had been appraised for, said Jeffrey C. Daniels, a partner with the law firm Daniels & Daniels.

The decline of home prices in the Northeast also put a squeeze on lenders' bottom lines (which started to improve somewhat during 1993). Congress has been trying to license the profession, something that has not happened as of this writing. The combination of foreclosures and the threat of licensing, experts said, has caused appraisers to become more conservative.

But appraiser Maurice Perkins said his profession hasn't become more conservative; rather, lenders are becoming more intelligent in selecting appraisers. When the market was overheated in many parts of the country, harried lenders started using anyone calling him or herself an appraiser. When real estate markets slowed around the country, lenders began employing only those with experience. "What you're seeing are true appraisals which are more thorough in research," Perkins noted. If there's a large discrepancy between the contract-of-sale price and appraised price, it's probably because the seller is asking too much, he added.

"Appraisals are very subjective," said Richard Hoesch, former president of the Long Island chapter of the American Society of Appraisers. "It's not an exact science." Accuracy will depend on the appraiser's experience, knowledge of the area and finding mirror images of properties that recently sold in the area to the home being appraised, he said. The more one-of-a-kind a home is, the harder the appraisal becomes. Instead of getting an appraisal, Fox said, a buyer is better off asking his or her broker for the most recent comparables of sales in the area.

Others suggested the buyer go down to the local county clerk's office and check the most recent homes sold. But, in doing this, you then have to visit each of those homes to make sure they are similar to the one you are purchasing. One other problem with this is that it takes several months for home prices to be recorded with the county clerk and, in a heated or depressed market, selling prices can already be higher or lower than past sales.

Hiring a Buyer's Broker

In Chapter 11, the pros and cons of hiring a buyer's broker were given. However, La Pointe said, in an area that does not have a multiple listing service—which lists the prices of recently sold homes—having a buyer's broker becomes more critical. Likewise, if you're buying a co-op, a buyer's broker is helpful. In most areas, co-op sales are not on public record because they are actually purchases of shares. Since no title changes hands, recent sale prices are not recorded. A broker working for the buyer, keeping track of these sales, is better able to come up with comparables so that the buyer can make an intelligent offer. For the buyer to rely on the seller's broker, La Pointe said, is wrong, because that broker's goal is to get the highest possible price for the seller. It should be noted, however, that no one had heard of any cases where selling brokers tried to hide or lied about comparable selling prices.

Additional Things a Buyer Should Do Before Making an Offer

Besides possibly getting an appraisal, as well as hiring an engineer to have the home inspected (see Chapter 12), there are other things a buyer should do before making an offer.

In his capacity of acting on behalf of a buyer, Dornheim always investigates how long a home has been on the market. The longer the home has been languishing with a "for sale" sign on its lawn, the more desperate the seller becomes, he said. He also looks at how many price reductions there have been on the home.

When Dornheim examines the condition of the property, he looks for other things that might help him negotiate the price down. For example, one bedroom found empty, with impressions in the rug of where furniture used to be, is an indication that someone recently moved out. It could mean a divorce has taken place or that the husband or wife has been transferred to another job, with the remaining spouse waiting for the home to sell before going along.

Information about the homeowner can be obtained in casual conversation with the seller's broker or by talking with the seller, Dornheim said. However, he added, remember that the seller's broker will not volunteer information that can intentionally harm his or her seller and help the buyer. The broker, for example, won't tell you that a low-cost housing development is being proposed for the area (something you should have found out in your walk around the neighborhood when you were deciding on where to live).

Likewise, when the seller's broker takes you to see the home, he or she won't drive past the garbage dump, if there is one, but rather go several blocks out of the way using the most scenic route. It's up to the buyer to personally research these things, Dornheim said. These negatives are all elements that will help in negotiating the price down.

Careful What You Say

A buyer usually spends more time with the seller's broker than the seller does, said attorney John Nappi. In many cases, buyer and broker actually strike up a friendship. There's nothing wrong with this, Nappi said. However, the buyer has to be careful not to reveal what he or she intends to do when it comes time to negotiate on price, he cautioned.

As has been mentioned before, the broker's fiduciary duty lies with the seller (unless you've hired a broker to represent you). If you casually say, "I think I'll offer $100,000 for the house, but I'm willing to go to $125,000," the broker has a duty to tell his or her seller what you intend to do, Nappi said.

Noted Lazar, this is a tough situation for some selling agents. Because of the code of ethics and legal responsibility the broker has to the seller, the agent really doesn't want to be in a position of knowing ahead of time what the buyer intends to do during the negotiating. "The less the buyer tells you, the better," she said.

The buyer, however, should be honest with the broker about other intentions so he or she isn't wasting the selling agent's time, Lazar said. If you're just browsing, with the intention of buying something three years from now, be honest with the broker.

Some buyers, Testa added, are too secretive. Knowing where the broker's fiduciary duty lies, they sometimes don't even want to offer information that will help the broker focus on the type of home that the buyer is looking for.

PRICING

The old rule of thumb that brokers tell sellers is to price a home 10 percent above what they want to get. This leaves room for negotiating. Many brokers still believe this and have their sellers price their homes accordingly.

But some, like Denise Quinn, believe that in a slow market, where home prices have been dropping, the best tactic is to price the home at what the owner thinks it will sell for. By pricing a home competitively from the start, she said, the seller isn't losing time on the market. The homeowner will see traffic from the beginning. Noted Barbara Fox, an overpriced home attracts few buyers and bids. With no bids, nothing happens.

Fair market value, Quinn added, increases traffic and with more people looking, the seller can dictate the terms he or she wants. When the buyer says, "I'll give you 10 percent less than you're asking," the seller can turn around and say to the buyer, "If you look at what's available in this area, you'll see I'm priced right."

However, Quinn added, most buyers are now looking at everything that's out there—even things they can't afford—so that they come into a deal knowing exactly what homes are worth. In other words, a buyer really has to know what similar homes recently sold for in the area to negotiate fairly and get the lowest price he or she can.

Usually the first offer a seller gets from a serious buyer is the best offer, Lazar said. Added Fox, the longer the home is on the market, and the more price reductions it's had, the more a buyer can use those factors as ammunition for getting the price down even further.

Value vs. Low Price

In a slow market with dropping prices, one thing Fox has noticed is that buyers become obsessed with getting the lowest price possible and begin overlooking good value. In a buyer's market, such as still exists in parts of the country, purchasers begin to pick up lesser-quality homes because they were able to negotiate a rock-bottom price. Many tend to ignore homes in good condition and in good locations that might actually be a better value, but cost a little more.

A buyer should always remember that this home will be sold later, Fox said. Better to pay a little more, if you can afford it, for a good value rather than to just purchase anything because you were able to talk the seller down to a below-market price.

Some brokers, however, will disagree with this, saying that if all a first-time buyer can afford is the rock-bottom-priced house, better to settle for this than to continue living in a rental. Value and location are important things to consider, but not at the expense of owning nothing.

LET THE NEGOTIATIONS BEGIN

You've looked over the home, studied the engineer's report and checked out what comparable homes in the area have sold for and are now ready to make an offer. How much lower you go than the asking price will depend on how overpriced you think that price is and how much ammunition you have to support a reduced price.

Brokers said that most initial offers average 10 to 15 percent below the seller's asking price. However, in a slower or depressed market, offers can be 30 percent below or more. "Some buyers are just interested in trying to steal a home," Testa said.

After the initial offer is made, there will be a back-and-forth volley of offers and counteroffers with buyers slowly creeping up in price and sellers coming down. There is no rule of thumb for how big these price reductions or rises should be, Dornheim said. Added Testa, "the negotiating process is really a meeting of the minds."

A successful negotiation, as La Pointe pointed out before, has to be fair for both sides. A buyer, Dornheim said, can't just ask that the price be lowered 20 percent. He or she has to back the reduction with facts, such as that the home is on a busy road, that there's a garbage dump nearby or that there's something physically wrong with the home. The buyer could use the engineer's report, pointing out that the roof has only five years' worth of life left or that the heating system is on its last legs. This means major out-of-pocket expenses are in store for the buyer shortly after taking over the home, Dornheim said. However, the buyer can't use the excuse of a worn rug or some other interior design feature to get a price down, Nappi noted. These are things the buyer would have replaced anyway. Counteroffers made by sellers should also be backed with facts.

Some brokers suggested going to the county clerk's office and finding out what the seller originally paid for the home. This way you know how much profit the seller is trying to make on the property, be it reasonable or outlandish.

Other Strategies to Use to Negotiate a Price Down

If there are a number of homes for sale on the same block, a buyer can use this fact to help drive a price down, Dornheim said. The buyer can point to the fact that there is ample product available for sale in the area, but that there are few purchasers. Noted Testa, if the home you are looking at has higher property taxes than the rest of the homes up for sale on the block, also use that for negotiating the price down. Remember, however, that if the property taxes are lower than those of surrounding homes, the seller will use this to help keep the price up.

One strategy taken by La Pointe in her capacity as a buyer's broker is to locate several suitable properties for her client and make an offer on all of them, letting each of the sellers know that she is doing this. Using this strategy, La Pointe managed to get a home, originally priced at $260,000, for less than $200,000, within her buyer's budget.

While the home's seller said that he was firm on his price of $260,000, after negotiating on several other properties, La Pointe went back to him for one final try. She showed him how she had prices in the $200,000 range for homes similar to his. Upon seeing that data, along with the fact that he was unable to sell his home at his original asking price in the interim, he accepted the deal. Making the deal even sweeter for her buyer, La Pointe learned later that a similar home, with 200 fewer square feet of living space, had sold for $240,000 a few weeks later. La Pointe credits her strategy for getting the cheaper price along with the fact that her client used a buyer's broker instead of trying to negotiate the deal on his own. A buyer's broker has allegiance to no single property and just keeps hammering away until he or she comes up with a deal that favors the client, she said.

If a buyer falls in love with one particular property, a second tactic La Pointe takes, after researching comparables and looking the home over, is to make a bid including a down-payment check and a contract of sale contingent on the buyer getting a mortgage and also seeing the financial reports of the building (if it's a co-op). This, she said, shows the seller that her client is a serious buyer.

When Negotiations Stall. Not all negotiations will go smoothly. Every so often a deadlock occurs, where the buyer insists he or she won't go up in price anymore and the seller refuses to come down another dollar.

If negotiations should stall, brokers suggested a cooling-off period of one or two days. But now comes the problem of ego and losing face, Nappi said. No one wants to admit that he or she gave in on price.

To get things going again, the seller might call his or her broker and ask what the broker thinks will entice the buyer to start negotiating again. A buyer can also ask the same thing of the seller's broker.

Sometimes, Nappi said, it may be necessary or even advisable to bring in third parties, such as the buyer's and seller's attorneys. These third parties can discuss what it will take to get things moving again.

Instead of lowering the price further, Nappi has found negotiations can sometimes be jumpstarted by having the seller offer to pay some of the buyer's closing costs or by leaving additional items in the home, such as outdoor furniture or a chandelier the buyer admired. Noted Fox, "When you run into a wall, you try to pull out all the stops to see what works to get things moving again."

Testa has often suggested bringing in an independent appraiser agreed to by both parties. Whatever price the appraiser comes up with is the price the parties will agree to.

Dornheim suggested that a buyer might suggest that, instead of an outright purchase at this point, both parties agree to the purchaser renting with the option to buy. This is where the buyer rents the home for a specified period of time with a certain percentage of the rent going towards the down payment.

When You Find a Truly Desperate Seller

A buyer will find that a seller is more willing to negotiate on price—enabling him or her to get a deep discount or a true bargain over the original asking price—when the seller is desperate, Testa said. If a seller is in the midst of a divorce or has been transferred to another area because of work, you can use either of these circumstances to get a lower price in exchange for a fast closing, he noted. This is an ideal strategy for a first-time buyer who has no other home to get rid of and who also has been pre-approved for a mortgage. If you can meet the seller's quick time frame, then a better price is often possible.

Even a nondesperate seller, Quinn said, will lower the price if he or she knows that a deal is not contingent on the buyer having to qualify for a mortgage or sell another home. Especially in areas where the market is slow, the quicker you can close on a deal, the more attractive a buyer you become and the more likely the seller will work with you so as not to lose a live prospect, she noted.

Never Knock the Property

During your negotiations, one thing a buyer should keep in mind is to never knock the property, but rather praise it, Testa said. A real estate transaction is a very emotional thing. Telling a seller (even through the broker) that the decor is ugly or that the place is a dump puts the seller on the defensive and bruises his or her ego. Contrary to what you may think, it will not help you chew the price down by being negative.

A better strategy, Testa advised, is to say that you like the property, but that its price is slightly more than you can currently afford. Then ask the seller if he or she can work with you on price. A positive approach keeps emotions from taking over the negotiations, he pointed out. And if the seller starts to like you and begins to think, "Hey, this is the guy or gal who I'd like to see live in the home where I raised my three kids," then he or she may help you with price, closing costs or other things, Testa added.

Should I Use a Buyer's Broker?

Chapter 11 went into some of the pros and cons of a buyer hiring a broker to represent him or her, but it's probably worth looking at this argument again from a negotiating point of view.

Dornheim argued that a buyer's broker is skilled in negotiating and knows what things to point out to get the price down. The broker is skilled at negotiating, unlike a buyer who is doing this for the first time. In fact, Dornheim pointed out, brokers' commissions are set up to encourage them to get the lowest price possible for their buyers. The broker gets 1 percent of the listed price plus $200 for every $1,000 he or she is able to get the price reduced.

Noted La Pointe, a buyer's broker is objective and doesn't have loyalty to any one property. In addition, having negotiated deals numerous times in the past, he or she knows how to read a seller's counteroffer better than a buyer doing this for the first time. Some buyers receive an offer and read it the wrong way, La Pointe said. They take it to mean "this is my final offer," then give up on the deal and walk away. "I never assume what's going on in the other person's mind," she said. "I just keep going at it, trying it from a different angle if necessary."

But Nappi believes that a buyer can do just as well handling his or her own negotiations. A buyer can get previous home prices in the area and other pertinent information about the homeowner from the seller's broker. Other things for getting the price down can be gathered from the engineer's report, Nappi said. Ultimately, the buyer is the best one to do the negotiating, he added, because only a buyer knows exactly how large a monthly mortgage he or she will feel comfortable with and how much he or she can afford and wants to spend on the home.

PASSING ALONG ALL OFFERS

A buyer's market doesn't always mean that the purchaser can call all the shots, Nappi said. If the seller starts with a realistic price and backs up that price with comparable area sales, then there's no reason why he or she can't get close to the asking price. Buyers should be willing to listen to reason and be fair. But there's no reason why you can't begin the negotiations with a really lowball offer; the most a seller can do is say no.

According to the broker's code of ethics and the laws of many states, brokers are supposed to communicate all offers to their sellers, Quinn said. Some brokers, however, take a protective attitude towards their sellers and don't pass along "ridiculous offers." But if a home has been on the market for awhile and a seller is getting anxious, what was ridiculous six months ago may sound good today, noted Lazar.

Another problem, Quinn said, is that some sellers will ask the broker not to pass along any ridiculous offers but won't define what is meant by "ridiculous." A good broker, Quinn said, will find out below what price the seller doesn't want to hear an offer and then convey everything else. When this sort of arrangement has been set up, the broker is working both within his or her code of ethics and within the parameters of the law.

However, if you feel that an offer that you've made has not been conveyed to the seller, there's nothing against your contacting the homeowner on your own, some experts advised. You can call, starting with, "I don't mean to bother you, but I was wondering if your broker conveyed my last offer to you of $100,000?" If the broker hasn't, and the seller finds this a good offer, then the seller will actually be grateful that you called. If the broker has conveyed the offer, just apologize for bothering him or her and continue to negotiate through the broker.

Binders

Once a price is agreed upon, a binder is usually signed, Nappi said. There are some areas of the country where the money put down on a binder is nonrefundable. But in most places, the buyer has a week to ten days to think about the deal he or she has made. If after that time the buyer doesn't want the home, he or she can get back the $100 to $500 fee that most binders require. (It should be noted that in some areas of the country binders are not taken, but the deal moves right to the contract signing.)

One thing to beware, Nappi said, is that some brokers will draw up a binder stating that if a buyer changes his or her mind and doesn't want to buy the home, that buyer loses the deposit placed with the binder. There's nothing illegal about this. However, Nappi suggested not signing such a document. If you are unsure about the wording of the document after reading it, show it to your attorney before signing it.

Another thing Nappi pointed out is that if you feel that after lengthy negotiations in coming up with a price you have received a particularly good deal, bypass the binder (in areas of the country that use this) and immediately draw up a contract of sale. Once this document is signed, the deal is binding, he said.

With a binder, a seller can think twice about the price he or she has agreed to, and if the seller feels a higher price could have been gotten, cancel the deal (which can be done without repercussions in most areas of the country), Nappi said. Sellers are even more likely to have second thoughts about a price when a market is hot. Right after you've signed a binder for $100,000, another person might come along offering $20,000 more. Wanting to maximize profits, the seller will accept the second deal and cancel yours.

If a contract of sale is signed, however, Nappi explained, it becomes much harder to get out of the deal. If the agreement is broken (by either side), there are usually monetary penalties to deal with, he said.

1989 Survey Of 1,800 New Home Buyers from Across the Country Conducted by the National Association of Home Buyers

THE FEATURES BUYERS DEEMED MOST IMPORTANT FOR BUILDERS TO INCLUDE IN THE BASIC PRICE OF A HOME:

1) Two-car garage—82%

2) Central air conditioning—76%

3) Separate family room—64%

4) Quality of carpeting—62%

5) Fireplace—61%

6) Quality of paint used—55%

7) Separate dining room—49%

8) Size of rooms—48%

9) Quality of floor tiles—48%

10) Basement—45%

11) Having a large lot—42%

12) Brick front—38%

THE SAME 1,800 BUYERS WERE ASKED TO RATE THE IMPORTANCE OF ITEMS THAT SHOULD BE INCLUDED IN THEIR NEXT HOME:

1) Smoke detector—82%

2) Two-car garage—82%

3) Central air conditioning—76%

4) Walk-in closet in bedroom—70%

5) Separate family room—64%

6) Separate guest room—64%

7) High-quality carpeting—62%

8) Storm doors—62%

9) Fireplace—61%

AVERAGE PROJECT REMODELING COST VS. RESALE VALUE

PROJECT	AVERAGE REMODELING COST	AVERAGE RESALE VALUE/ PERCENTAGE
Major kitchen remodel	$20,641	$18,167/88%
Bath addition	$10,151	$ 8,586/85%
Minor kitchen remodel	$ 7,892	$ 6,617/84%
Master suite	$21,074	$16,620/79%
Family room addition	$31,223	$24,327/78%
Replace siding	$ 7,789	$ 5,776/74%
Bath remodel	$ 7,568	$ 5,499/73%
Add skylight	$ 3,385	$ 2,280/68% (1989 stat)
Deck addition	$ 5,109	$ 3,447/67%
Reroofing	$ 3,964	$ 2,432/61% (1989 stat)
Sun room addition	$15,368	$ 9,389/61%
Replace windows	$ 6,577	$ 3,739/57%
Replace doors	$ 1,541	$ 655/42%
Add a swimming pool	$20,692	$ 7,776/39% (1989 stat)

The survey was done in 1990 by the National Association of the Remodeling Industry. (Some figures, however, are from the 1989 chart.)

Chapter 15 ——————————

THE CLOSING

Pat yourself on the back. You're in the home stretch.

Once the contract of sale is signed and a mortgage has been approved, all that remains left to do is close on the property. "A closing is the culmination of the home buying process where all the parties get together and everything is signed," explained real estate attorney C. Jaye Berger. Once the mortgage has been lined up, a closing date can be set.

But before buyers and sellers meet face to face for the closing, there are a number of things that should be done (you didn't think this step was going to be THAT easy, did you?). "Unless you have some experience with this," said attorney Michael Cohen, "when a person gets to the closing, he or she finds a foot-high pile of papers placed in front of him or her. There's a look of befuddlement on the buyer's face over what to do. It's a complete mystery to most. A vast majority of people don't know what they're signing even after their lawyer explains it to them."

It should be noted here that in a few areas of the country, especially the West Coast, a closing is called a settlement. Instead of lenders, attorneys, the real estate broker, the buyer, the seller and others getting together, escrow agents meet (sometimes in the title company's office) and close the deal. The steps detailed below leading up to a closing should also be followed leading up to a settlement.

SET UP A REHEARSAL PRIOR TO CLOSING

Because of the unfamiliarity most people have with the closing process, Thomas Szczepaniak, a vice president with American Savings Bank, recommended that an attorney and buyer get together a few days before the closing and have a sort of rehearsal. This way, he said, there won't be any surprises about charges due or papers the buyer will be asked to sign. "Things will go more smoothly," he noted.

Cohen concurs, saying that he keeps a list so he can show the buyer the checks and documents being signed at the closing. A day or two before the closing, he has the buyer come into his office and he goes over each of the items on the list, explaining what they're for. Then, at the closing, as the buyer signs each of the checks or documents, Cohen crosses them off his list. He believes this helps a buyer understand what he or she is doing.

In addition to all these pre-closing meetings, Szczepaniak also recommended buyers read the booklet entitled "Closing Costs and You," put out by the Department of Housing & Urban Development and given to buyers by most lenders when they first apply for a mortgage. Szczepaniak said the booklet runs through everything that will happen at the closing, listing all costs that the buyer will encounter. This includes everything from what the bank will charge to settlements that have to be made with the seller, such as paying for any fuel that remains in the tank if the home is heated with oil.

"Closings are all about dollars and cents," said Scott Lanoff, a manager for the GMAC Mortgage Corp. This is why he also suggested meeting with the person at the bank who made your loan sometime before the closing to go over each fee being charged line by line. Lanoff then recommended reviewing the fees again with your attorney. "The borrowers I respect the most are the ones who even ask what the lender takes in the way of real estate taxes for escrow at the closing," he said.

Line Up People and Inspect the Home Before the Closing

You've arranged to meet with your attorney and loan officer a few days before the closing to comprehend what will be going on. However, there are a few things that need to be taken care of in advance of showing up.

The buyer and his or her attorney, Berger said, "should make sure that all the appropriate people come to the closing." Besides the buyer and seller, there will be the respective attorneys for each, the bank's attorney and someone from the title company who has made sure the home's title is free and clear of any liens or other persons claiming to be the owner of the property. If the present owner has an existing mortgage on the home, a representative from his or her bank may also be there, Berger said. That lender's job is to receive the balance of principal from the seller's present mortgage.

The purchaser should also make a final inspection of the property as close to the closing date as possible, said Daniels. The contract between buyer and seller usually states that this can be done 72 hours prior to closing as long as the purchaser gives the seller proper notice that he or she is coming over. In Michael Cohen's judgment, buyers don't inspect the home they're buying close enough to the closing. He prefers it be done within 24 hours of the signing of all the papers.

This inspection is done, said Daniels, to make sure the home is still in the condition that it was when the buyer signed the contract of sale. Some buyers are continually going back to the house after the contract of sale is signed to take measurements or mull over decorating ideas. But other buyers don't return until after the keys and title are in their hands. Not inspecting the home right before the closing is a big mistake, experts agreed.

If something is found to be wrong with the home, it has to be addressed before the title changes hands, Daniels said. For example, if the present owners accidentally put a hole in a wall while still in possession of the home or removed a light fixture that they promised to leave behind, these things should be addressed prior to the closing so the problem item can be either replaced or fixed. If the problem is found the morning the home is scheduled to change hands, then in order for the whole deal not to be held up, at the closing an agreed-upon sum of money (to make the repair or replace the missing item) would be placed in escrow, Daniels said. This money would then be used, after taking possession of the home, to fix or replace whatever was found to be faulty with the home.

Make Sure COs Are Brought Along

One reason Donald Henig, president of Island Home Funding, has seen closings delayed is because sellers have forgotten to bring along COs (certificate of occupancies) for the home. If a seller is missing a CO for either the home or any addition that was made, this can be a real problem, Cohen said. The bank won't give the mortgage to the buyer without a certificate of occupancy.

Noted Daniels, COs are issued by the municipality that the home is in to show that the property is in compliance with all building codes. A buyer should make sure that all renovations and additions to the home have a CO. Sometimes these certificates are overlooked by the title company and the closing still takes place, but this can cause problems for the buyer down the road, Daniels said. Years later, when the buyer goes to refinance the mortgage or sell the home, the next purchaser (or new lender in a refinancing) may question where the CO for a deck or dormer is. If you can't produce one, the headache of getting a CO from the building department will be yours.

To grant a CO, a building inspector usually has to come to the home. Sometimes plans for the alterations or addition are requested. If you don't have them, an architect has to be hired to draw up a set of plans—at additional cost to you. Daniels noted that he's seen cases where a porch, for example, was later found not to have been built in compliance with existing building codes and had to be torn down. This, of course, will then affect the selling price of the home, because it's no longer coming with everything the buyer thought he or she was getting.

Cohen also recalled a personal experience with a house that he was buying. In the municipality of the home there was an ordinance that fences could not be higher than four feet. However, the home that Cohen had signed a contract of sale for had a fence that was six feet high. The building department would not grant a variance for the higher fence. Before Cohen could close, the seller had to take care of the fence problem.

There are cases, Daniels added, in which a home was built prior to when COs were needed. In such cases, all the seller needs is a letter from the municipality stating this and that everything is in order. (Some areas of the country, however, might have a different procedure; check with your attorney.)

Make Sure You Have Homeowners Insurance, Certified Checks and Other Items

Another thing that the buyer will need to get before the closing is a homeowner's insurance policy for the property, Daniels said. At the closing, the lender making the mortgage will ask to see a paid receipt for this policy. All banks require a policy be secured before they will close on the mortgage. The policy must be for at least the amount of the mortgage that the lender is making on the home.

Daniels also noted that if a seller who heats his or her home with oil should have the fuel company come to the home and take a final reading of how much oil is left in the tank before the closing. The reason is that at the closing, the buyer gives the seller a check for the amount of oil left in the tank. With the price of oil today, few people are going to make 200 gallons of oil a gift to the purchaser, Daniels said.

In addition, certified or bank checks will be needed to pay a number of costs at the closing, Berger noted, such as the balance of the home's purchase price (not covered by the down payment or mortgage). These have to be arranged ahead of time. The buyer's attorney should let his or her client know how many checks will be needed, whom they should be made out to and for how much each should be written, she said.

If one of the buyers closing on the home can't be present the day the home changes hands, someone can be tapped to take that person's place. However, in order to do this, the buyer will need a properly executed power of attorney form, Berger said. This gives that person (or persons) the right to fill in for the absentee buyer. The seller's attorney should be notified this will be happening ahead of time, Berger added. The closing could be adjourned right after getting underway if the power of attorney form were found to be filled out incorrectly.

When Closings Are Adjourned or Delayed. No one wants to see a closing adjourned for any reason, Cohen said, noting, "You try to use creative problem-solving to prevent an adjournment." If a document or certified check is missing, send someone out to get it.

An adjournment can be costly for both the buyer and seller. The buyer runs the risk of losing the mortgage commitment and promised rate of interest, Berger said, because these are issued for only a certain period of time. The seller is usually buying another home and probably has a closing scheduled later that day for the new property, Daniels said. In addition, both the seller and the buyer probably have moving vans lined up and ready to take their furniture to their respective new homes, he noted.

While an attorney tries to anticipate any problems that might occur, there are times you don't find out about something until the closing, Daniels said. Donald Henig recalled a client who was closing on a property that the buyer said was to be owner occupied. When the attorney presented the paid insurance receipt at the closing, it was found to be for a landlord policy, indicating that the buyer had lied to the lender and was going to use the home as investment property. The closing was adjourned, Henig said, because using the house for investment meant different terms were required for the loan. If you try to pull a fast one and get caught—as many do—it delays the whole deal and could even cost you more in the way of higher interest if your commitment runs out and interest rates are on the rise.

If the closing is adjourned because of something the seller was responsible for and the buyer loses his or her mortgage rate, the seller may have to compensate the buyer. Likewise, if the buyer has caused the closing to be adjourned and this costs the seller money—such as by having to reschedule a moving van coming to the house—then the buyer would have to compensate the seller, Cohen said.

Because of the hardships adjournment could cause both of the parties, those connected with closings said they try to do whatever they can to bring these sessions off on schedule. Henig suggested that both buyers and sellers maintain good communication with their attorneys, especially in the days prior to the closing, so they can keep up to date on any changes and additional items being requested of them.

THE DAY OF THE CLOSING

According to GMAC's Lanoff, the most important item a buyer can bring to the closing is his or her checkbook.

While this comment was made in jest as he discussed what happens on that exciting but bewildering day, in reality, Lanoff's joke couldn't be truer, attorneys and lenders said. Both groups of professionals had chilling tales of closings adjourned halfway through because buyers had miscalculated costs and simply ran out of money in their checking account. As was discussed in previous chapters, closing costs generally run between 6 and 8 percent of the mortgage amount being borrowed.

Henig recalled one buyer who, upon learning prior to the closing how much he would need in the way of closing costs, realized he wouldn't have enough funds and went out and got a loan to cover the costs. The problem was that this loan gave the borrower added debt, which made him ineligible for the mortgage he had applied for. The closing had to be delayed while the man paid off the loan and arranged for a cash gift from his parents to go through with the closing.

While your lender and attorney should give you a detailed list of costs prior to the closing, there are always unexpected charges that pop up during the one-hour to 90-minute session, Berger said. She recommended buyers put extra funds into their checking accounts before attending the closing. Other attorneys also advised that buyers bring along enough checks. Don't expect to be able to write one check to cover all the bills and charges put before you.

What Actually Occurs During Closing Day for the Seller

So what takes place at this mysterious ritual?

For the seller, there are few things to do, Cohen said. If a broker was used, a check is written to cover his or her commission. Another check pays the balance of any mortgage principal remaining on the home being sold. The seller's attorney will also present the buyer with a payoff statement or letter from the lender holding the seller's existing mortgage, showing that the principal has been paid off, Daniels said.

In addition, a check is written to cover the seller's fee for his or her attorney and to cover any state or local transfer taxes on property that may exist (not all areas have these). From that point, the seller can sit back and watch you, the buyer, do the rest of the work, Cohen said.

The Buyer's Part. The buyer's attorney should begin his or her part of the closing by reviewing the mortgage note and making sure the terms and rate match those on the commitment letter, Cohen said. Sometimes the terms don't match up, and the lender has to make some quick calls to find out where the error is and then fill in the correct numbers.

It's important to catch any mistakes beforehand, Cohen said. Once the papers are signed and the closing is history, getting an incorrect rate or term corrected can take forever.

It's also during this review that the buyer sees for the first time the amount of interest he or she is being asked to pay over the life of the loan, Cohen said. This amount has been listed on other documents before, but he finds this is the point when the interest amount really sinks in with a buyer. "Most people fall out of their chair when they see the overall interest they're paying," he said.

The Checks You Will Sign

It's then time for the buyer to begin signing checks. Note that not all of these costs will pertain to every buyer, and some states have additional costs that are not listed here. In general, however, the following is a list of costs you will sign checks for on the day of your closing:

LENDER CLOSING FEES—This covers any origination fees, such as points, not paid for at the time of commitment. It also covers other fees including those for credit checks and appraisals, underwriting fees and document fees, Daniels said. All are spelled out in advance in a good-faith estimate that the buyer receives within three days of applying for the loan, he added. There could, however, be other fees that are not listed on the good-faith estimate, Cohen noted. For example, you might be asked to pay for any overnight letters that had to be mailed on your behalf.

MORTGAGE BROKER—If a mortgage broker is used to secure the loan, closing day is the time the broker will be present to collect his or her fee.

PRE-PAID INTEREST—Many closings don't occur on the first day of the month. But the lender will still want to collect the interest on the mortgage money that you are using between the closing and the time of your first mortgage payment.

For example, assume you close on March 15. Your first mortgage payment won't have to be written and sent to the lender until May 1. Interest is paid by a borrower retroactively—in other words, April's interest is collected from your May 1 payment. But there's still the interest to be settled and collected from March 15, the closing date, to March 31.

Companies servicing loans are set up only to collect equal payments each month, said American Saving's Szczepaniak. Instead of a separate charge later on, the lender requires you to pay the March 15-to-March 31 interest in advance at the closing, he noted.

PROPERTY TAX ESCROW ACCOUNT—Many banks insist that they pay the property taxes on the home they are issuing a mortgage on to make sure the taxes get paid, Daniels said. Of course, the money they are using to pay these taxes is yours. It's gotten from an escrow account (called an impound account in the West) that's put together from funds built into the mortgage amount you pay each month. If you close in March, and your first town tax comes due in June, for example, not enough money will be accumulated in your escrow account to cover this. So at the closing, the lender will ask you to pay four or five months of property tax escrow in advance.

HOME INSURANCE—As previously mentioned, the lender will ask the buyer to present a receipt showing that he or she has paid a full year's fire insurance premium. The lender may then also ask you to write a check for escrow money so he or she can pay the following year's insurance premium when it comes due, Berger said. However, Daniels added, an increasing number of lenders are allowing buyers to pay this premium on their own.

ATTORNEY'S FEE—During the closing you will pay the agreed-upon fee to the attorney representing you.

BANK ATTORNEY'S FEE—Besides paying your own attorney, as a buyer you also have to pay the bank's attorney a fee that runs anywhere from $350 to $600, Cohen said. You are paying for the attorney's time for being at the closing and for preparing the papers.

Many experts, including Paul Havemann, vice president of the mortgage research firm HSH Associates, have begun questioning why the buyer should have to pay for someone looking out for the bank's interests. He suggested questioning the lender and seeing whether this fee can be removed.

GMAC's Lanoff said the reason for the fee is tradition. It could be eliminated under the label of "bank attorney fee," he said. But it is a cost of doing business for the lender and would probably show up somewhere else, such as in higher points.

ADJUSTMENTS TO THE HOME'S SELLING PRICE—This is where you pay the seller for any home heating oil left in the home's fuel tank or for any property taxes that the seller paid in advance that overlap the time that you will be residing in the home. Additionally, if you asked to buy some of the seller's furniture or lighting fixtures, this is the point at which those items would be paid for.

BALANCE OF PURCHASE PRICE—This check is for the balance of the purchase price that is not covered in the down payment (which was paid when the contract of sale was signed) or in the mortgage amount being borrowed.

TITLE CHARGE—Some states have a title charge or mortgage tax that is collected by the title insurance company for the state. The tax varies (and usually rises over the years as governments look for extra revenue to fill their budget gaps). It is usually based on the mortgage amount being borrowed, such as one-half or one-quarter of 1 percent of the amount.

BUYER'S TITLE INSURANCE—This is to insure you for any problems that might arise in case the title company has incorrectly cleared the title on the home for transfer.

LENDER'S TITLE INSURANCE—This is insurance for the bank that covers any part of the loan not made in case you, the borrower, default. The bank won't make the loan unless this insurance is bought, Daniels said. And it's you, the buyer, who must pay it. In some areas, if both lender and buyer's title insurance are taken out at the same time from the same company, a discount is given, Daniels added. (Note that some attorneys also refer to the lender's title insurance as mortgage insurance.)

TIPS FOR THE TITLE CLOSER—In many areas, it is also tradition for the buyer to tip the title closer. To determine how much, and whether a tip should be given at all, ask your attorney.

In addition to all of the checks listed above, Cohen pointed out, the buyer will have to sign some forms and documents that vary from area to area. Some will be so the municipality has a record of when the property changed hands (listing for how much, from what seller and to what buyer). The mortgage note will also be signed. Your attorney should be able to tell you about any other forms that will cross your path prior to the closing.

One curious form that some lenders present at the closing, Cohen said, is a document stating that if the buyer forgot to sign any forms at the closing, he or she agrees to sign them as soon as possible after closing. Fortunately, he added, despite the number of forms that must be signed during this title or property transfer session, at least these forms are standardized so that an attorney can keep track of them.

Parting, but Important, Advice

One last piece of advice passed along by Lanoff is to make sure that the title being transferred has your correct name (or names, in the case of a married couple) on it. "If you use a middle initial, make sure that it's in place," he noted. An incorrect name on the title might cause you problems later on.

THE CLOSING'S FINALE

At the closing, in most areas of the country, you will receive a photocopy of the deed or title along with the keys to the home. The original deed will be taken, usually by the title company, to be recorded at the county clerk's office. Several weeks or months later (depending on the backlog), the original will be sent back to your attorney, who will mail it to you.

Because the buyer can lose track of what he or she has written checks for during the closing (even if he or she was prepared for the day in advance), many attorneys follow up the closing with a statement. This form explains everything that transpired that day and what each of the checks you wrote was for. Appropriate documents are also sent along.

And while the closing will drain you, both emotionally and financially, the nicest thing about the follow-up letter from your attorney is where it's sent—to the address of the home that's finally yours!

Index

A

Adjustable rate mortgages (ARMs), 91–94
  40-year loans, 93–94
  index on, 91
  teaser rates, 93
  Veterans Administration (VA), 135
Affordability formula, 31
Alabama loan programs, 139
Alaska loan programs, 140
American Society of Home Inspectors, 229, 232–33
Annual percentage rate (APR), 105, 108
Application fees, 103
Application for mortgage commitments, 109–11
Appraisals
  buyer, 258–60
  short, 111–12
Arizona loan programs, 141
Arkansas loan programs, 142
ARMs. see Adjustable rate mortgages (ARMs)
Assets, for down payments, 120
Assumable loans, 108, 131, 136
Attics, 65
Attorneys
  contract review, 251–52
  fees, 241, 244–46, 282–83
  finding, 242–44
  hiring, 240–46
  interviewing, 244, 246–47
  for purchase money mortgages, 194
  selection, 239–53
  use of, 102
Auction homebuying, 77, 79–81, 83–85

B

Balloon mortgages, 193
Bank attorney's fees, 282
Bar association referral services, 242
Bargains, homebuying, 67–86
Basements, 65
Bathrooms, 64
Bedrooms, 63–64
Binders in negotiation, 270
Board of directors, residence, 50, 54–55
Borrower's protection from lender's fees, 105
Borrowing limits, 29
Brokers
  being your own, 225–26

Brokers *(continued)*
  buyer's, 223-25, 260-61, 266,
    268-69
  defined, 220
  discount, 221-22
  duty, 217-19
  hiring, 260-61, 268-69
  mortgage, 98-99, 101, 281
  real estate, 100
  selection of, 223-26
  seller's, 262
Builders
  incentives on new homes,
    123-24
  workouts, 209-10
Building conversions, 210-11
Buydowns, 200
Buyers
  appraisals, 258-60
  features most important to, 271
  title insurance, 283
Buyer's brokers, 223-25, 266
  hiring, 260-61, 268-69
Buying Real Estate Foreclosures,
    80

C

Cable TV, 65
California loan programs, 143-44
Camcorders, using in home
    shopping, 62-63
Cash
  gifts for down payments, 28
  required at commitment, 110
Certificates of occupancy (COs),
    194, 250-51, 276-77
Certified checks, 277
Changes, making to residence
    unit, 250
Checks at closing, 281-84

Closets, 65
Closing costs, 106-7, 274
  lenders, 281
  mortgage without, 122
  in saving for home, 121-22
"Closing Costs and You," 274
Closing dates, 249
Closing rehearsals, 274-79
Closing statements, 284-85
Closings
  adjourned, 278-79
  for buyer, 280-84
  day of, 279-85
  home inspections before,
    274-76
  money purchase mortgages,
    192
  for sellers, 280
Co-operatives, 49-65
  buying, 58-59
  inspection, 232-33
  selling, 56
Colorado loan programs, 144
Commitments
  application fees, 109-11
  conditional, 110-11
Community Associations Institute,
    50
Community Home Buyer's
    Program, 96
Commuting time, 37-38
Conditional commitments, 110-11
Condominiums, 49-65
  buying, 58
  inspection, 232-33
  selling, 56
Connecticut loan programs, 146
Contract for deed sales, 125-26
Contract listing of items left in
    home, 251
Contract of sale, 240, 247-52
  certificate of occupancy (CO),
    250-51

Contract of sale *(continued)*
    financing clause, 248-49
    home inspection clause, 248
Contract sales, 125-26
Contract vendee, 126-27
Conversion bargains, 210-11
Convertible mortgages, 94-95
Costs
    of home inspections, 231
    of loans, 103-7
Counteroffers, 264-65
Creative financing, 187-200
Credit checks, 27-28
    purchase money mortgages,
       193
Credit ratings, 26-28
Credit reporting agencies, 27
Crime in neighborhoods, 42-43

D

Debt, 25-26
Deductions, 32-33
Delaware loan programs, 147
Desperate sellers, 267
Dining rooms, 64
Discount brokers, 221-22
Down markets, 208-11
Down payments, 24-25
    from assets, 120
    builder incentives for, 123-24
    contract sales, 125-26
    contract vendee, 126-27
    from employers, 121
    on FHA loans, 131
    how much, 114-15
    from 401(k) savings plans, 123
    locating, 115-21
    from parents, 127
Drive-around tests, 216

E

Earnest money, 77
Economy, depressed, strategies
    for, 213-15
Emotional element in
    homebuying, 215
Employers, as source of down
    payments, 121
Equity
    shared, 195-98
    sweat, 70-74
Errors
    in credit reporting, 27
    first-time buyers, 3-4
Escrow accounts, 108-9, 282
Estate sales, 74-77
Estate taxes, 76-77

F

Fannie Mae (Federal National
    Mortgage Association), 25,
    95-96
Federal government loan
    programs, 129-37
Federal Home Mortgage
    Corporation (Freddie Mac),
    25
Federal Housing Administration
    (FHA) loans, 129-33
Federal National Mortgage
    Association (Fannie Mae),
    25, 95-96
Fees
    application, 103
    attorneys, 241, 244-46, 282-83
    junk, 104-5
    maintenance, 53-54

FHA (Federal Housing
    Administration) loans,
    129–33
Financing, 24–26
  choices, 188–200
  renting with option to buy,
    188–90
  seller, 190–95
Financing clause, contract of sale,
    248–49
First-time buyers, 1–2, 9–21
  common errors, 3–4
  favoring, 2–3
  ownership types, 59–61
  tips, 21
Fixed-rate mortgages, 90
Florida loan programs, 148
Foreclosures, 82–83
  government, 77–83
  lenders, 79–80
40-year loans
  adjustable rate mortgages
    (ARMs), 93–94
401(k) savings plans, for down
    payments, 123
Freddie Mac (Federal Home
    Mortgage Corporation), 25

G

Garages, 64, 257
Gentrified neighborhoods, 68–70
Geographic differences in
    markets, 212–13
Georgia loan programs, 149
Gifts
  for down payments, 28, 116–19
  limitations, 119
  taxes on, 116–17
Government foreclosures, 77–83
Government loan programs

  federal, 129–37
  state, 138–86
Graduated payment mortgages
    (GPMs), 198–200

H

Handyman specials, 70–74
Harvard study on
    homeownership, 2
Hawaii loan programs, 150
Home affordability, determining,
    23–35
Home improvement for resale,
    258
Home inspection clause
  contract of sale, 248
Home inspections
  before closing, 274–76
  co-operatives and
    condominiums, 232–33
  cost, 231
  not revealed, 234–38
  professional, 227–33
  reports, 235–37
  self, 227–33
  termite, 249
Home inspectors
  selection of, 229–31
  what they do, 233–34
Home insurance, 24, 277, 282
Home moving, 85–86
Home offices, 64
Home prices, median, 2
Home resale, 258
Home shopping checklist, 63–65
Homebuying
  at auctions, 77, 79–81, 83–85
  bargains, 67–86
Homeowner's associations
    (HOAs), 49–65

Homeowner's associations
  (continued)
    buying, 59
    inspection, 232-33
    selling, 56
Homeowners insurance, 277
Homeownership study, 2
Homes
    builder incentives, 123-24
    changing mind about, 250
    important features to buyers,
        271
    selecting type, 49-65
Houses vs. locations, 44-45

I

Idaho loan programs, 151
Illinois loan programs, 152
Incentives on new homes, 123-24
Income, 28-29
Index on ARMs, 91
Indiana loan programs, 153
Insurance
    home, 277, 282
    mortgage, 283
    PMI, 24-25, 29-30, 108
Integrated neighborhoods, 43
Interest, 24
    deductions, 32-33
    prepaid, 281-82
    rates, 30-31
Interior remodeling, 57
Investments of borrowers, 29-30
Iowa loan programs, 154

J

Junk fees, 104-5

K

Kentucky loan programs, 155
Kitchens, 64, 258
Kollen, Melissa S., 80

L

Lawsuits, 249-50
Lenders
    closing fees, 281
    foreclosures, 79-80
    institutions, 96
    questions to ask, 108-9
    selecting, 99-103
    title insurance, 283
Lending institutions, 97-99
    mortgage bankers, 98
    mortgage brokers, 98-99
    where to borrow, 96
Living rooms, 64
Loan annual percentage rate
        (APR), 105, 108
Loans
    assumable, 108, 131, 136
    costs, 103-7
    no-down-payment from sellers,
        124
    secondary market, 30
Locations, 37-47
    vs. houses, 44-45
Long distance moves, 45-47
Louisiana loan programs, 156

M

Maine loan programs, 157
Maintenance fees, 53-54
Maintenance on homes, 51-52

Markets
    determination, 215-16
    extremes in home buying,
        205-8
    geographical differences,
        212-13
Maryland loan programs, 158
Massachusetts loan programs, 159
Median home prices, 2
Merrill Lynch Credit Corp., 96-97
Michigan loan programs, 160
Minnesota loan programs, 161
Missouri loan programs, 162
Montana loan programs, 163
Mortgage bankers, 98
Mortgage Bankers Association, 100
Mortgage brokers, 98-99, 101, 281
Mortgage payment factors, 34-35
Mortgages
    adjustable rate (ARMs), 91-94
    ceilings, 129, 133
    convertible, 94-95
    Fannie Mae, 95-96
    fixed-rate, 90
    graduated payment (GPMs),
        198-200
    locating, 97-99
    low interest, 137
    procedures, 24-26
    purchase money, 190-95
    refinancing, 90
    self-insuring, 25
    where to get, 89-112
Moving homes, 85-86
Multiple Listing Service, 216, 221

N

Names of buyers on titles, 284
National Association of Home
    Builders, 257-58

National Association of Home
    Buyers, 271
National Association of Realtors, 2
National Association of the
    Remodeling Industry, 258,
    272
Nebraska loan programs, 164
Negotiations, 255-72
    beginning, 264-65
    binders in, 270
    lower price strategies, 265-66
    stalling, 266-67
Neighborhoods
    crime in, 42-43
    decaying, 69-70
    improving, 69-70
    integrated, 43
    locating right one, 40-44
    priorities, 38
    property taxes, 43-44
    questions about, 46-47
Nevada loan programs, 165
New Hampshire loan programs, 166
New home buyers survey, 271-72
New home incentives, 123-24
New Jersey loan programs, 167
New Mexico loan programs, 168
New York loan programs, 169
North Carolina loan programs, 170
North Dakota loan programs, 171

O

Occupations, 28-29
Offers, 269
    before making, 261-62
Ohio loan programs, 172
Oklahoma loan programs, 173
$125,000 tax exclusion, 190
Option to buy, renting, 188-90
Oregon loan programs, 174

P

Parents
    down payments from, 127
    financing, 116-20
    lending program, 96-97
    neighborhoods of, 39-40
Parking, 65
Payment factors, 34-35
Pennsylvania loan programs, 175
PMI. see Private mortgage
        insurance (PMI)
Points, 105-6
    on FHA loans, 131
Porches, 64
Prepaid interest, 281-82
Prices, 263-64
    median, 2
    negotiation, 255-72
    residence units, 60-61
    selling, adjustment, 283
Principal, 24
Priorities in neighborhoods, 38
Private mortgage insurance (PMI),
        24-25, 29-30, 108
Property taxes, 24
    deductions, 32-33
    escrow accounts, 282
    neighborhoods, 43-44
    on residence types, 52
Purchase money mortgages,
        190-95

Q

Quality in neighborhoods
    schools, 38-39

R

Rates
    ARMs, 93
    APR, 105, 108
    interest, 30-31
Real estate brokers, 100
Real Estate Settlement Procedures
        Act of 1974 (RESPA), 105
Realtors, 219-20
Recreational facilities, 65
Refinanced mortgages, 90
Religion, 42
Remodeling costs vs. resale value,
        272
Rentals, buying, 28-29
Renting with option to buy,
        188-90
REOs (real estate owned) buying,
        81-82
Resale value vs. remodeling costs,
        272
Residence types, 49-65
Resolution Trust Corporation
        (RTC), 78-79
Rhode Island loan programs, 176
Riders, 240
Right of first refusal,
        condominiums, 55
Right to rent residential units, 55

S

Sales associates, 220
Schools, 38-39, 42
Self-inspection of homes vs.
        professional, 227-33

Self-insuring mortgages, 25
Sellers
    broker, 262
    desperate, 267
    financing, 190-95
    fixing homes, 257
    of HOAs, co-operatives,
        condominiums, 56
    nearing age 55, 190
Selling price adjustments, 283
Shared equity, 195-98
Short appraisals, 111-12
Single-family homes, 49-65
Size of homes, 64
South Carolina loan programs, 177
South Dakota loan programs, 178
State government loan programs,
    138-86
Sweat equity, 70-74
Swimming pools, 258

T

Tax benefits of homeownership,
    32-33
Taxes
    estate, 76-77
    gifts, 116-17
Teaser rates, ARMs, 93
Tennessee loan programs, 179
Termite inspections, 249
Texas loan programs, 180
Time
    best to buy home, 203-16
    for sweat equity, 71-73
    winter, 204-5
Timing in housing market, 207-8
Title charges, 283
Title insurance, 283
Titles, buyers' names on, 284

28/36 formula for qualifying
    buyers, 24-25, 119

U

U.S. Dept. of Housing & Urban
    Development, 77, 274
Utah loan programs, 180

V

Value of homes
    adding to, 257-58
    figuring, 256-57
    vs. low price, 263-64
Vermont loan programs, 181
Veterans Administration (VA)
    ARMs, 135
    loans, 134-37
Virginia loan programs, 182

W

Warehousing fees, 107
Washington loan programs, 183
West Virginia programs, 184
Wintertime, 204-5
Wisconsin loan programs, 185
Withholding deductions, 32-33
Workouts, builder, 209-10
Wyoming loan programs, 186

Y

Yards, 64-65